DATE DUE

Christian:
Celebrate
Your
Sexuality

By Dwight Hervey Small:

DESIGN FOR CHRISTIAN MARRIAGE
AFTER YOU'VE SAID I DO
CHRISTIAN: CELEBRATE YOUR SEXUALITY

Christian: Celebrate Your Sexuality

DWIGHT HERVEY SMALL

A Fresh, Positive Approach
to Understanding
and Fulfilling
Sexuality

15176

Fleming H. Revell Company
Old Tappan, New Jersey

Unless otherwise identified, Scripture quotations in this volume are from the Revised Standard Version of the Bible, copyrighted 1946 and 1952.

Scripture quotations identified KJV are from the King James Version of the Bible.

The Scripture quotation identified as PHILLIPS is from The New Testament in Modern English translated by J.B. Phillips, copyright J.B. Phillips, 1958. Used by permission of the Macmillan Company.

The Scripture quotation identified as NEB is from The New English Bible, © The Delegates of the Oxford University Press and the Syndics of the Cambridge University Press 1961 and 1970. Reprinted by permission.

Excerpts from *The Ethics of Sex* by Helmut Thielicke, © 1964 by John W. Doberstein, are used by permission of Harper & Row, Publishers, Inc.

Excerpts from *Sexual Ethics* by Sherwin Bailey, © 1962 by Sherwin Bailey, are used by permission of the Macmillan Publishing Company.

Excerpts from *A Christian View of Sex and Marriage* by Andrew Eickhoff, copyright © 1966 by The Free Press, a division of Macmillan Publishing Co., Inc., are used by permission.

Excerpts from *Love and Will* by Rollo May, copyright © 1969 by W. W. Norton & Company, Inc., are used by permission.

Excerpts from *The Natural History of Love* by Morton M. Hunt, copyright © 1959 by Morton M. Hunt, are used by permission of Alfred A. Knopf, Inc.

Excerpts from *The Family In Search of a Future* by Herbert A. Otto, ed., Virginia Satir, and Edward Hobbs, © 1970, are used by permission of Prentice-Hall, Inc., Englewood Cliffs, N.J.

Excerpts from *Sex and the Christian Life* by Seward Hiltner, copyright 1957 by Association Press, are used by permission.

Excerpts reprinted from *Sex in History* by G. Rattray Taylor by permission of the publisher, The Vanguard Press, Inc. Copyright 1970, 1954 by G. Rattray Taylor.

Excerpts from *It's a Playboy World* by William S. Banowsky, copyright © 1969 by Fleming H. Revell Copany, are used by permission.

Excerpts from *Creation and Fall* by Dietrich Bonhoeffer, copyright © SCM Press Ltd. 1959, are used by permission of Macmillan Publishing Co., Inc.

Library of Congress Cataloging in Publication Data

Small, Dwight Hervey.
    Christian: celebrate your sexuality.

    Includes bibliographical references.
    1. Sex (Theology) I. Title. [DNLM: 1. Religion and sex. 2. Sex behavior. HQ61 S635c]
BT708.S6   241'.6'6   74-11161
ISBN 0-8007-0661-7

TO
my students and colleagues
on the faculty of Westmont College,
Santa Barbara, California

Contents

Preface

This book is the product of many years' involvement in two special ministries: first, college conferences and marriage workshops across the land, and second, college teaching, begun part-time at Wheaton College and now the writer's occupation as a professor at Westmont College, California. The book represents a search which for years has failed to turn up an adequate volume on human sexuality solidly based on evangelical theology. The manuscript was written to fill the gap which still exists. Quite frankly, it is intended for those who are prepared to think more seriously, perhaps, than they have ever thought before on this fundamental biblical subject. And while such a study by its very nature must combine the approaches of sociology, psychology, history, and cultural anthropology, the key to it all is biblical theology. Even a Christian ethic cannot be built except upon an adequate theology. This book seeks to meet that concern.

The writer is indebted to numerous others for assistance and encouragement: Ned Divelbiss, Director of the Library at Westmont College, who secured numerous books and dissertations through the inter-library loan service; the two college deans under whom I am privileged to work, Dr. George Brushaber and Dr. William Lindberg, who made possible a reduction of responsibilities while the writing was undertaken; Mrs. Phyllis Hobe, who once again served as editorial associate, adding her expertise in making the manuscript more precise and enjoyable reading. Not least, I'm indebted to my wife, Ruth, with whom I have constantly discussed the developing chapters, and who contributed her own suggestions and carefully assisted in the final preparation of the manuscript.

Introduction

When speaking of the contemporary preoccupation with sex in American culture, one quickly inclines toward Rollo May's expression, "the banalization of sex," or Harvey Cox's—"the trivialization of sex." If the writer of Ecclesiastes were living today, he might well be crying, "Banality, banality, all is banality." For our culture has succeeded in squeezing sex into a mold that is too small for it, making it less than the Creator intended it to be. If man's relationship to his own sexuality determines whether he becomes more human or less, then man seemingly is becoming less. The record of our time displays the growing bankruptcy of inner values in our society, and nowhere is this more visible than in our national attitudes toward sex. With greater availability has come greater meaninglessness; this meaninglessness touches all of life, for we are sexual beings, and sexuality is basically the power to relate as persons. May points out that our preoccupation with sex performance and technique has obscured the fact that in terms of inner values and meaning, we have been brought to an existential crisis. He says that "the assumption that the ultimate goal of existence is the satisfaction of impulses has led sex into the cul-de-sac of tedium and banality."[1]

Sexuality is an expression of the whole person; it belongs to the symphony of human existence. It cannot be compartmentalized, but is the music of the body, complete with rhythms and melodies and harmonies. Throughout the relationship of marriage there plays, as it were, the obligato of sexual love. To quote Rollo May again:

"Consider, as an analogy, Mozart's music. In some portions of his music Mozart is engaged in elegant play. In other portions his music comes to us as pure sensuous pleasure, giving us a sheer delight. But in other portions, like the death music at the end of Don Giovanni or in his quintets, Mozart is profoundly shaking; we are gripped by fate and the daemonic as the inescapable tragedy rises before us. If Mozart had only the first element, play, he would sooner or later be banal and boring. If he presented only pure sensuality, he would become cloying; or if only the fire and death music, his creations would be too heavy. . . . Sexual love similarly can not only be play. . . . The same is true of sensuality, obviously an element in any gratifying sexual love; if it has to carry the whole weight of the relationship, it becomes cloying. If sex is only sensuality, you sooner or later turn against sex itself."[2]

Compared to contemporary views, the biblical view of sex is radical and unconventional. It is impatient with the simplistic come-ons of twentieth-century hedonism. On the other hand, it is cordial to the principles derived from humanistic psychology and sociology for the most part, affirming all the while that neither is capable in itself of the whole vision. Man is infinitely larger than the current theories of human sexuality take him to be. For if human sexuality is less than the mystery of human selfhood—including the mystery of man's relationship to God—then it is less than thoughtful men know it to be. The meaning of sexuality is the meaning of man himself.

The Christian affirms that sexuality belongs to the mysteries of divine revelation. In consequence, its ultimate meanings can be known only by revelation. To the non-Christian this is exasperating nonsense; to every committed Christian believer it is fundamental to knowing the truth. As it turns out, however, Christian realism in the sphere of sexuality is greatly enhanced by the expanded consciousness that revelation brings to it. Thus we have a promise, an anticipation at the very outset: Christian conceptualization is the larger, freer, and more fulfilling view. To demonstrate this is our central task.

That we are living in a time when sex attitudes and behavior are in revolution, no one will deny. Daily we are reminded how far and how fast the nation is going in the direction of permissiveness in all things sexual. That basic American institution—the Gallup Poll—recently issued its 1973 nationwide survey of American attitudes on sex. The tired title tells us that these attitudes are changing profoundly—as if we hadn't guessed. The significance of the poll is that it traces the change over a four-year period, and it also compares United States' attitudes with those of several other countries. The results are as follows:

Fewer Americans today than in 1969 say they would be offended by pictures of nudes in magazines—55 percent compared to 73 percent in 1969. Those who would object to actors and actresses appearing in the nude in Broadway plays have declined from 73 percent to 44 percent, while the proportion who would be offended by topless nightclub waitresses has declined from 76 percent in 1969 to 59 percent in 1973.

In terms of attitudes toward premarital sex, two out of every three Americans four years ago held the view that premarital sex relations "are wrong." Today the public is closely divided, with 48 percent believing sex before marriage is wrong and 43 percent holding the opposite opinion. Evidence of a generation gap is seen in the fact that only 29 percent of young persons, eighteen to twenty-nine, believe that premarital sex is wrong. A far smaller proportion of single persons—27 percent—than married persons—51 percent—think it is wrong. A large majority of people over the age of thirty continue to hold that premarital sex is wrong, even as they say they would be offended by nudity in magazines, in the theater, and by topless waitresses.

It is interesting to note that youths in the United States are far more liberal than their elders, but at the same time more conservative than their peers in many other nations of the world. For example, a larger proportion of American youths say premarital sex is wrong than do their counterparts in the United Kingdom, France, Switzerland, West Germany, and Sweden. Inasmuch as there is continuing discussion in the United States as to the values and responsibility involved between premarital sex with affection or without affection, the following percentages are significant. Whereas 57 percent of American youths polled endorsed premarital sex with affection, only 19 percent endorsed it without affection. The greatest difference was found in the United Kingdom, where 68 percent endorsed premarital sex with affection, only 15 percent premarital sex without affection. The closest, as might be expected in what may be the most liberally oriented Western nation, Sweden, represents an 18 percentage point difference between endorsing premarital sex with or without affection. But what is surprising about this sexually free country is that the percentage of youths endorsing premarital sex with affection was third lowest of the ten nations polled, just above India and Brazil. Perhaps the experience of Swedish young people has not been as acceptable as we have been led to believe.

There is an understandable dichotomy between the traditional views of orthodox Christians and a predominant array of humanistic psychologists and sociologists who populate our college and university faculties. Joined by the media, the entertainment world, and much of contemporary literature, academia is quite overwhelmingly aligned against traditional Christian sex ethics. Many an introductory chapter in a college text dealing with human sexuality and marriage briefly describes the Christian tradition or some distortion thereof, leaving it thus indicted and in need of no further elaboration. Refutations of the Christian position are generally brief. Rarely is any part of the Christian tradition shown in a favorable light. Sometimes it is damned by mere slight. An example from recent reading will illustrate:

"A central question in contemporary social and legal thought has involved the right of the society to have laws against abortion, homosexual and sodomous acts, adultery, fornication and other acts in which persons willfully engage as a result of their personal morality. Laws against such acts have behind them the Judeo-Christian model of the sex act as procreative and the fulfillment of its function through marriage. The circle which this model draws around man's sexual nature and which defines the forms in which he can morally exercise his sexual powers and those in which he cannot depends for its authority on a metaphysical and scriptural view of the nature of things and man's place in it. . . . The Judeo-Christian view of sexual morality has as its justification its theology of the ultimate nature of God and the world. The moral doctrine is overlaid with a spiritual doctrine and underlaid with legal codifications."[3]

Having thus stated what purports to be the Christian model—far too brief and segmented to be truly descriptive—the writer proceeds to set in counter-distinction the contemporary view:

"Counter to the Judeo-Christian model of sexual morality in contemporary Western society is the view that regards sex and sexual pleasure as natural to man and does not regard man's sexual activity as having intrinsically moral and immoral forms. This view does not derive its authority from a theological interpretation of the nature of things. It establishes its concept of moral and immoral actions through the evaluation of the effects any action has on others. This view is founded on the notion that persons in a society should be allowed to maximize the satisfaction of their desires and act as they see fit as long as their actions are not detrimental to the society as a whole or to the well-being of other individuals."[4]

One of the obvious faults in this kind of description is that it fixes on a stage of the Christian tradition as an ultimate interpretation, or leaves it stated in an oversimplified way without any recognition of nuances that may be highly significant to a real understanding.

What incredible shifts have taken place in the history of Christian thought with reference to human sexuality! From the early emphasis upon celibacy to the now-emerging emphasis upon celebration—how far has the church of Jesus Christ come! The rather recent, distinctly Christian idea that sexuality is a gift of God to be celebrated as part of man's worshipful response to Him, is a concept above and apart from all secular versions of human sexuality. Though it may appear an excitingly innovative approach to biblical psychology, it is rooted in the earliest biblical revelation, as future chapters shall set forth.[5]

One cannot speak of celebration without conjuring up such related ideas as those of a valued gift, of grateful response to the giver, of joyful participation in the benefits of the gift, of consummate happiness in the nature of the gift. Indeed the term *celebration* is presently undergoing a major mutation in contemporary Christian usage. In his recent book *The Feast of Fools*, Harvey Cox says, "Porpoises and chimpanzees may play. Only man celebrates. . . . Man is by his very nature a creature who not only works and thinks but who sings, dances, prays, tells stories, and celebrates."[6] He goes on to suggest that celebrative affirmation is "saying yes to life." And this is truly Christian.

The Apostle Paul said in 1 Corinthians 10:31, "So, whether you eat or drink, or whatever you do, do all to the glory of God." Whenever the Christian celebrates God's gifts, he is doing so to the glory of God. And the "whatever you do" includes man's rightful sexual activity. The apostle is more explicit in 1 Corinthians 6:19,20, "Do you not know that your body is a temple of the Holy Spirit within you, which you have from God? You are not your own; you were bought with a price. So glorify God in your body." And to glorify God in one's body and its every function is to celebrate God's goodness and grace, to say yes to life as His gift. It recalls Paul's word in Romans 12:1, "I appeal to you therefore, brethren, by the mercies of God, to present your bodies as a living sacrifice, holy and acceptable to God, which is your spiritual worship." Spiritual worship includes the offering of one's body and its functioning to God in a veritable sacrifice of living wholly unto Him. Thus does the Christian celebrate. And in a deep sense, sexual intercourse between husband and wife establishes and nurtures the one-flesh relationship which the apostle says is a union representative of the covenant union between Christ and the church. Thus, in a very real way, the mystery of our relationship with Christ, which mystery is typified by the husband-wife union, is a celebration. Such celebration, as Harvey Cox suggests, links us both to the past and to the future. Yes, and it links us in Christ to the human and the divine. That which takes place on the human, bodily plane is elevated in dignity as it is representative of the intimate bond between Christ and His bride, the church of the redeemed.

In my role as a sociology professor, I find that Christian young people resonate with the idea of sexuality as God's gift to be received with thanksgiving, offered in faith back to Him in its fulfillment, and celebrated in His holy presence. Here is a radical shift in emphasis from all that was typical of the centuries of Christian tradition in sexual thought. It opens the way toward willing and joyful commitment to a transcendently worthy view of sexuality for the Christian. It incorporates sexuality as an expression of man's total being, affirming and celebrating its humanness. Sexuality is seen as a gift from a bountiful and loving Creator, a gift for man's enjoyment and for the fulfillment of his highest welfare and happiness.

A major intention of this book is to get behind sexual behavior to sexual being. Behavior builds upon being, and to understand sex is first to understand sexuality. What one *does* is dependent upon what one *is.* The vast majority of books on this subject might be classified as behavioral studies —*doing sex.* In Christian terms, ethics builds upon theology. And any understanding of what is functional about man must be incorporated within a view of man's total being. If evangelical Christians have suffered from a cultural deprivation in their understanding of sexuality, they have suffered a like deprivation in their theological understanding. Thankfully, there is surfacing within the Christian church a new breed of theologians and ethicists who see man in holistic and relational terms. They are attaching entirely new values to man's sexuality as God's gift. We celebrate their presence in the church and welcome their company in the ongoing theological investigation. Too long has the church been building retaining walls when it was called to build bridges. And it is all too true that Christian writers have largely majored in moral warnings, neglecting to present sexuality in positive, self-affirming terms. But before we yield too much too quickly to the social critics of the church's teaching, let us remember that the insights of psychology and sociology are of recent refinement, even as the medical aspects of sexuality are a matter of relatively recent knowledge. While the church was in poor company with the philosophers and medical men and moralists of the past, today the church is in good company with the psychologists and sociologists whose work casts light upon the subjects at hand.

It is within the new tradition which is combining faith and learning that this book seeks to make a contribution. Its aim is to fill the need for a semitechnical book oriented toward theological ethics, yet readable to the average layman. Ample references and technical notes are supplied at the end for students who wish to pursue the subtopics in greater depth and refer to the primary sources directly.

In view of the church's largely negative stance in the past, this book is a mild protest and positive restatement. It is also meant to be a challenge to the validity of secular ethics. We dare to affirm that *only the informed and committed Christian can truly celebrate his sexuality!* As secular ethics seems obsessed with what man is being freed from, so Christian ethics is concerned with what man is being freed for. If the writer senses his commission rightly, the subject demands a review of the present sex scene in America, a close look at the history of twenty centuries of Christian thought, a theological examination of the chief writers who are ranking theologians, and an attempt to adapt theology to a viable ethical system. Really, ethics is implicit in theology.

In our transition from a traditional society to an open society, the accelerated social change has brought with it a dissolution of religious restraints in society. We live in an era of sexual normlessness—or rather, *anomie*—a plethora of conflicting norms in which none is predominant. Yet, as Harvey Cox points out, sex is one of the last spheres of truly private, intimate, and nonmechanical activity left to modern men and women. It is most painfully evident that the contemporary church has abdicated its role of providing dependable models of sexual identity. Nor does it have an unconfused rationale for what norms it has succeeded in maintaining. Speaking of the church, Cox says, "Until we have developed a model of responsible and joyful sexuality for the modern world, contemporary man will continue to go elsewhere to find his models. . . ."[7] The words of Emil Brunner, written before the Second World War, are even more to the point today:

"The crisis in marriage presents the Christian ethic with the most serious and the most difficult problem with which a Christian ethic has to deal; indeed, in comparison with this problem even the questions of economic and political justice are of secondary importance. For not only are we here dealing with the foundations of human existence, but here too all the ethical problems are condensed into a complex at one point, so that we are compelled to say, what an ethic has to say on *this* question shows whether it has any use or not."[8]

This book is addressed to the college mind first and foremost, as it represents material given in lecture form in the college classroom. The writer can identify quite perfectly with Dr. Robert Osborn of Duke University, who said, "As a member of an undergraduate faculty I cannot escape the impression that, sophisticated as he is, the average undergraduate student is at a loss to give an account of his sexuality." The writer assumes the same stance as Osborn when he adds that "sex is the decisive dimension of existence, and for theology to address itself to this question and make contact at this point is to meet man as man, in the very essence of his humanity."[9] This leads us to a preliminary observation. It may not be apparent to the reader that most Christian books on sex belong to the category of Christian ethics. One generally looks in vain for any substantial biblical theology in such books.

What you are about to read in this book is, first, a history of Christian thought along with an outline of today's sexual milieu. Second, the major chapters are devoted to a biblical theology of sexuality. This is not a book on sex ethics, although ethical considerations are necessarily scattered throughout. And what is the rationale for such an approach? Quite simply this: ethical debate can take one of a number of directions depending upon the theological premises of the debator. Our concern is not with those ethical directions primarily, but with the fundamental teaching of Scripture on the nature and purpose of sexuality. When valid theological foundations are laid, then much of the ethical discussion becomes unnecessary. Where essential agreement is sorely needed today is at the theological level, more so than at the ethical level. This is the distinctive nature of this book within the evangelical enterprise.

We turn, then, to our first concern—setting the stage through examining the sexual mores of the twentieth century in the United States. It becomes immediately apparent that the Christian lives within a particular social milieu. He must understand the secular nature of it for what it is if he is to know the mind of God as to his own individual behavior. He is inescapably a part of a minority group, a *subculture* whose world-view and life-style are often at odds with the secularism surrounding him. An intelligent response to the dominant sex culture demands of him the discipline of thorough study, that his might be an informed response worthy of the One who called him out of this world's darkness into His marvelous light. This requires giving careful attention to the origins and development of Christian thought from biblical times to the present, and then plumbing the depths of biblical understanding.

But enough for the preliminaries; let's get on with our journey. Hopefully, the reader has a taste for history, and will profit from an understanding of the background which makes our theological study a compelling one. For the theological task today is largely a corrective one, and the reader owes it to himself to know just why this is.

Part One

SEX, YESTERDAY AND TODAY

1
Sex Options in Today's Scene

American culture with increasing frequency refers to itself as the "Post-Christian Era." Our society is struggling against a residual Christian sexual tradition, seeking to emancipate itself from a Christian ethic which derives from a theology it does not espouse. It is to be expected that such a society will choose a humanistic ethic—asking what seem to be the best, most acceptable options for individual persons in their own chosen relations of intimacy, with sensitivity as to the congruence of these relationships with the welfare of a changing society. It is in such a context that secular sex ethics are person-oriented, not fixed in any particular tradition of values, and ever seeking viable alternatives to the present.

I was reminded of the premise of today's most popular sex slogan, "Permissiveness With Affection," by a bumper sticker which caught my attention. As a stop signal brought traffic to a halt, I drove up to the rear of a stopped vehicle to note the bumper sticker which read, DON'T GET TOO CLOSE; WE HARDLY KNOW EACH OTHER. The secular rationale for changing sex norms is, however, much more sophisticated. But the contention of this book is that the Christian rationale is also far more sophisticated than it is generally credited with being. As Reuel Howe once sighed, "Thank God there are only two sexes, complicated as things are now!" There are acknowledged legalisms and limitations which the Scriptures impose upon God's people. It is understandable that secular man wishes to discard all such restrictions, especially with regard to his sexual life. It should be equally understandable that the committed Christian turns duty into delight, accepting God's declared will in these respects—not because he is bound by legalisms, but rather because he loves to do the will of the God he knows through Jesus Christ. He also believes that the rationale behind God's declared purposes for him is good and right, whether he fully understands or not.

It is the purpose of this initial chapter to show that we are being confronted today by an amazing potpourri of sexual attitudes, concepts, and life-styles. The secular expression is multifaced. In *Life* magazine you have Derek Wright suggesting correctly that the much-vaunted sexual liberation is turning out to be a new bondage, a tyranny under the authority of the "experts." As he says, "It is so easy to build a prison around a man by convincing him he is a prisoner." And here we might add our own interpretation: young people today are being convinced that they are prisoners of "the old morality," meaning, of course, rigid puritanical codes. We are to hold nothing but contempt for our unknowing, moralizing predecessors. The experts gain our sympathy by saying that sexologists have sought to liberate us in our sexual relationships, but liberation in sex means being able to take it or leave it—and this is not what sexologists mean—hence today's sex addicts and all the new anxieties which have replaced the old ones. But then *Life* exposes a nation of readers to this: "In the first place, we must rid our minds finally of the idea that there are any special moral rules for sexual behavior. Sexual pleasure is never wrong. . . . True sexual liberation occurs when the sexual is dissolved into the fully personal and when sexual ideologies are discarded for the tedious pedantries they are."[1] Those for whom *Life* magazine is the final authority have it unambiguously!

In a somewhat more sophisticated source, this theme is found espoused by John Petras of Central Michigan University in his book *Sexuality in Society:*

"The grand illusion regarding sexuality and morality has been the myth that the two have a causal relationship. This began with the idea that although morality existed independently of sexuality, it could nevertheless define the rightness or wrongness of sexual beliefs, attitudes and behavior. A later myth, still prevalent today, is that which reverses the causal priority and defines morality as the result of sexuality. Much of what is happening today is related to the shattering of this myth and the security that it offered. We are beginning to accept sexuality and morality for what they are—emergent phenomena that reflect our present situations, the ways in which we define our pasts, and the projections we make of ourselves into the future."[2]

If the Christian is to understand the changing view of morality which bids well to dominate our time, he must grasp the modern attitude toward what the sociologist refers to as "deviant behavior." In the early decades of this century social scientists equated deviant behavior with what is morally or socially pathological. This is still the way Christians view such behavior, because for them it represents a deviation from a moral standard which God has set. But social scientists recognize no such moral standard as a universal "given." They see behavior as cultural patterning. Howard Becker, a leading proponent of the new view, says that we ought not to consider deviant behavior as something unique in the sense of depraved action, but simply as behavior which some disapprove and others value. We are to forsake the value orientation and study the various processes by which either or both perspectives emerge and are maintained in society. From this amoral approach there arose those who went further, claiming that deviance may support, not undermine, social order. Among the most eloquent of these advocates is Kai Erikson:

"Deviant behavior . . . may be, in controlled quantities, an important condition for preserving the stability of social life. Deviant forms of behavior, by marking the outer edges of group life, give the inner structure its special character and thus supply the framework within which the people of the group develop an orderly sense of their own cultural identity."[3]

It is from such premises, more and more inculcated in the university setting of America, that young people generally derive their greater toleration of nontraditional forms of sexual behavior. And of one thing Christians must be perfectly clear: from a secular standpoint this reasoning is sound. The Christian, however, belongs to a very special subculture—a subculture with minority status, if you will—and his view of morality, of deviant behavior, of sex ethics is determined from a diametrically opposite position. He sees all things in relation to God their Author, and in respect to the purposes and governing laws which He has determined. There really is no rational middle ground; one takes either the Christian or the secular position.

If one adopts the Christian position—sex ethics determined by the authority of God's revealed purposes and laws—then such behavior as nonmarital sex, whether premarital, mate-swapping, group sex behavior, or simple adultery is wrong. It is proscribed by Scripture and that settles the question. But if one has no such authoritative proscription, then one is plunged into a highly sophisticated realm of social ethics with the attendant responsibility of weighing theories and research data with respect to interpersonal relationships. Granted, this pursuit is most attractive and intriguing. It holds out high promise; it is the way of the humanist. Two illustrations of this latter view will suffice to make the point.

David Pivar, in his history of the Social Purity Movement in the United States, claims that the moral crisis that shook Western civilization in the final decades of the nineteenth century was the development and spread of prostitution. Moralists expressed alarm that this would lead to a general decay in morality. Christians would have been the first to agree. But in 1937 Kingsley Davis published a paper advancing what has come to be known as the "safety-valve" model of deviance. He developed the idea that "the attempt of society to control sexual expression, to tie it to social requirements, especially the attempt to tie it to the durable relation of marriage . . . or to base sexual expression on love, creates the opportunity for prostitution. It is analogous to the black market, which is the illegal but inevitable response to an attempt to fully control the economy. The craving for sexual variety, for perverse satisfaction, for novel and provocative surroundings, for ready and cheap release, for intercourse free from entangling cares and civilized pretense—all can be demanded from the women whose interest lies solely in price."[4]

Another social implication in Davis's argument is that since the prostitute by "virtue" of her profession is, for the most part, excluded from the ranks of potential spouses, the risk of romantic involvement which may threaten a man's marriage is greatly reduced. As we shall see later, this is an approach that Augustine and Aquinas also adopted. It is society providing certain institutionalized outlets for forms of behavior which are condemned by the prevailing moral system. It is regarded as the lesser of two evils, the implication being, as Murray Cohen put it, that otherwise "frustration and discontent may lead to an attack on the rules themselves and on the social institutions they support." Presumably, prostitution in a secular society is supportive of monogamous marriage. Ned Polsky recently claimed pornography to be a functional alternative for similar reasons.

There can be no questioning the fact that in the area of sexual understanding and behavior vast changes are taking place in our day. This is spoken of as the "Sexual Revolution," or the "Sexual Renaissance." What has been written about the changes in theological perspective, however, is the proverbial drop in the bucket, in the sea of secular writing. The result is that most sociologists and psychologists are quite unaware of, as well as out of touch with, the changes in Christian thought in this century. But they are painfully aware of the influence of past Christian thought, and this is their constant target. It is important that we understand this. A few illustrations may help to put it in perspective. We can begin by observing an apparently innocuous statement of Herbert Otto: "It is only with the advent of modern anthropological research and sociological theory that man has recognized his institutions, not as eternal verities, but as defined ways of being social."[5] This says, of course, that marriage is not a divinely ordained institution.

In the same highly respected volume *The Family in Search of a Future*, a liberal theologian says that "from a theological perspective there can be no justification for continued insistence on the forms of marriage and the structure we have inherited. . . . It would be quite possible to meet the demands of Christian theology and Christian ethics with other structures. . . ."[6]

Again, in the same volume Virginia Satir sounds the same note in writing: "The marriage contract in the Western Christian world has no provision for periodic review or socially acceptable means of termination. I would offer that this contract, as it stands, is potentially inhuman and anti-human, and works against the development of love, trust, and connectedness with other human beings. It is made with the apparent assumption that the conditions present at its inception will continue without change for eternity. This asks people to be wiser than they can possibly be. It is made at a time in the lives of the respective parties when they have the least preparation in fact with which to make this contract."[7]

It is interesting to note that the core chapters in this book were presented as part of a symposium at the American Psychological Association's 1967 Annual Meeting. The book I now quote, with its more virulent attacks upon the Christian position, is also a collection of distinguished papers, a number of which were presented to the 1969 annual meeting of the same association. This is not to indict the American Psychological Association, but simply to point out a prevailing mood. The following, then, are illustrative of this mood:

"Before a scientific approach to sex arose, the dominant stance toward sex was a religious one, and, in our culture, it was the Christian religion. This traditional Christian religious stance was, essentially, that sex was bad, a sin (the 'worst' sin, in some eyes), something evil and dirty. Sex, in this view, could (and usually did) lead mankind to hell and damnation. In some religious leaders' views, the sexual act itself was the specific act that led to the downfall of all mankind. . . . Wayland Young has shown that the basic reason sex (or eros) has been denied in our culture can be traced back to the Christian religious scheme. We must, ultimately, reject this whole religious scheme as inert, sanctimonious and obsolete. . . . As Lawrence Lipton has concluded, 'If we are ever to be delivered from the strait-jacket of the Judeo-Christian anti-sexual moral code, it will have to *begin* in the schools. . . . The implication of the foregoing pages is, hopefully, quite clear: the anti-sex values of orthodox Christianity should not be allowed to survive in this age of increased scientific knowledge about sex, which we have attained and are attaining.' "[8]

"Although in this century religion as a social force has lost much of its impact, in many cultures and subcultures religion does still exert a strong influence, primarily on people who have deep needs for approval from the community, people who fear making internal evaluations of their own behavior, or people who rely on rules to maintain impulse control. The religious viewpoint, by and large, claims that the meaning and direction of people's lives is derived from adherence to the tenets of the religion, and most religions then evaluate the individual and judge his morality, worth, and integrity by his performance according to their particular standards. Thus the evaluative processes and life-style do not develop from within the individual but are dictated to him by the religious authority, and the meaning of his life ultimately is not defined by the individual himself. The significance of his life becomes a matter of 'being good' or 'doing the right thing.' In this context there is little room for accepting one's sexuality. . . ."[9]

"And yet most of us have had our consciences on sexual matters solidly molded early in our uncritically childhood states by parents and others who have taken as inexorable truth the limited teachings on sex attributed to such doubtfully qualified behavioral scientists as Saul of Tarsus and Jesus of Nazareth."[10]

One of the tasks of this book is to sort out those criticisms of traditional Christian thought which are legitimate and those which are not. Another task will be to launch our own criticism of those liberal Christian views which concede too much to the new sexuality. But more immediately we need to set the scene for our historical review of Christian thought by tracing, albeit briefly, the attitudes and practices of our American culture since the midpoint of this century. To do this we shall begin with the rise of the Singles' Culture in the past decade. This phenomenon has explosive dimensions, even a new "class" consciousness.

There are over 41 million single adults in the United States. This includes 15.5 million males who have never married and 3.5 million divorced and widowed males. There are 12.5 million females who have never married, but only 1.5 million in the divorced and widowed category. Or one can look at the statistics in this way: 12.7 million single adults are between the ages of 20 and 34—an incredible jump for that age group since 1960. The number of single adults under 35 who have been divorced and have not remarried (1.3 million) is more than double the figure of a decade ago. The accelerating divorce rate is not only dumping hundreds of thousands more into the singles' fold, but they now tend to remain here for longer periods. An enormous percentage of migrants to New York and California are singles, many drawn by a new life-style. For the most part these singles are office workers or professional people. Singlehood has become an attractive end in itself, a life-style built on the premise of living life to its fullest in the most unencumbered way. To many observers it appears as a prolonged phase of postadolescence. But whatever it is called, there is no obscuring the fact that there is today a large singles-oriented society with all that is required to make it self-contained. This potential, of course, could not long have escaped the American entrepreneur—not when the post-Pepsi generation has an annual spending power of some $40 billion! In less than eight years a growth industry has risen, aimed at satisfying the unwed's every need and wish. There are singles' housing complexes, bars, clubs, tours, resort hotels. According to an article in *Newsweek*, while many singles' apartment colonies would vie as "sexual supermarkets," the unchallenged pacesetter is Marina del Rey, south of Santa Monica. In such complexes you will find doctors, lawyers, stewardesses, actresses, writers, secretaries, and accountants living in what has been described as "like a coed dormitory," where the only problem is keeping people *out* of your apartment, never luring them in. And the fact that the West Coast areas of California, Arizona, and Nevada have taken over the "swinging singles" (known as "swingles") role is no coincidence. Hot weather is conducive to less clothing, and this in turn is conducive to the "meet marts" (or, as some call them, "meat marts"), for maximum mingling. Since all of this is part of a rising market, as might be expected the media is providing the seductive imagery to go along with it and sell, sell, sell. As one bar owner put it, "For city dwellers, the bar fills the singles' social vacuum. People don't meet at church anymore."

The enormous amount of sexual hustling at the core of the new singles' life-style may well be, as some assert, an attempt on the part of the economically independent and domestically emancipated to find "wholeness" in singlehood. Certainly, for women today, economic and sexual liberation has diminished the need for the "sacred halo of marriage." In other words, the fruits of the Industrial Age are being spelled out in the new independence of the American woman. She can live her life in segments, each segment offering new options her mother and grandmother never had. The Women's Lib movement of the past decade is having its effect upon the single woman—and, as a college professor I might add, upon the college woman as well. The search for self-identity in particular is a luring quest for the single adult, a quest that seems necessary to many a single person in view of the role-confusion of our time. Dr. Joyce Starr feels that this quest for self-identity may, in the lives of many single women, be placed above the quest for a mate. But when this quest includes free and frequent sex—permissiveness with or without affection—it is trying to have one's cake and eat it, too. No wonder a backlash is evident on the singles' scene —"Sex has gotten so cheap." It all begins to appear empty, contrived, monotonous. It no longer seems to be the real world, the world of promise. As Rosalyn Moran expressed it:

"As one selects a career, so can one select a way of life—a life-style. This too, if unacceptable, can be changed. A single person is a human being with drives and desires like everyone else. Before, he had to sublimate some of these desires in order to conform with society. Today, society has made a place for him, albeit a lesser role for the single female. Now, there is a choice for all. How one chooses is a strictly personal thing; and that, after all, is the way it should be."[11]

But it isn't quite so simple. As *Newsweek* observed,

"The longer that many 'swinging' singles play their roles, the harder it seems to unlearn the script, to break off the quest for new conquests and the conditioned adjustment to a paucity of communication and commitment. . . . Inordinately indulged, prolonged singlehood tends to deaden the emotional and sexual palates, freezing its disciples in a state of suspended adolescence."[12]

So, what do the disillusioned do? What is the next step on the road? This leads us to a second life-style that is gaining popularity on the American scene today, a life-style that is not only appealing to the working single adult, but is attracting college young people by the thousands. It is the alternative that seems to promise the best of two worlds: living together without the benefit of marriage. In the view of many a single adult, this is the way that provides emotional, sexual, and economic benefits without causing either party to feel trapped. It offers a degree of responsible living and loving but without the sticky conditions of a contractual relationship, and certainly without the painful anticipation that a break would involve the divorce court. It is this mode of sexual coupling that we must look at next.

Morton Hunt made the passing remark, "Saint Paul said it is better to marry than to burn; today, feeling the glacial chill of the world we live in, we find it better to marry than to freeze." But many a single young adult is contending that the answer to the glacial chill of the world we live in is simply to find a congenial partner and live together. The basic philosophy is that such relationships are like all friendships; they last only as long as they are valid, as long as the major bonds are need-satisfying. With the changing needs of the young, this is not expected to be a forever thing. The rewards are greater, nonetheless, than living singly, and the pain of breaking up is less than divorcing. Is this not, indeed, a reasonable option? And so far as the sexual dimension is concerned, the attitude supposedly character-istic of enlightened young people today is that sex practices between con-senting adults are no longer the concern of anyone but the individuals involved. In fact, this is expressed by Herbert Otto in his Epilogue to *The Family in Search of a Future:* "If it is admitted that individuals do, in fact, have the right to the 'pursuit of happiness,' so long as they do not infringe upon the rights of others, then it follows logically that alternative marriage and family forms which do not injure others should not only be permitted but encouraged."[13]

Harold Greenwald suggests that because we are becoming a pluralistic society, many individuals within our society may need forms other than state-sanctioned and state-enforced monogamy. It is this kind of reasoning toward which many young people gravitate. They say that if state registra-tion were eliminated, people would stay together for the only reason that makes marriage really viable—because they wanted to. They ask, "How can marriage be fulfilling or authentic to mates or to children when it is maintained by legal fiat, not by the desires of the partners to the relation-ship?" And lastly, we might add, common-law marriage has long been recognized in states like California. This and other considerations have materially reduced the objection of deficient legal standing for the woman. As for the stigma of parenthood, Otto says, "I know of no child whose friends demand that he produce his parent's properly-executed marriage certificate before accepting him as a playmate."

A few at least would agree with Mervyn Cadwallader that "Contemporary marriage is a wretched institution. It spells the end of voluntary affection, of love freely given and joyously received. Beautiful romances are transmuted into dull marriages; eventually the relationship becomes constricting, corrosive, grinding and destructive. The beautiful love affair becomes a bitter contract."[14]

There are not a few college students today who are living as couples without marriage. Their parents grudgingly go along and continue to send the monthly check. For some it is seen as an economic benefit to share resources, and emotionally stabilizing to have a semipermanent relationship during the years when study must take first place. One learns from such couples that the possibility of a break is not so serious a matter, for, as they say, the experience of having lived together will be valuable in preparing them for another such arrangement, or perhaps for marriage itself in time. We who look on must recognize that to a generation exposed to the Norman Mailers, Henry Millers, John O'Haras, and James Baldwins of our time, sexual exclusiveness is no "big deal." In this our whole culture has adequately supported them. Celebrities continually extol and illustrate the virtues of serial monogamy, and repeatedly exclaim, "We have such a beautiful relationship, but we're afraid marriage will spoil it." And in unnumbered instances marriage does indeed seem to "spoil it." In a day when affluence has made life relatively easy for the broad spectrum of the American middle class, there is little attraction in the marital challenge of constant adjustment, accommodation, compromise, and sacrifice. It is the day of instant happiness, not the struggle to grow and achieve. In the devaluation of values and the loss of traditional symbols, the marriage certificate represents for some no more than a scrap of paper. And to make a commitment that reaches into the future is unthinkable to the generation that has grown up to regard all things as tentative. This is the Now Generation for whom "til death do us part" seems but poetic license.

So far as commitment to any religiously authoritative base for the permanence of marriage goes, there are no ultimate authorities anymore. The individual is his own authority in such matters as concern his personal life. Or, if one is to look to parental models for guidance, the observed bickering and brawling, the infidelity and hypocrisy, the convenient living alongside each other when love has long since disappeared—all this causes anxious young adults to seek alternatives with a higher promise. Surely, in an age when man has demonstrated his ability to devise solutions to every imaginable problem on earth and in space, he can innovate alternatives to what appears a failing marital system. In the meantime, the safest thing is just to live together without legal bonds.

Ira Reiss is one prominent investigator who believes that the more permissive code is not indicative of a moral breakdown, but rather that young people are assuming more responsibility for their own behavior. He sees the general permissiveness in the adult cultural environment as largely determinative of how much sexual permissiveness is considered acceptable in a courtship group. "The potential for permissiveness derived from parents' values is a key determinant as to how rapidly, how much, and in what direction a person's premarital sexual standards and behavior change."[15] It is in attitude, he says, rather than in behavior that changes have come. In fact, attitudes and behavior seem closer today than for many generations. And David Riesman was right in pointing out that the responsibility for character formation in our society has shifted from the family to the peer group to the mass-media, peer-group surrogates.

Evidently we've passed the generation of boys and girls who felt they must be swept into sexual experience by something "bigger than both of us," but now we have another kind of problem on our hands. Harvey Cox summarized it concisely:

"Remember also that dating (and with it various types of petting) now reaches down to the sixth grade. Youngsters are thus exposed for a longer period and much more intensely to the mutual exploration of erogenous regions, which is the American courtship pattern. The only advice they get is 'Don't go too far,' and it is usually the girl who is expected to draw the line.

"By the time a girl who begins petting at thirteen has reached marriageable age, she has drawn an awful lot of lines. If she is especially impressed with her religious duty to avoid sexual intercourse, she will probably have mastered, by twenty-one, all the strategems for achieving a kind of sexual climax while simultaneously preventing herself and her partner from crossing the sacrosanct line."[16]

The next alternative to traditional marriage to be considered is that known as trial marriage. This assumes several forms, recent forms being referred to as "contract marriages." Judge Ben Lindsay proposed trial marriage in 1927, the first American to do so. Bertrand Russell, teaching in New York at the time, approved of Lindsay's companionate marriage, and both were ostracized by American culture at that time. It is a sign of today's changing sexual attitudes that Margaret Mead could revive the idea in 1966 without causing a national stir, and others have elaborated on it, making it the focus of marriage discussions in the late sixties. The notable advance in the seventies is the best-selling book *Open Marriage* by George and Nena O'Neill.

It is important that we understand the proposal of Margaret Mead. She envisions two kinds of marriage, individual and parental. Individual marriage would be "a licensed union in which two individuals would be committed to each other as individuals for as long as they wished to remain together, but not as future parents. As the first step in marriage, it would not include having children."[17] Obligations would be ethical, not economic. The legality of the relationship would consist in a "registration" of the union with the civil authorities. Thus, individual marriage would be "a serious commitment, entered into in public, validated and protected by law and, for some, by religion, in which each partner would have a deep and continuing concern for the happiness and well-being of the other."[18] If the individual marriage proved untenable and unfulfilling, the contract allows either partner to terminate the relationship without stigma. In other words, divorce would be easy and nonjudgmental.

The second step, termed "parental marriage," must be preceded by individual marriage; it is this aspect that makes it trial marriage. "Every parental marriage, whether children were born into it or adopted, would necessarily have as background a good individual marriage. The fact of a previous marriage, individual or parental, would not alter this. Every parental marriage, at no matter what stage in life, would have to be preceded by an individual marriage."[19] Parental marriage would anticipate a lifelong relationship, although in the event of failure it may terminate by divorce. Divorce in second-step marriage would be a serious matter, however, and would be subject to legal codes and procedures. Since parental marriage involves a broader scope of responsibilities and commitments, the preceding individual marriage provides a significantly lengthy period of time for the couple to shed unrealistic expectations and romantic idealizations, learn new roles, and gain marital identity and experience.

Mead's rationale is clear. Sex, now considered a normal need in youth, often drove couples into premature and unwise marriage, frequently leading to unhappiness and divorce. Divorce should be granted before any children are conceived, so that only wanted children in stable marriages are brought into the world.

Vance Packard concluded that the first two years of marriage are the critical ones. He recommended a two-year confirmation period, after which the marriage would become final or would be dissolved. A more sophisticated scheme was proposed by philosophy professor Michael Scriven: "We try to make one institution achieve three aims . . . sexual satisfaction, social security, and sensible spawning. The solution would be to create three types of marriage arranged so that any combination would be possible: preliminary, personal, and parental marriage. The first would simply be legitimized cohabitation . . . a prerequisite for other kinds, and would impose a period of a year's trial relationships before the possibility of conversion to personal marriage. . . ."[20]

In "Marriage as a Statutory Five Year Renewable Contract," Virginia Satir, well-known West Coast family therapist, said: "Maybe there needs to be something like an apprentice period . . . in which potential partners have a chance to explore deeply and experiment with their relationship, experience the other and find out whether his fantasy matched the reality. Was it really possible through daily living to have a process in which each was able to enhance the growth of the other, while at the same time enhancing his own? What is it like to have to undertake joint ventures and to be with each other every day? It would seem that in this socially approved context, the chances of greater realness and authenticity continuing would be increased, and the relationship would deepen, since it started on a reality base."[21]

Another variation of the renewable contract was proposed by sociologist Mervyn Cadwallader: "Marriage was not designed to bear the burdens now being asked of it by the urban American middle class. It was an institution that evolved over centuries to meet some very specific needs of a nonindustrial society. . . . Marriage was not designed as a mechanism for providing friendship, erotic experience, romantic love, personal fulfillment. . . . Its purposes . . . have changed radically, yet we cling desperately to the outmoded structure of the past. . . . Why not permit a flexible contract, for one or more years, with periodic options to renew? If a couple grew disenchanted with their life together, they would not feel trapped for life. . . . Instead of a declaration of war, they could simply let their contracts lapse and while still friendly, be free to continue their romantic quest. . . . If the bitter and poisonous denouement of divorce could be avoided by a frank acceptance of short-term marriages, both adults and children would benefit."[22]

How attractive this seems when one's philosophy of life is wholly concerned with personal happiness! Under the guise of increased responsibility, it diminishes responsibility. It utterly fails to recognize that ultimate happiness is something achieved through struggle, through sacrifice, through harvesting the fruit of long-term commitments which cost something. But like any supersell technique, the idea of trial marriage is proposed in all of its theoretically attractive aspects without a balancing list of liabilities. How, for instance, can two people learn trust and experience full complementarity on a temporary basis? If, indeed, marriage is a total commitment, then trial marriage is a contradiction in terms. But the lure of the new, the adventuresome—especially when it includes risks and the rejection of convention—is peculiarly great for the young. Little wonder, really, that *The Harrad Experiment* caught the imagination of college people across the land. In Robert H. Rimmer's novel, college students lived with computer-selected roommates of the opposite sex. Unlike the totally informal arrangements now made by college students on their own, the Harrad Experiment was controlled and guided by a husband-wife team of sociologist and marriage counselor. The essential structure follows Mead's two-step marriage contract theme.[23]

Sociologist John Crosby of Indiana University makes the following prediction: "Trial marriage will probably gain definition and structural form through an evolving process, with innovations along the way, until a cultural pattern is established, much as in earlier eras the betrothal became the accepted pattern, and in more recent times the engagement. What seems to be evolving is an alternative to traditional marriage based on a two-step marital commitment, the first step being a trial relationship unburdened with legal, financial, or child-related matters, and the second step being akin to traditional marital definitions, responsibilities, and patterns. If the legal-ecclesiastical establishments do not endorse this change in marital patterns, or at least seek to deal with it in an honest, forthright manner, the trend will undoubtedly continue without them."[24]

The most widespread nontraditional marital pattern in the United States is permissive monogamy. This is adultery in whatever variation it is found, but it is not considered to be infidelity in some of its forms. It may not have legal sanction, but it is a cultural reality involving vast numbers of Americans. George P. Murdock estimates that only 5 percent of the societies known and studied make no legal provision for sexual intercourse outside of marriage. The United States is among the 5 percent. Clellan Ford and Frank Beach state, in *Patterns of Sexual Behavior*, that less than

16 percent of 185 societies studied by anthropologists had formal restrictions to a single mate, and of these less than a third wholly disapproved pre- or extramarital sexual relations.

It is interesting to see infidelity through the eyes of the unfaithful themselves. This has been researched by Robert Whitehurst, John Cuber, Albert Ellis, Morton Hunt, and others. In general, they agree that perhaps a majority of the unfaithful are not seriously dissatisfied with their marriages or their mates. Perhaps less than a third seek extramarital sex for neurotic motives. Perhaps even a majority do not feel that they, their mates, or their marriages have been harmed. Of course, it is still true, says Hunt, that many a "deceived" husband or wife, learning about his mate's infidelity, feels humiliated, betrayed, and unloved. Many are filled with rage and perhaps a third of all divorces are caused by infidelity. Studies reveal another dark side to this story: more often than not, deceived spouses never learn of their mate's infidelity and the marriage status does not change because of it.

Edward Hobbs, theologian at the Church Divinity School in Berkeley, feels that to expect to find one's sole sexual relationship in marriage is an impossible dream for most married couples. He decries what he feels is the abandoning of the permanence of marriage in order to maintain sexual exclusiveness. He says, "We may seriously ask whether something approaching a reversal of these two attitudes toward marriage might not promote a healthier and happier model for American family structure."[25] In essence, he thinks that we ought to preserve the marital union and permit sexual relationships outside it. In sum: "Marriage would be, as in all societies, the institution whereby men and women are joined for the purpose of founding and maintaining a family; the special kind of dependence, however, would be limited to reproduction of offspring by the couple. Sexual relationships would not be limited to the marriage bond in any special way whatever, except of course that pregnancy control would be utilized at all times . . ."[26]

Crosby's assessment is summed in these words: "Hobbs' stand in favor of familial stability over sexual exclusivity seems to make sense in view of what is known today about child development and the importance of security and love needs. But it must also be asked, what effect does sexual permissiveness have on the solidarity and emotional health of the marriage?"[27]

A second type of permissive monogamy is receiving wide attention with the publication of *Open Marriage* by Nena and George O'Neill. The O'Neills point out that the purpose of open marriage is to achieve a nonpossessive, nonmanipulative, and nonintrusive relationship. Open marriage maintains a mutually satisfying growth relationship. Trust and fidelity are viewed in a nontraditional light. If the partners trust each other to be open and honest in their total relationship with one another, they can give each other the freedom to be a human being instead of a role-performer. Marriage will no longer be built upon role expectations. In such a relationship the traditional vow of fidelity is considered out of place, discarded as part of a closed contract. Freedom to have intimate friendships outside the marriage is an inherent right in open marriage.

The problems in such a relationship are obvious to most social critics, for the initial writing of an open contract is no guarantee that the needs will be met or that negative reactions to such permissiveness are precluded. If it is legitimate to question the value of the traditional marriage contract, it is equally valid to question the effectiveness of an open contract.

Another alternative to traditional monogamy is called *progressive monogamy, serial monogamy,* or sometimes *monogamous polygamy.* This is the common American way of marriage followed by divorce and remarriage. It has both legal and cultural approval. Granted, each relationship may have its own intrinsic value. Nevertheless, the value of a total configuration that is possible in a sustained relationship is often lacking; usually it is recognized as important only when people enter the later stages of the life cycle. And when partners enter into a marriage with the idea that they probably will be married serially through life, then the prospects of forging a strong entity through adjustment and sacrifice diminish materially. Just how immature this can be is illustrated by the cartoon in the *New Yorker* showing a young couple leaving what is evidently the home of a justice of the peace. The bride, dressed in her wedding apparel, turns brightly to her young man and says, "Darling! Our first marriage!"

As a nation, we are playing, as Ethel Alpenfels says, "a gigantic game of marital chairs." One out of four who marry this year will divorce, and three out of four of those will remarry within the next three years. Interestingly, the chances for divorced persons of whatever age to remarry are higher than for any other category. At age thirty, for example, remarriage is more frequent among divorced than among widowed persons, and higher than first marriages for singles. Note this analysis by Morton Hunt:

"Divorcing people, however, are seeking not to escape from marriage for the rest of their lives but to exchange unhappy or boring marriages for satisfying ones. Whatever bitter things they say at the time of divorce, the vast majority do remarry, most of their second marriages lasting the rest of their lives; even those whose second marriages fail are very likely to divorce and remarry again and that failing, yet again. Divorcing people are actually marrying people, and divorce is not a negation of marriage, but a workable cross between traditional monogamy and multiple marriages. . . . Despite its cost and its hardships, divorce is thus a compromise between the monogamous ideal and the realities of present-day life."[28]

The great value of marriage—and its chief risk—is that marriage remains one of the few human institutions in which personal autonomy can function and in which the individual still has a sense of personal choice. In this light, sociologists tend to view progressive monogamy as an alternative in the face of cultural disaster. As with every other alternative, the Christian must ask deeper questions as one who seeks above all else the will and purpose of God.

A relatively minor phenomenon in America is group marriage, which seems always to have existed during man's history. What little is known about them suggests that group marriages do not remain viable for any considerable length of time, but keep breaking up for one reason or another, with some members who are devoted to this ideal seeking to found other group marriage arrangements. Albert Ellis has quite thoroughly outlined the positive and negative features of this form of marriage, expressing doubt that there is much future for it.[29]

Is it true that "the family that swings together clings together"? The term *swinging* refers to mate-swapping, or, as it currently is called, *co-marital sex*. This is a phenomenon that has gained an incredible number of adherents in recent decades. Researchers believe that it has followed in the wake of the growing understanding that women experience sexual desire as strongly as men and want to have that desire satisfied. The current conception of female sexuality coupled with the greater opportunity for women to pursue sex without unwanted pregnancies, seems to have opened a new era in the active movement of women toward sexual variety outside marriage. Interestingly, mate-swapping appeals to some couples as the least threatening relationship and the one most compatible with monogamy because the sexual activity that takes place is fully known to both partners. There are no subterfuges, each exercising surveillance over the extramarital activity of the other. There is an atmosphere of mutual approval and control, and so the danger that the sexual relationship will become a romantic involvement is minimized. This, of course, is facilitated by the brief and segmented nature of the encounter.

The definition of Carolyn Symonds is the best: Swinging is a husband and wife's "willingness to swap sexual partners with a couple with whom they are not acquainted and/or to go to a swinging party and be willing for both he and his mate to have sexual intercourse with strangers." It is a husband-wife activity—sexual togetherness, if you will!—but with the added twist that it enhances their own sexual interest in each other.

In a study made by Duane Denfeld and Michael Gordon, swingers who advertise and attend swinging parties do not conform to the usual image of the deviant. They have higher levels of education than the general population, and are disproportionately found in the professions and white-collar occupations. They tend to be generally conservative. The study made by James and Lynn Smith found religious affiliation to be quite low, with 56 percent of the respondents claiming no religious affiliation. Some 92 percent reported a history of premarital intercourse, certainly significant to their later sexual freedom. A total of 76 percent reported that they had witnessed or observed the sexual activities of others present, particularly their own mates. Sixty-four percent reported engaging in private heterosexual intercourse at parties, while 57 percent reported engaging in public intercourse. Fifty-two percent reported engaging in what they perceived to be group sex—an orgy involving many, either one at a time, or, as they call it, a "daisy chain."

The research team of William and Jerrye Breedlove estimate that roughly eight million couples have at one time or another exchanged partners, while between two and three million couples exchange partners on a somewhat regular basis, that is, three or more times a year. The swinging club magazine market has over fifty national publications. A recent issue of *Select* shows 3,500 advertisements of couples seeking exchanges. Part of the excitement is the discretion which must carefully hide the activity from family, friends, and business associates. Part of the adventure is traveling some distances to meet a new couple. So apparently it is true that for a certain type of culturally-conditioned American couple, to swing together is to cling together. Sex is regarded as something other than the deepest aspect of their own interpersonal complementarity, the basis and nourishment of a unique union. In this respect, of course, swinging strikes at the very heart of the Christian concept of sexuality and marriage.

The rationale begins at a different point altogether from either God's purpose or His law. Rather, it is expressed in the question, "Why should a married couple express the entirety of their recreational and erotic lives exclusively toward each other?" The premise is clear; swinging has to do only with recreational and erotic aspects of sex. It represents the new attitude which accepts the moral and practical propriety of a variety of sexual life-styles. As John Cuber analyzes it, there is a difference between someone who breaks the rules and someone who does not accept the rules: one is a transgressor, the other is a revolutionary. Many contemporary college students look upon themselves as revolutionaries, and thus sexual activity is no longer in the realm of morality. Morality for them has more to do with social justice, exploitation of the environment, and business ethics. Leave sex to the individual, they say; if that's their thing, live and let live. Anyway, who has the authority to make value judgments about other people's personal relationships? Thus the secular argument builds its mighty edifice.

The heart of the issue is expressed by Lester Kirkendall, who says that nonmarital sexual relations have become more acceptable if entered in a responsible manner, and contained within a relationship characterized by integrity and mutual concern. The shift is from an emphasis upon an act —as in traditional ethics—to emphasis upon the quality of interpersonal relationships. Kirkendall cites liberal religious leaders as providing the most striking illustration of this change. We shall undertake an examination of these views in a later chapter when the new morality shall come under consideration. In anticipation of this, and for those who may not be familiar with situation ethics, one illustration of this point of view will suffice for the present. John A. T. Robinson, Bishop of Woolwich, asserts:

". . . nothing can of itself always be labelled 'wrong.' One cannot, for instance, start from the position 'sex relations before marriage' or 'divorce' are wrong or sinful in themselves. They may be in ninety-nine cases or even one hundred cases out of one hundred, but they are not intrinsically so, for the only intrinsic evil is lack of love."[30]

In some quarters, sex is looked upon as a new art form. It is the way to improved sensitivity, to personal identity. The change in attitude is expressed by Herbert Otto who points out that it has taken over a hundred years since the bed sheet came into general usage to change this companion of our most intimate moments from sterile white, where every spot pointed to the user's "dirtiness," to today's sheets of brilliant colors and patterns so beautiful we can fantasize ourselves lying amidst fields of flowers. How far our culture has moved can also be illustrated by pointing out two simple facts: As late as 1937 it took tremendous pressure for the surgeon general of the United States to win the right to use the term "venereal disease" on the radio. In 1970, less than thirty-five years later, sex play and actual copulation between men and women were staged in a number of "legitimate" bars, nightclubs and theaters, in Los Angeles and New York City, while topless and bottomless waitresses adorned many an establishment whose primary business was selling food. There is indeed a sexual revolution —a revolution in overtness.

Attitudes were once reflective of the church's authority and voice in national life, but not now. The attitude-makers employ the media, and what shapes national attitudes is good for business. Sex is the biggest business of the century. Having turned sex into a commodity, countless entrepreneurs are taking enormous profits.

But the current sex boom represents something very different from what twentieth-century philosophers had in mind. Instead of liberating man from taboos and unrealistic conventions, the involvement of Eros in consumer-goods fetishism has produced a new alienation. Contraceptive know-how has resulted in the divorce of sex from responsibility toward both the individual and society. A further unexpected consequence of contraceptive know-how is that women have a kind of freedom formerly enjoyed only by men. Like men, women can now channel feminine aggression into the sexual sphere, where it can be used as a weapon. Sex thus becomes a ruthless form of mutual aggression.[31]

The sexual reality of our culture is replete with improvisations and potentials little dreamed of in past generations. It is hardly news when an elderly film producer tells journalists that girls over eighteen no longer interest him, when male TV and movie personalities marry girls younger than their own daughters by previous marriages, enjoy them for a while, and then get divorces and begin all over again. The Lolita complex denotes man's boredom with women of his own age, his retreat from woman as a life companion, his obsession with the media's image of the girlish playmate.

Another consequence of absolute sexual freedom is the increasing demand for the sanctioning of homosexuality. This fits into the formula that says that whatever consenting adults do in the privacy of their own lives is beyond moral judgment and is not to be repressed by society.

Substantial reforms have recently been enacted in Britain and Germany with reference to the laws against homosexuals.

Now, it is true, of course, that among the ancient Greeks, particularly the Spartans, homosexuality was firmly anchored in the culture. But we must remember that there pederasty served the interests of militarism. In that male-dominated society, where children were taken from their mothers at the age of seven, education consisted almost entirely of preparation for military service. Men lived, not with their families, but in tent communities—eating, sleeping, and exercising together. The male sex was considered the beautiful sex, and an adolescent boy's goal was to find favor with an older male lover. Even so-called platonic love, far from being "platonic" in the contemporary sense, was a philosophical idealization of sexual relationships between men. This is what Plato had in mind when he wrote in the *Republic:*

"If it were possible for a whole state or a whole army camp to consist of lovers and their favorites, no better community could possibly be imagined, because out of consideration for one another they would abstain from every bad vice and continually vie with each other in noble competition. When it came to battle they would triumph over every adversary even if they were outnumbered. For a lover would rather the whole world should see him running away than that his beloved should."

While the debate continues as to the origin and development of homosexuality, the vast majority of cases are thought to be psychogenic in origin—at an early stage of psychosexual maturation, the object-orientation of the sex impulse becomes fixed at the like-sex level, for any number of possible causes. Homosexuality, in this view, is a learned defect.

Certainly the cry for absolute sexual freedom, and the fact that sex is one route of social protest in our time, has a destabilizing effect and leads to the demand that all variations from the norm be accepted. Abram Kardiner is among those who see the more taxing demands upon men in professional life as making it more difficult for men to assert their masculinity successfully. The sexual competition of emancipated women intensifies the situation in which men feel themselves sexually inadequate. Homosexuality is sometimes a consequence of the flight of men from women, the fear of the masculine role. Be this as it may, there are societal complications arising from the overt homosexuality in the alienated culture of twentieth-century America. One of the more bizarre manifestations is the homosexual church, found in many cities under the designation "Metropolitan Community Church." The Christian protest may be summed up for the present by simply saying that the full biblical requirement is for a sexual relation that is complementary in the fullest sense—and this requires heterosexual marriage union as God designed the sexes to fulfill.[32]

Jessie Bernard, distinguished researcher in the field of marriage and family for over forty years and respected analyst of sociological trends, believes that the future of marriage is as assured as any human social form can be, that men and women will always want intimacy and the many ways in which they can share and reassure one another. But she distinctly sees the future as one of marital options; the real question being, not the future of marriage, but the marriage of the future. No one kind of marriage will be required of everyone, because there will be a full recognition of the enormous difference among human beings which modern life demands and produces.[33]

Freud came out on the side of Saint Paul in his sexual conservatism in personal life, and also in his view of the restriction of sexual activity. He writes, in *Civilization and Its Discontents,* that we have to restrict sexual activity in order to get people to work. Freud said that civilization is built up on renunciation of instinctual gratification. He insisted that restrictions on sexual life are among the reinforcements the culture needs in order to erect barriers against the aggressive instincts of men. Well, of course, Freud was arguing from the perspective of the development of industrialism. Today, Herbert Marcuse challenges this position. In *Eros and Civilization* he points out that the inevitable decline in the need for work in modern societies renders Freud's identification of civilization with sexual repression invalid. He concludes that work relations actually would be improved rather than impeded by freer instinctual relations. In a somewhat different frame of reference, Aldous Huxley, in his *Brave New World,* sees sexual freedom as obligatory. He says that as political and economic freedom diminishes, sexual freedom tends to increase.

Jessie Bernard does not see any intrinsic limits to the forms of marriage either in human nature, or in the nature of society itself, but more from the nature of changing cultural configurations. As far as human nature is concerned, men and women have demonstrated that they can accept any kind of relationship if properly socialized into it. Almost every kind of relationship has occurred somewhere at some time—monogamy, polygyny, polyandry, exogamy, endogamy, arranged marriages, self-selection of mates, and the like. All these variations seemed quite natural to those who lived in them. Edward Westermarck opted for monogamy in the nineteenth century on the basis of male jealousy. But Kingsley Davis argued just the opposite on the same grounds: for him, monogamy produced jealousy, not jealousy monogamy. This, we saw, was the point of view and the claimed experience of the swinging mate-exchangers. And this is expressed in such novels as John Updike's *Couples.*

The Christian recognizes that God did not place the ultimate good of monogamy within the confines of human nature, but in the dictates of His own will and purpose. This involves a decision and a commitment which are not relevant to the non-Christian. Any commitment, however desirable, imposes restraints and conflicts. Human beings make incompatible demands on life—for freedom, adventure, excitement on the one hand, and for security and stability and intimacy on the other. They cannot have it both ways. Marriage, in whatever form it takes, is always a compromise between conflicting impulses. Some will choose one form of marital commitment over another simply because they find the cost of another type of commitment too high. Modern life offers these options. But for the Christian it is basic above all things to accept the forms of life which God the Creator and Ruler asks of His redeemed own if they are first and foremost to live out their commitment to Him.

We will continue to see that the changing nature of cultural patterns have their direct effect upon marriage forms. Sociologist William J. Goode has shown that, with industrialization, marriage in all parts of the world tends to converge toward the form that prevails in the industrialized West. But as the technological innovations that created the Industrial Revolution had to do with production, they have to do now with consumption. As this particularly affects the role of women, so the institution of marriage is similarly affected. Women are no longer restricted to the domestic role. In every conceivable way their lives have been emancipated by the advances of technology. Thus, as Bernard concludes, the forms of marriage will be as much related to technology in the future as to either human nature or the nature of society. The Christian can agree with her estimate that no amount of tinkering with the social system can overcome the inherent contradictions involved in marriage itself. Even if we could eliminate all the extrinsic barriers to happiness, marriage would still fall far short of perpetual bliss. God never intended that marriage be everything to all people. Nor will modern libertines find all satisfaction in sexual license.

Enlightened Christians can affirm the biblical premise that sex was made for man, not man for sex, whereas contemporary society has reversed this to read that man was made for sex. For many moderns it is enough that sex is reciprocal, not complementary in the fullest possible sense that God created and intended. And herein lies the challenge to evangelical Christians. Has God His own purposes for sex? Has He indeed set laws to conform the expression of sex to His purposes? Is there a primary responsibility to divine law and a secondary sensitivity to situational demands? Is there an unambiguous scriptural way acceptable to committed Christians?

We have tracked the sexual milieu in which Christians find themselves today. There are competing ideologies, humanistically attractive and logical within the confines of secular life. Only a convincing theology can inform a Christian ethic, and that is the challenge of this book. And before we can undertake the theological and ethical task, it is necessary to get some historical perspective. After all, the Christian church has spoken on these matters for twenty centuries. What it has said is hardly a positive, affirming word. But if we are to be thorough in our pursuit of what is truly biblical, then we cannot evade the painful distortions of history.

2

Don't Blame the Puritans!

Ashley Montagu, in *Man Observed*, tells the delightful story of the Bishop of Worcester who, upon returning from the Oxford meeting of the British Association in 1860, informed his wife at tea that the horrid Professor Huxley had declared that man was descended from the apes. Whereupon the dear lady exclaimed, "Descended from the apes! Let us hope it is not true! But if it is, let us pray it will not become generally known!"

The history of Christian thought on the subject of sexuality is a long, dark journey. The story, while at best intriguing, at worst is downright dismal. Contemporary young minds must find it incredulous. Prior to the beginning of our own century it cannot be termed in any true sense positive. In imagination we might recast Montagu's story, placing it in the ecclesiastical setting of the fifth century of the Christian era. There we can see a local cleric returning from a solemn assembly to report to a fellow monastic (he would not likely have had a wife to report to): "Dear brother, I hate to so say, but that controversial Bishop of Hippo, Augustine himself, declared to our solemn assembly that man is a sexual being." Whereupon the fellow cleric, duly taken aback, exclaimed, "Man a sexual being! Do pray God it is not true! But if it is, let us earnestly beseech heaven that it will not become generally known!"

The story must be told if only to see how far Christian thought has progressed in our century. Unfortunately, Christian leaders have for the most part had no exposure to this history in their formal training, and the only thorough treatise, written in 1959, is out of print.[1] If nothing else, the reader should no longer blame the Puritans for the climate of sexual thought which prevailed until early in our century.

In the preface to *The Nature and Destiny of Man*, Reinhold Niebuhr reflects: "There are resources in the Christian faith for an understanding of human nature which have been lost in modern culture." However, these resources necessarily had a limited utility in prescientific ages. The understanding of the human body and its functions that prevailed in the early centuries of the Christian era, the superstitions concerning sexuality and procreation—these influences were bound to shape the thinking of early Christian theologians. And what they as individuals brought to the subject out of their own experiences was equally significant. Greek dualism and the competing Hellenistic philosophies show their impact. The resources of the Christian faith remain unchanged, indicative of their divine origin, but the ability to utilize them adequately has paralleled advances in the sciences and humanities. And this is no different from what we should expect. Prescientific cultures saw human nature—sexuality in particular—through a glass darkly.

It is with these considerations in mind that we can appreciate the attacks made in recent times upon the Christian tradition with respect to its teaching on sexuality. Those attacks are not without grounds. However, it is only fair to say that the Christian tradition must not be made to carry the whole responsibility. For this reason the present chapter outlining the Christian tradition in the Western world over the past twenty centuries is followed by a glimpse at the parallel philosophical development. We must keep in mind that a mature theological ethic has been coming of age only within the past century.

The early Christians inherited from the Jews a rigorous condemnation of sexual irregularity. In earlier times this was penalized only when it infringed on a husband's property-right in his wife or, by contaminating a virgin, reduced her chances of matrimony and obliged her father to be content with a smaller bride price. The dominance of the procreative motif in Hebrew sexual thought was doubtless partly responsible for the fact that the common Jewish view of woman seems to have risen but little above the low estimation of most Eastern peoples. The woman was respected, however, and her life was not as servile as that of her Greek or Roman counterpart. The Jewish sexual ethic and conception of marriage, despite limitations, were never surpassed in antiquity by those of any other culture.

As with the Jews, so with both Greeks and Romans, the declared purpose of marriage was procreation, the production of legitimate offspring for the service of the state. To this end laws enforced a formal monogamy, while custom sanctioned a double standard of morality which encouraged male promiscuity. The sexual ethic of the Hellenistic world contrasted strongly with that of Judaism, the Greeks displaying a certain insensibility to the notion of moral purity in sexual matters. The baser elements of Greek sexual life made their way into Roman society to undermine earlier Roman tradition. Yet, against the moral laxity, the philosophies of the age proclaimed an ascetic ideal which inclined toward mortification of the flesh. This was chiefly the product of a pessimism which abandoned the realm of the material as the irreclaimable domain of evil. The Cynics interpreted their master, Diogenes, as repudiating marriage and family life. This was true of Stoicism as well. Neo-Pythagoreanism inclined toward a dualism which regarded coitus as a defilement calling for continence. This rigorist strain, both in the noblest speculative thought and in the more popular mystery cults, created an atmosphere conducive to the development of asceticism within Christianity, an asceticism markedly sexual in its empha- sis. Along with this was the revulsion from the immorality of the times which called forth the denunciations of the church. The Christians were children of their times as they shared many of the assumptions and atti- tudes universally current in antiquity. From the teaching of Jesus on mar- riage, however, asceticism is almost wholly absent. In the saying concerning those who "made themselves eunuchs for the kingdom of heaven's sake," (Matthew 19:12 KJV), Jesus merely gives validity to the fact that the service of God may demand, in some instances, a self-imposed continence. Our Lord's choice of the single life as a necessary condition for the fulfillment of His messianic vocation likewise led to early, false impressions. Paul, too, does not conceal his own preference for the single state, although his commendation of it is "by reason of the present distress" (see 1 Corinthians 7:26), and because it is less a hindrance to the service of the Lord. In one passage, he represents marriage as a concession to human frailty—a means whereby those not endowed with the gift of continence can avoid the sin of fornication. Still, he does commend wedlock and disapproves ascetic practices save when devotion may be thought to require a brief period of abstinence. The married are forbidden to defraud one another of the coitus which is their due, and are reminded that they have conceded to each other the power over their own bodies. In his Epistle to the Ephesians, Paul exalts marriage as the symbol of the relation between Christ and the church. There he makes no mention whatever of its negative utility in providing relief for incontinence. Paul certainly did not accept the pessimistic dual- ism of Hellenistic philosophy.

The early church did not inherit from the apostle any comprehensive or systematic treatment of sexual matters. Even the seventh chapter of First

Corinthians, so often misunderstood as a definitive statement of the apostle's position, is simply a collection of answers to questions of the church at Corinth, designed to give guidance for specific matters relevant at the time. Paul does not go beyond the scope of these questions, and in places distinguishes between the commands of the Lord and his own opinions. He is concerned to counsel these unstable Greek converts in the most immoral city of antiquity. It is futile to seek in this chapter for any exposition of a complete Pauline theology of sexuality and marriage. The early church, however, seemed to dwell more on Paul's counsel to the Corinthians than to the exalted passage on marriage in the Epistle to the Ephesians. One can see how easily a tension could develop in the early church between those who reveled in the new liberty proclaimed in Christ and the rigorists who saw only evil in sexual behavior.

From New Testament times on, a tradition emerged from such individual thinkers as Saint Augustine, Thomas Aquinas, and Martin Luther, among others. In assessing each of these Christian theologians, the philosophical setting of their time is important. In general, Augustine, who was the first major thinker to relate Christian doctrine to philosophical thought, had his roots in Platonic philosophy. Aquinas, also joining the ideas of Scripture with Greek thought, reflects a Christian interpretation of Aristotle. Thus these monumental thinkers represent two benchmarks of the Christian tradition which must be evaluated according to their times and within the philosophical setting unique to each.

Augustine was specifically concerned with the moral aspect of sex, as were Aquinas and Luther in their time. The concept of sin—both original sin and the particular sins which man commits—caused these thinkers, perhaps with undue stress, to concentrate upon the distinction between moral and immoral forms of sexual behavior. Augustine was troubled that the sexual act, performed within marriage and hence licit, and performed for the purpose of procreation as God appointed, nonetheless depends upon lust (or "the strivings of obscene heat"). For though Christian morality involves controlling one's bodily appetites through one's will, and though the Christian can thus resist the temptations to illicit sexual relations toward which his bodily appetites may incline him, yet he must submit to those lusts if he is to engage in sexual action in its licit form—the having of children in marriage. The true Christian, says Augustine, "would prefer to beget children without this kind of lust." This irreducible element of lust in the sex act, and hence in the very continuation of the species, is viewed by Augustine as part of original sin. With the focus of attention upon such problems as these, it is hardly to be expected that Augustine could devote attention to the positive relational aspects of sexual behavior. It is equally appropriate, within the context of psychological and philosophical systems of our day, that Christian tradition now places full emphasis upon that relational aspect.

Thomas Aquinas quite largely provides the intellectual basis for the doctrines of the Catholic faith. From a much different historical and cultural period, he writes about the problem of man's sexuality with emphasis upon man's relationship to God. Central to the doctrine of Aquinas are such prevailing ideas in modern Catholicism as: (1) sexual intercourse should only be engaged in for the purpose of procreation and not simply for pleasure; (2) contraception by artificial means is sinful and not to be engaged in.

Contemporary writers seeking to present a clear and cogent view of the nature of sexual relationship in the light of the Scriptures are called upon to undertake a radical reconsideration of the church's long tradition. Sherwin Bailey suggests the position to be taken: "Study of the tradition demands an exercise of the historical imagination that is sympathetic as well as critical; sometimes what is branded as obscurantism or bigotry is simply a reflection of a climate of ideas wholly alien from that of our own time."[2]

Even as the Scriptures present no comprehensive and systematic theology of sexual relation, neither did the early church. What did emerge was a tradition which was consolidated by the end of the fifth century, modified somewhat by the Schoolmen of the Middle Ages, modified again in a few essentials by the Reformers in the sixteenth century, and rather uncritically held until early in the twentieth century. It is the temptation of social critics to fix the Christian tradition by exhuming the views of Augustine in the fifth century, Aquinas in the thirteenth, or Martin Luther in the sixteenth century. But this ignores the later progress of thought, especially that of such twentieth-century theologians as Karl Barth, Emil Brunner, and Helmut Thielicke. To apply the critical insights of our time to the theology and ethics of antiquity is inappropriate. There is much in that tradition which contemporary theologians reject. The remarkable feature of the emerging Christian tradition is that the earliest voice of the church is the Word of God. Its relevance to modern formulations commands our fullest consideration.

It must be kept in mind that the early church was comprised of three human strands: Jews, Greeks, and Romans. This is particularly important in terms of the cultural inheritance of the Christian church. In antiquity, the Jewish sexual ethic and conception of marriage was rooted in the Old Testament. Hellenistic thought, however, was perhaps even more dominant, for Greek philosophy was by that time highly developed. There existed, too, the cultural milieu of the Greeks and Romans against which the church reacted. Thus, both directly and indirectly, the combined forces of tradition and social environment played a significant part in molding the sexual thought of the church.

It was the pessimistic Greek dualism, setting the material and spiritual in opposition, which formed the basis for the Christian understanding of human nature. It is well that we recognize the dependence of early Christian theologians upon Platonic and Aristotelian categories, the strength of long-standing and universally held tradition, and the cultural conditioning from which later Christian thinkers have had to extricate themselves. A comparable process is not to be found in the other sciences which concern themselves with the understanding of human sexuality. Sherwin Bailey provides an excellent summary:

"But the Christian sexual tradition, though it owed something to both its Jewish heritage and the influence of Hellenistic asceticism, did not originate merely in a synthesis of elements drawn from these two sources alone. In the writings of the New Testament, distinctive as well as familiar features can already be discerned. Jesus himself did not, of course, proclaim any new sexual ethic as such, and any apparent novelty in his teaching upon sexual matters is due largely to its contrast with the prevailing spirit and practice of the time."[3]

As Bailey points out, in His condemnation of infidelity, Jesus implicitly disclaimed any intention to innovate, recalling His hearers to the first principles of sex and sexual relation set forth in the orders of Creation: "On the other hand, his insistence upon the paramount obligations of love and forgiveness had profound implications in the sexual realm, as men and women began to discover when they exchanged the bondage of the Jewish Law for the freedom of the Spirit, or when they stepped from the darkness of paganism into the light of the kingdom of Righteousness. However imperfectly they grasped them, however ineffectually they put them into practice, Christians recognized from the first that certain sexual truths belonged to the Gospel—the spiritual equality of man and woman in the sight of God, the high theological significance of marriage, the impartial

application of the rule of chastity to both sexes."[4] His concluding statement is equally worthy of quotation: "Thus the original element in the
Christian sexual tradition consisted, not in any novel code of morals or
behavior, but rather in a different and higher conception of Man than that
taught even by the philosophies—and above all, in the conviction that the
new life offered to men and women in Christ through the power of the
Holy Spirit was able to transform and redeem both persons and institutions."[5]

One looks in vain among the early church fathers for a controversy in
which a thorough examination of Christian sexual thought might appear.
For the most part, theoretical analysis yielded to the urgency of more
practical issues.

Through the influence of Greek dualism, and the misreading of several
of Paul's statements, virginity came to be equated with a more spiritual life
and hence to be preferred above marriage. This exaltation of virginity, as
Bailey comments, is one of the regrettable legacies of the Patristic Age.
Inevitably, by the end of the fifth century, celibacy was enforced upon the
clergy in the Western church, for from them a higher life was expected.
Marriage, relegated to secondary status, was more concession than commendation. The negative factor derived from Paul's declaration, "It is
better to marry than to burn with passion" (see 1 Corinthians 7:9). Marriage, at best, legitimized sexual desire, providing the necessary context for
procreation and subsequent child-rearing. Sexual intercourse was perceived
more as a bodily function than an expression of personal relation. Since the
same act was performed in marital intercourse as in fornication, intercourse
became intrinsically evil.[6]

In the first five centuries, the church's interest in sexuality was occa-
sional, limited, and more of a practical than a theoretical nature. But the
rigorist tendency, strongly noted in the Apostle Paul, came to full development during the Patristic Age in an asceticism which sought, much like its
Hellenistic counterparts, to attain perfection through renunciation of the
world and subjection of the body. To this end every means was employed
—fasting, prayer, solitude, mortification; but always the decisive test was
that of sexual continence. Origen, greatest of the Hellenistic theologians,
had a theory of the Fall in which the serpent is represented as having
seduced Eve and having physically infected her, a theory in which original
sin is defined as an inclination to "wantonness." As a consequence, Origen
consistently regarded all sex activity as inherently wrong and as the ground
of all actual sins. So with its first theologian, the church got off to a bad

start in its conceptualization of the sexual relation.

The cult of virginity came early. To Christians who felt called to a "higher" life, a special standard was set, the chief feature of which was abstention from coitus and even from all forms of association with members of the opposite sex. Little surprise, therefore, that Patristic literature devotes space to a vindication of celibacy against marriage, and of widowhood against remarriage. Yet marriage had been instituted and blessed by God and sanctified by Christ, therefore it could not be treated as something impure or evil. Still, Tertullian voiced the opinion of the early church when he declared, "We do not reject marriage, but simply refrain from it."

John Chrysostom maintained that the wedded state is not per se an obstacle to salvation or to the performance of religious duties. Yet he could not regard it as the perfect state, for it hinders the freest possible service to God. In this view Ambrose concurred. Methodius allowed that those who had lived chastely with their wives and had refrained from excessive embraces would not be denied entrance to the marriage feast of the Lamb.

While the fathers did not yield to the dualism which denounced marriage as intrinsically evil, they continued to regard marriage as a concession to the inordinate desires of fallen humanity and as a refuge for those weaker souls who could not bear the discipline of celibacy. Because the end of the age drew near, as they presumed, marriage was no longer necessary for the increase of the race, and it served now to provide sinful man with a remedy against concupiscence. Indeed, John Chrysostom seems to have regarded this as its principal purpose.

Gregory of Nyssa dismisses marriage as a "sad tragedy." Jerome (noted translator who gave the church the Latin Vulgate Bible) praised it solely because it produces virgins! More facetiously, Jerome conceded: "I do not condemn wedlock. Indeed, I should like everyone to take a wife who cannot manage to sleep alone because he gets frightened at night." Ambrose considered marriage "a galling burden," bidding his brethren reflect upon the oppressive bondage into which wedded love too often degenerates. Clement of Alexandria was more moderate. While allowing that celibacy was the way of higher merit, he commended marriage as best suited to the majority of men. He argued that it offered better opportunities than virginity for attaining perfection, because it involved greater temptations and therefore more occasion for the exercise of self-discipline. He also suggested that avoidance of wedlock might in some cases proceed from cowardice rather than love of continence.

It was left to Augustine to compose the treatise *De bono conjugali*, defending the view that virginity did not require for its justification any denunciation of marriage. Meanwhile, in Rome, Siricius was the first pope who attempted to invoke apostolic authority to prohibit all married presbyters and deacons from coitus with their wives. Given this developing attitude in the church, a rule of celibacy was only a matter of time. In the East, custom established from earliest times what later became canon law—namely, that while a married man might proceed to ordination, an ordained man might not proceed to marriage. Presumably, behind this practice lay the principle of 1 Corinthians 7:17-24. In A.D. 325, at the Council of Nicea, an absolute rule of clerical celibacy was rejected, but the mood was alarmingly favorable. The Council of Trullo in 692 established a modified version of the custom enabling a lawfully married man to become a deacon or priest. But the church did not sanction the marriage of a man who, prior to ordination, gave notice of his intention to marry. Furthermore, the wife of a man advanced to the episcopacy was required to separate from him and to retire to monastic life.

In the West an attempt was made at the beginning of the fourth century to impose a rule of abstinence upon all bishops, presbyters, deacons, and others employed in the service of the altar. A hundred years later a succession of synods more or less established the principle. Clerics were forbidden to enter second marriages upon the death of a partner, and none who had married widows were admitted to the ministry. The Eastern church imposed a mild penitential discipline upon those who thus remarried: the crowning was omitted from the wedding ceremony, and presbyters were expected to show their ecclesiastical disapproval by refraining from attending the nuptial festivities.

The most remarkable manifestation of sexual asceticism in the early church was the phenomenon of spiritual marriage—the cohabitation of the sexes under conditions of strict continence. A couple might share the same house, perhaps the same room, and sometimes the same bed, yet they conducted themselves as brother and sister. (Presumably Paul's allusion beginning in 1 Corinthians 7:36 and references by Hermas confirmed the great antiquity of the practice.) Spiritual marriage followed several forms. Certain of the desert ascetics were accompanied each by a female hermit who served as a maidservant to the holy man. In a curious reversal, some wealthy young women or widows, having refused marriage and thus acquired the reputation of virginity or continence, sought out clerics to share their homes. In these equivocal relationships the woman played the dominant role, reducing the cleric to anything from house steward to domestic chaplain to spiritual lover. Tertullian, predictably unpredictable, not only approved such marriages but recommended a plurality of spiritual wives! With the passage of time, however, spiritual marriage lost its original character and eventually became an open scandal demanding the discipline of the church. From the beginning of the fourth century onward, councils enacted against the custom, insisting that no women should reside in the houses of the clerics except mothers, sisters, daughters, and other near relatives. In numerous instances action had to be taken against those of the clergy who refused to part with their virgins. The practice only disappeared, however, with the abandonment of asceticism and when clerical concubinage arose in its place to engage the attention of ecclesiastical moralists.

Gnosticism, with its dualistic premise that matter is inherently evil, provided a theoretical justification for sexual asceticism on the ground that marriage and coitus only serve to entrap more souls in the prison house of the body. Continence was a means of mortification to bring the flesh into subjection to the spirit. Both wedlock and procreation were condemned by some Gnostics as the works of Satan. Others simply taught that coitus is a sowing to the flesh from which man reaps corruption. There was, strangely, an antinomian as well as an ascetic tendency in Gnosticism—due to the same contempt for the body, but also to the notion that physical actions are indifferent to the soul. Thus sexual licentiousness became in effect a demonstration of this conviction. If not that, it demonstrated the freedom of the Gnostic from the bondage of the Demiurge, the Evil One who had created all things material.

A certain Hieracas taught that Christ had come to preach absolute continence, and that since His advent no married person could inherit the kingdom of heaven. The Montanists evolved their rigorism in sexual matters from a mistaken striving after perfection and in expectation of the approaching End; theirs was not a reprobation of the body as such. The various apocryphal *Acts* purporting to recount the evangelistic endeavors of the Twelve abound in passages which display an uncompromising rigorism toward every aspect of sexual relation. Extraordinary beatitudes are put into the mouth of Saint Paul in which four of the blessings pronounced are upon those "who keep the flesh chaste, for they shall become the temple of God," or upon the continent, "for unto them shall God speak"; upon those who "possess their wives as though they had them not," etc. The spirit of these apocryphal romances had a popular impact. Even Pelagius,

Bishop of Laodicea, reportedly employed his wedding night in persuading his bride to share with him a life of continence.

While there was no denying that procreation was good in itself, there was nevertheless a general disposition to deplore the means appointed by the Creator to that end. One recalls the remark of Karl Olsson about this general attitude of the fathers: "In them and in many of their followers the love of the Creator often looks like a hatred of his creation." Coitus was regarded on the whole as an unfortunate necessity to which the Christian should descend with regret. The devout man, said Gregory of Nyssa, would not be overly concerned with such "trifling debts of nature." Tertullian assured his wife that none of the improper and voluptuous acts of their wedded life will be resumed in heaven, for God has not prepared things so frivolous and impure for His own. It was for these reasons that there would be no marriage in heaven, in accordance with Jesus' Word, but all would be as the angels. In fact, the genital organs were regarded as an unsightly disfigurement. Moreover, the allusions to Christ's birth of a virgin carry the implication that so holy a birth must of necessity be somehow free of carnal intercourse. This same logic led to the notion, later to become dogma, not only of the perpetual virginity of Mary but also her own Immaculate Conception.

Inevitably, these notions found expression in disciplinary requirements such as prohibition of coitus during penance, while preparing for baptism, and after receiving the Holy Communion. A man was not to enter the church after coitus until he had washed—and then not at once, for his mind was still occupied with lewd feelings of wrong desire and unfit for spiritual things. However, if the act had been performed solely for the purpose of generation, and not for pleasure, he was not to be denied the Communion—provided he had surely made his ablutions.

None of the fathers made a deeper impression upon Christian sexual ideas and attitudes than Tertullian, Jerome, and Augustine. In all three, published confessions invest their teaching with unusual psychological significance. As Bailey points out, all three brought a personal background of experience which colored their attitude toward all things sexual.

Tertullian dwelt somewhat morbidly upon his extravagant sin prior to conversion. He contrasted his former adultery with the continence he now strove to attain in the same flesh. As Bailey notes, "The excesses for which he reproaches himself afford their own explanation of the vehemence with which he repudiates his coital experiences in marriage."[7]

Jerome, who also led a licentious life prior to baptism, deplored the loss of virginity and the sinfulness of his youth. Bailey again takes note: "His extravagant laudation of celibacy and his crude and violent outbursts against marriage, no less than the lascivious thoughts and visions which tormented him in his desert retreat, show that he never succeeded in coming to terms with his own sexuality. Even in the midst of his austerities he burned with desire as the scenes of his student dissipations arose before him, and a feverish imagination filled his cell with bevies of seductive girls. Both his confessions and his controversies proclaim a psychological unfitness to act as a guide in sexual matters, and his influence upon Christian thought in this respect can only be regretted."[8]

Augustine's confessions reveal something of the emotional conflict which accompanied his intellectual and spiritual quest. Conflict arose from his inability either to reject sexuality entirely or to integrate it into his life and thinking. He was one with the spirit of his age in holding that the highest conception of the holy life involved the ideal and discipline of continence. But he was attached to sensual pleasures, and realized that the settlement of his intellectual and spiritual problems depended partly upon a renunciation which eventually had to be made, but which he wished to defer as long as possible. Hence his constant agonizing prayer, "Give me chastity—but not yet."

For thirteen years Augustine pursued his search for a faith that would answer his needs, spiritual and sexual. Meanwhile he acquiesced uneasily to concubinage with the mother of his son Adeodatus. When he was thirty and settled with his mother, a woman of exemplary faith, in Italy, he was persuaded by her to think seriously of marriage. Augustine concluded that the lawful satisfaction of his sexual desires through marriage might pave the way toward the resolution of the intellectual and spiritual problems. A seemingly suitable engagement was arranged, though the wedding had to be put off until the bride reached marriageable age—legally twelve, but in custom fourteen. Meanwhile Augustine sent his mistress back to Africa so that her presence might not deter his marriage plans. But before long he had taken another mistress.

Then one day in the seclusion of the garden, he heard a voice, "Take up and read," and opening a volume of Saint Paul his eyes fell upon the words of Romans 13:13,14, "Not in reveling and drunkenness, not in debauchery and licentiousness, not in quarreling and jealousy. But put on the Lord Jesus Christ, and make no provision for the flesh, to gratify its desires." This he interpreted as a call to celibacy, and in those decisive moments he found the conclusive answer to his quest.

The psychological factors involved in Augustine's conversion are significant for the light they throw upon his sexual thought as a Christian theologian. As Bailey sums it up: "The direct connexion between Augustine's personal experience and his theological speculation appears most clearly in his anxiety to attribute the present character of human sexuality to the Fall. He was particularly offended and embarrassed by the act of coitus, with its intensity of venereal emotion and its uncontrollable orgasm, and he blushed to think that even the good work of generation cannot be accomplished without 'a certain amount of bestial movement' and a 'violent acting of lust.' He believed that it could not always have been thus, and that the shameful copulations which men and women now endure in the discharge of their procreative functions are not natural to our kind, but result from the transgression of our first parents."[9]

Augustine maintained that Adam and Eve were naked and unashamed in Paradise because their genitals, like their other members, were wholly under the dictates of the will. "Away the thought," he exclaims, "that there should have been any unregulated excitement, or the need to resist desire." Libidinous stimulation would have been unnecessary, and ejaculation would have occurred in psychological tranquility. (Whether such an exercise would have been pleasurable in Paradise, he does not venture to say.) He held that the sexual consequences of this original transgression still persist in us, shown by the inability of the will to govern the genitals, and also by the shame generally aroused by coitus—so that the act is always veiled in secrecy, and even parents blush to think of what they have done together. Every child is literally conceived in the "sin" of the parents, and for this he assumed the support of his interpretation of Psalms 51:5, "Behold, I was brought forth in iniquity, and in sin did my mother conceive me." He reasoned that since generation cannot occur unless the carnal union of husband and wife is motivated by the seductive stimulus of fleshly lust, neither can it occur without sin.

Can Augustine then defend marriage as an honorable estate? Yes, because a distinction is to be drawn between the state of matrimony and the carnal act to which it gives opportunity, even sanction. Wedded chastity consists in transforming coitus from the satisfying of lust to a more objective performance of a necessary duty, so that when the act is employed for generation it is excused of inherent sinfulness. There is the further negative consequence, however, that coitus is still the means by which concupiscence and its guilt is transmitted from parents to children. Hence the need for baptismal regeneration for the newly born, by which the guilt of lust is washed away—though the impulse of lust remains, and with it the sense of sexual shame.

Institutional and legal validity Augustine regarded as immaterial to the reality of marriage. He held that if a man and a woman came together "by reason of their incontinence," but preserved mutual fidelity in a permanent relationship, then their union is one of true wedlock. He insisted that it is sinful to have sexual intercourse when its intention is not expressly procreative, and that sin is aggravated if it is accompanied by any attempt to thwart the natural consequences. This Augustine denounced as an "abominable debaucher." Thus, we are driven to conclude that Augustine must bear no small measure of responsibility for the idea, still widely current, that Christianity regards sexuality as something peculiarly tainted with evil.

Gregory the Great modified Augustinian theory slightly, introducing the idea that the evil element in coitus is not in the act itself, nor in the concupiscence by which men and women are compelled to mate, but in the sensual pleasure which accompanies the act. It is the acquiescence of the will in such pleasure that is sinful. Clement of Alexandria had proposed the idea that the Fall was a falling "under the power of pleasure, for by the serpent pleasure creeping on its belly is in a figure signified."

Aristotle is accountable for the view that woman is a deficient man, but in early Christian thought she was seen as inferior on several grounds. She was last formed, first fallen. It was she who beguiled Adam and became the temptress of men. In her sexuality some of the fathers saw a "daemonic" quality, and failed to realize that the emotional disturbance which she appeared to provoke was in fact due, not to her seductive influence, but to the male's susceptibility to venereal stimuli. Because woman was seen as the beguiler, the fathers repudiated cosmetics and adornments of every kind. Tertullian, as one might suppose, carried it to the point of saying that "even natural beauty ought to be obliterated by concealment and neglect, since it is dangerous to those who look upon it." In church a woman should be veiled, lest by uncovering her face she should invite another to sin. In such attitudes the church witnessed to its embarrassment and fear in the face of physical sexuality.

It was Tertullian again who inveighed against women as the guilty sex upon whom the sentence of God still abides. "Do you not know that each of you is also an Eve?" he said, and that "you are the devil's gateway, you are the unsealer of that forbidden tree, you are the first deserter of the divine law, you are the one who persuaded him whom the devil was too weak to attack. How easily you destroyed man, the image of God!" Augustine, predictably, supplied the refutation in his observation that if woman is dishonored in Eve, she is correspondingly honored in Mary. He said, "Since through a female death had occurred to us, through a female also life should be born to us."

As an institution in society, the church found it necessary in the common interest to regulate the sexual relationships and behavior of its members. During the first three centuries there was little legislation to this end, although from earliest times a high standard of moral conduct was inculcated, with threats to the delinquent of ecclesiastical sanctions or divine retribution. The Council of Elvira in A.D. 305 was the first such council to occupy itself extensively with questions of moral discipline.

One of the earliest regulations pertaining to marriage is that laid down by Ignatius who says, "It is fitting that when men and women marry they should unite with the consent of the bishop, that the marriage may be according to the Lord, and not for the sake of lust." Validity of the marital union did not require, however, the episcopal approval nor any ecclesiastical rite or blessing. The nuptials of the faithful continued to take place with the formalities customary at the time. In fact, not until the ninth century do we find any account of the rite of Christian matrimony in the West. Even then it was identical with the old ceremony of pagan Rome in every respect save that of the sacrifice and divinations, which were replaced by the Eucharist.

One must remember that marriage, according to Roman law, was simply a contractual relationship established by consent, and voidable, like any other contract, by a mere revocation of consent. And this could be either by mutual agreement or by unilateral action. Since both Christians and their pagan contemporaries looked upon marriage as designed principally, if not exclusively, for the procreation of children, the church and Roman law were identical at one significant point: the right of a husband to put away an adulterous wife. Adultery on the woman's part, by risking the confusion of progeny, defeated the chief end of matrimony as they saw it, namely the production of legitimate offspring. It was of cardinal importance that a man be in no doubt concerning the paternity of the children borne by his wife. No such consideration restrained a husband from fornication, a factor which contributed to the establishment of a double standard. With such reasoning, the church continued to approve, and occasionally required, the dismissal of an adulterous wife.

Rather strangely, divorce did not affect the status of a couple, so that while secular law sanctioned remarriage, the church prohibited it. The mutual surrender of physical sexuality continued to impose upon husband and wife a moral duty which separation could never annul so long as both were alive and might possibly resume cohabitation and thus fulfill their matrimonial obligations.

Additionally, Augustine regarded marriage as sacramental inasmuch as it represented the union between Christ and the church. For this reason the nuptial bond ought never to be severed, resulting as it would in the destruction of the supernatural union. Oddly enough, uninterrupted cohabitation was not considered essential to the sacramental aspect. It was of course desirable, but the sacramental nature of marriage was sufficiently exhibited in a demonstrable and exclusive adherence of one man and one woman. The intrinsic virtue of the sacrament could not then be vitiated by divorce—which was actually separation—but only by remarriage. Death, on the other hand, destroyed the symbolism which owed its reality to a legal rather than to a spiritual and personal relationship.

Other church fathers regarded marriage as the tie which joins a man and a woman as partners in a common domestic life of responsibility and cohabitation. This bond is severed by divorce, disrupting the cohabitation and breaking the yoke which held them together. But to all the fathers, whatever theoretical position they took, the remarriage of a divorced Christian during the lifetime of the other partner was inadmissable under all circumstances.

At the close of the Patristic age, and within six centuries of the beginning of the church, most of the typical features of the Christian sexual tradition were already firmly established. We have noted that the attitudes of the fathers toward physical sexuality ran the gamut from embarrassment to suspicion to antipathy to abhorrence. It included an excessive exaltation of virginity (and the Virgin Mary), which encouraged many extravagant notions—among them the theory that a consecrated female virgin had contracted a special, quasi-nuptial relationship with Christ which gave to any subsequent lawful marriage the character of adultery! It led also to the injudicious advocacy of matrimony at an early age in order to avoid youthful lusts.

During the first great age of the church the Christian attitude toward sexuality was profoundly affected by the ascendancy of Hellenistic dualism which regarded the good life as essentially one detached from all that might impede the rational exercise, and sexuality as something not only emotionally disturbing but in some sense defiling. As Bailey concludes: ". . . the achievement of the Fathers and Doctors of the early church in the realm of sexual relationship must be measured by the fact that most of the basic presuppositions of the tradition which they developed (such as the superiority of virginity to marriage, the binding force and spiritual symbolism of matrimony, the incompatibility of wedlock and holy orders, and the contamination of coitus with a certain taint of evil) were never challenged in principle, and underwent only minor modification, during the succeeding millenium."[10]

Seward Hiltner, reflecting on this period of the church's history, makes the following evaluation: "By the fourth century of our era, the suppression of any sex life was considered by many Christians to be a positive good in itself, better pleasing to God than the married state. Although marriage was not held to be contrary to God's will, it was felt to be inferior to celibacy. Many church leaders after the third and fourth century, unlike those of the New Testament, held or implied that abstinence from sexual expression was itself a kind of road to salvation. This was, as the Protestant Reformers later pointed out bluntly, attempting to achieve salvation by a form of 'works'."[11]

And what a strange form of works it was! Whereas in the Old Testament period marriage was the accepted pattern of life, and celibacy and asceticism were practically nonexistent, the reverse is true of the early fathers. Whereas the teachings of Christ reveal no change from the Old Testament acceptance of sex as a God-designed part of natural life, now there is a marked change. Sex is viewed with distaste, suspicion, and antipathy. Connubial intercourse was considered one of the "works of the flesh," and little more than a lawful substitute for fornication. The nonbiblical asceticism which entered the church's thinking in this period served to color its views of sex in human life for centuries to come.

This, then, was the age that countenanced a Jerome who told husbands, "If we abstain from coitus we honor our wives; if we do not abstain, well—what is the opposite of 'honor' but 'insult'?" It was the age that began the long, dark journey, the succeeding age that was to see a Peter Lombard warn that the Holy Spirit left the room when a married couple engaged in sexual intercourse. The marriage of widowers was frowned upon because the death of a spouse was looked upon as God's call to sexual abstinence—a "second chance" as it were, for a life of celibacy. Such, in brief, is the story of the strange developments that spanned the next one thousand years.

We would not do justice to the early church were we to neglect entirely the origins of this attitude in the culture which flourished in the centuries preceding the Christian era. The time has come to put the picture in a wider perspective.

In the Mediterranean world preceding the birth of Christ, there were three patterns of religion and sexual practice. The most familiar was the Jewish, known to Christians through the Old Testament portion of their Scriptures. There the sexual code is according to God-directed sanctions. In contrast with this, Graeco-Roman sexual regulations had only civil force. In the words of G. Rattray Taylor, author of the extensive work *Sex in History*, "The gods on Olympus are not much interested in how men behave, in sexual matters or in any other, though they too seem bound in principle to obey similar sexual rules." Then there was a pattern of thought in which the sexual act was felt to have magical and even divine significance: it was to be performed with reverence, and only after carrying out the appropriate purifying rites. It constituted, in fact, an act of worship.

This view of sex as a sacred mystery can be traced to various levels of sophistication. In its most primitive form, the sexual act is seen merely as having potent magical properties. During the long winter season when nature seems dead, what is it that one should do to ensure that the seeds in the ground will quicken and bring new growth? What but perform the generative act oneself? Thus, in earliest times, even as among some preliterate peoples today, the sexual act is the culminating point of a ceremony of rebirth. Even in modern times, in the remoter parts of Europe, peasants copulate in the fields in order to ensure a good crop.

Similarly, the sexual organs have served as a symbol to remind man that everything depends upon the vital generative power. And so, in the earliest days of Greece and Rome, we find the phallus exhibited outside shops, inscribed in the design of pastry, hung around children's necks, and exhibited at places of worship. In the same way that the cross is exhibited as a Christian symbol, the phallus was symbolically displayed in religious processions.

Primitive people believed that all fertilization was caused by the god himself, man being merely the vehicle. Curiously, as Philo and Plutarch record, it was thought that sleeping with a god could actually restore virginity. In the belief that all women should, at some time or other, offer themselves to the deity, many women would, in a spirit of holy awe, present themselves at the temple. In some cases, it was a priest who, as the god's representative, came to them in the darkness; in others, the women waited in the temple grounds until some men chose them. It was clearly understood that, whoever the man was, he was the representative of deity. Each temple also had priestesses who performed a similar service to male worshipers. This was the temple prostitution which was so notoriously represented to the Christians in Corinth where one thousand vestal virgins were kept for this purpose. But one must be careful not to regard this practice as ordinary prostitution. To the participants, it was a sacred and uplifting experience, an act of commitment and communion with deity.[12]

The Greeks attributed to the actions of the gods anything that was otherwise inexplicable. Hence, whenever a man was seized by some force compelling him to act otherwise than he normally would or could, this was explained as possession by a god. Such states were called *mania*. Plato says that "in reality the greatest blessings come to us through madness, when it is sent as a gift of the gods." The Greeks used the word *theos*, god, for the moment of excitement when one made a new discovery or had a new and especially mysterious experience. They spoke of a man as being *entheos*, whence our word *enthusiasm*. In those states where God was thought to have seized man, the action was known as *theolepsy*. The Greeks thus looked with special interest on any process which induced this theoleptic awareness of divinity working in them. They knew that music and dancing could cause it, and they found it present in the climax of the sexual act, when one's personality seemed to lose its independent existence and was merged with the infinite being of the deity. Thus from earliest times in certain parts of Greece, people climbed the mountains once every two years, danced wildly, and ended the rite by performing the sexual act. The moment of orgasm was their way of merging with the deity. In time this became the worship of Dionysius. Originally the rite ended with a living kid torn to pieces; at a later time reportedly it was the priest himself who was torn to pieces. Death and rebirth was symbolized, and strangely the sexual act was taken up as that symbol.[13] Sexual detumescence has often been called "the little death." The French refer to orgasm in this way.

This experience of theolepsy was distinguished from another state which was very similar. The Greek word here was *ecstasis*, from which we derive the word *ecstasy*. Literally, it means "to stand outside." We echo this when we say that a person "is beside himself." We refer to a kind of madness, a detachment from the rational, and we usually think of it as an emotional orgy of some kind. It is typical of present-day Pentecostal experiences of the ecstatic, and has always accompanied religious fervor, whether Christian or non-Christian. The Greeks distinguished *ecstasy* from *theolepsy* in terms of the movement: ecstasy could be passive, as in the trance, or it could be active, as in an orgiastic form. In *theolepsy*, it was the deity that possessed the individual; in *ecstasy* the individual went out of himself to become wholly immersed in the deity. Plato called the orgiastic form "divine frenzy," and it is to this form that we give the word *orgy*. Sexual orgasm was thought of as a divine vital force uniting the individual with divinity through the means of theolepsy or orgy.

The early Greeks and Romans regarded sexual behavior of all kinds as natural. Civil enactments were only for the purpose of protecting citizens from abuses such as rape. Because husbands had property rights in their wives, a wife's adultery was severely punished by the husband, partly because it made the paternity of his children doubtful. A husband, on the other hand, could have what sexual experiences outside marriage he liked, subject only to the possibility that he would incur the wrath of another husband if he seduced a married woman, and might be killed for so doing. An unmarried man was equally free. There was no admiration of virginity as such, and a woman was free to sleep with a man at her own discretion. In Rome, the daughters of knights were forbidden to take money for sexual favors, but that was their only restriction.[14] Horace recommended brothels, saying that "young men, when their veins are full of gross lust, should drop in there, rather than grind some husband's private mill." A marital relationship was recognized in common law whenever a couple had lived together for a year and it could easily be dissolved because it was a simple contract. Plato makes it clear that homosexuality was as acceptable as heterosexuality, and this was suitably institutionalized. The Greek love of boys is best seen in terms of the Greek ideal of beauty. In Doric custom, there evolved a system of relationships between older men and boys in which the older man undertook to cultivate and train the boy in the arts of life. This involved conversation, physical exercise, and sexual activity. This latter was not considered in Greek society as incompatible with marriage or heterosexual sexuality. For Plato and Aristotle sex was not a moral issue, hence they seldom discussed it. Instead they were concerned with the nature of love and sexual friendship.

There were two classes of women in ancient Greece, wives and hetaerae. In addition there were prostitutes and domestic slaves. Greek wives spent their time bearing and rearing children and managing their households. They had no part in public life and lived in their own quarters of the house. The hetaerae were a special class of mistresses regarded for their education, wit, and personalities, as well as for their sexual talents. Such women were publicly honored in statues where they stood next to famous men. Female homosexuality was also common, the primary example being Sappho, whose love poems describe the delights of female homosexuality and whose homeland was the island of Lesbos, from whence comes the term *lesbian.*

Classical thought moved from Athens to Rome, from Plato and Aristotle to two schools of thought: the Stoics, and the poets such as Ovid and Catullus. The Stoics maintained a doctrine of self-denial and cultivation of the powers of the will over the pleasures of the body, and the poets praised the erotic and endorsed sensual pleasure and sexual love. Epictetus saw sex as a problem for the moral will, while for Ovid sex was a delight of the senses. For Epictetus, the desire for sexual pleasure was to be overcome because it involved man with his brutish nature and represented a loss of self-control. For Ovid, sexual love was not brutish, but was part of man's humanity. Animals engage in sex acts but not in sexual love; sexual love can be experienced only by humans as only humans raise their bodily functions to the level of an art. Interestingly, there is a certain equality of the sexes implied in Ovid's concept of the art of love. It would not be altogether dissimilar to the concepts of the biblical *Song of Solomon,* and not all that far removed from the naturalism of the Jewish people.

D. P. Verene poses the following: "The views of Epictetus and Ovid raise one of the most sweeping and fundamental questions relating to the philosophical theory of sex: Is man to regard his sexual nature as part of his animal nature which must be overcome if he is ever to be a moral being? Or, is man to regard his sexual nature as a positive part of his humanity; a bodily function that is to be raised to the level of a human art?"[15]

At the time of Christ there was a parallel development in sexual attitudes. Josephus reports of the Essenes: "They reject pleasure as an evil, but esteem continence and conquest over the passions to be a virtue. They neglect wedlock." Among the Jews there was the naturalism of the Old

Testament people, as well as a growing asceticism. Among the Greeks and the Romans there was the naturalism associated first with Plato and Aristotle, later with the poets such as Ovid, yet a growing asceticism represented by Epictetus and the Stoics. From our present study of the early church we have seen the triumph of asceticism, a triumph that shall stretch over the centuries up to our own. For it has been only within the past quarter century that the dominant asceticism has turned back toward a truly biblical view. From celibacy to celebration—this has been a long, dark journey, as we shall see in the chapter to follow.

Now, lest we leave the attitudes of the early church with too biased a view, a slight corrective is in order. Perhaps we should simply say that the church overreacted. After all, the immorality of ancient civilization was closely related to its sexual practices. In *Satyricon*, Petronius describes the revolting exhibitions of gross carnality at the feasts, and others have described the sadism of the circus which released inhibitions and invariably turned to the erotic. Disrobing and public copulation are not unique to American theater; it was common in the Roman circus. It would perhaps be more to the point of our wonderment if the church had *not* overreacted.

And lastly, an important observation is made by Eickhoff: "It should be remembered, too, that after A.D. 70, when the temple in Jerusalem was destroyed and the Jewish culture in Palestine ceased to exist, the only Jewish influences in Christianity were through the Old Testament as part of the Christian Bible. Therefore, the ascendancy of Hellenistic dualism over Hebraic naturalism, relating to sexual relations especially, was much more easily accomplished, perhaps, than it would have been had the Hebrew culture continued to exist as an independent unit. Whatever the case, the more rapidly Christianity spread outside the Hebrew community in Palestine, the more rapidly the new religion had to adapt its message to new modes of thought. By the beginning of the second century responsibility for the ongoing development of Christian thought was in the hands of non-Jewish Christians, and acceptance of at least some of the contemporary ideas was probably inevitable."[16]

While it is not easy to overcome a bad beginning, the greater tragedy lies in the apparent inability of some segments of the church to recognize a bad beginning. The story that follows serves to dramatize the depths of distortion from which the modern Christian has had to extricate himself in order to formulate a truly positive, biblical perspective on the sexual relation. If there are truly redeeming features—and there most certainly are

—then perhaps the positive word of Ernst Troeltsch ought to close our chapter:

"From the very beginning the Church set before its members a high and strict ideal; it required them to observe the ideal of monogamy, of chastity before marriage (for both husband and wife), of conjugal fidelity, to exercise an ethical and religious discipline in the care of children, to reject all regulation of the birth rate by the exposure of children or by artificial sterilization; and after the Church was established by the State, as far as possible this ideal was made a general principle of Society, partly by the influence of the Church upon ecclesiastical law, penitential order and discipline, and partly by its influence upon the law of the State. According to the religious philosophy of the Church, which was based upon that of the Bible, the monogamous family is the basis of Society and of the State, which has itself been formed by the expansion of the family; among pagans the idea of the family had become most confused and perverted by its false ideas of sex, and it was radically purified by the Christians in order to serve as the foundation of a purer and better order of life."[17]

3
Long, Dark Journey

During the early part of the medieval era, the question of divorce and remarriage assumed a more prominent place than in the thought of the fathers. The first clear departure from the traditional view of the Western church is to be found in the Penitential attributed to Theodore of Canterbury, a collection of disciplinary rulings composed during the early eighth century. In it the dissolution of marriage with the right of remarriage is allowed in a variety of circumstances. Reflecting the turbulent times, the cases include: (a) the adultery of a first wife, in which case the husband may remarry forthwith, and the divorced wife after five years' penance; (b) remarriage forthwith if the partner enters the monastic life; (c) a wife captured with violence and with no possibility of redemption, in which case the husband may remarry with the bishop's approval and after one year; (d) a husband reduced to slavery for theft or fornication, in which case a first wife may remarry; (e) capture of a wife by pirates or in war allows the husband to remarry forthwith, and if the wife returns, the second marriage stands.

The influence of Theodore's Penitential spread to the Frankish church in the latter part of the eighth century. There the *Lex Romana Visigoth* allowed a husband to divorce his wife for adultery, poisoning, and procuring. A wife could divorce her husband for homicide, poisoning, *and tomb robbing!* A wife might also divorce her husband for homosexual practices, or if he forced her to commit adultery. As for the husband, some codes allowed a man to divorce his wife if he was compelled to emigrate and his wife refused to accompany him. Again, if one partner contracted leprosy the union could be dissolved by mutual consent, allowing the other partner to remarry. Nonetheless, Pope Nicholas I declared Rome's uncompromising opposition to remarriage, regardless of provincial warrant.

The spirit of Theodore's Penitential continued to influence ecclesiasti-

cal practice in the Frankish and German churches until the latter half of
the eleventh century. At that time Gregory VII finally placed the whole
question at rest for the next four centuries; no exception was allowed to the
universal prohibition of divorce and remarriage. Pope Innocent III concluded that pagan and mixed marriages are not per se absolutely indissoluble, but that on conversion the Christian spouse, though free to separate,
may only remarry if the unbeliever refuses cohabitation, blasphemes the
deity, or incites the converted partner to sin.

The qualitative difference between Christian and non-Christian marriage was finally ascribed to the former's sacramental character. In the
twelfth century a new theory of the nuptial sacrament gained ascendance,
according to which Christian marriage was one of seven efficacious signs
expressly instituted by Christ whereby sanctifying grace was imparted to
the faithful. Thus a profound distinction was established between Christian
and non-Christian wedlock; the latter, not possessing sacramental meaning
necessarily lacked immutability, and so could be dissolved. For the Christian couple, no longer was it held that matrimony *ought not* to be dissolved;
it was simply asserted that it *could not* be dissolved.

Marriage suits, at first handled by civil courts under the Roman system,
were more and more given over to the quasi-judicial authority of the bishops
through legislation by Christian emperors. Under the Anglo Saxons,
offenses were tried by a common tribunal on which both the bishop and
the secular magistrate sat. When William I separated the secular from the
spiritual judicatory, there was nothing to impede the church from gaining
control of marriage in England as it had already done on the Continent.
By the beginning of the twelfth century its authority was virtually uncon-
tested.

The question of how marriage was formed now became a legal question
of some urgency to medieval divines. The means by which the relationship
came into existence had never concerned the fathers. According to Roman
jurisprudence, consent alone sufficed to create a marriage union, and the
church followed the Roman pattern. This simpler determination of the
matrimonial bond was preferred over that of the Germanic peoples for
whom it was effected by transmission of the authoritative guardianship of
the bride from father to husband, confirmed by an oath of payment—the
bride price.

The sacramental character of Christian matrimony signified the union
of Christ and the church. Marital indissolubility was considered established

by sexual consummation. Thus marriage was effected, not by consent alone, but by consent and sexual consummation. But medieval theologians were reluctant to attribute such sacramental importance to anything sexual. Their dilemma was that they were committed to the idea that the one-flesh relation alone possesses the earthly sign of the mystical marriage of Christ and the church.

Is coitus now to be regarded as essential or merely an accessory to marriage? The problem of physical sexuality which had so troubled the fathers now arose in a new form. There was no question that Paul taught that coitus is the specific act by means of which man and woman became one flesh (1 Corinthians 6:16). Eventually the famous dictum of Ulpian, "consent, not coitus, makes marriage," won universal acceptance as a concise expression of the church's doctrine.

This doctrine was developed in more subtle ways by Gratian and Peter Lombard. Two forms of nuptial relationship were acknowledged. Gratian held consent to be the efficient cause of marriage, but allowed that the union resulting from sexual consummation alone had the properties of indissolubility and sacrament which belong to the perfect marriage. Lombard claimed the sacramental symbolism of Christ and the church no less for consent than for consummation. In other words, one sacrament is exhibited in two complementary aspects. This synthesis established a conclusion towards which Christian thought had been gradually moving for many centuries—namely, that coitus, though a normal feature of marital life, is not an intrinsic element in matrimony itself. The one-flesh union was at last displaced from its proper centrality in the theological conceptualizing of the sexual relationship. In its place was established a purely consensual union—an innovation quite alien to the Scriptures. The determining reason for the triumph of the consent theory was not theological, however. Rather, it best served to provide the ecclesiastical courts with a simple test by which the validity of a marriage could be ascertained. Medieval marriage unions were not infrequently formed in circumstances of doubtful validity. Child bethrothal, or alliances dictated by expediency or contracted under duress, required a test vastly superior to the proof of coitus —not readily proved or disproved! Thus, legal requirements were largely determinative in deciding the church's doctrine of how marriage was formed. But we may suspect something more; considering the climate of theological opinion which persisted from earliest times, any doctrine which minimized the importance of coitus was emotionally more acceptable.

Pope Alexander III settled certain aspects of the continuing dispute when he ruled that all that is needed to establish a marriage is the exchange of mutual consent in words of the present. He declared that coitus following betrothal is sufficient to create a valid matrimonial union. He also acted on the assumption that where there had been no consummation—as testified to by both partners—there was no indissolubility. Hence dispensation from all the effects of consent was permissible. In a negative sense, the failure of coitus overturned the validity of consent.

Peter Lombard modified the concepts of Augustine and Gregory by repudiating their theories that intercourse is sinful, either in itself or in its accompanying pleasure. Distinguishing between sin and evil, he maintained that intercourse always contains an element of evil though it is not individually sinful. It was left for the greatest of the medieval theologians to develop and qualify this idea. Thomas Aquinas denied that coitus had been so corrupted by the Fall as to contain no trace of goodness, for since a good God created man's bodily nature, nothing pertaining to that nature can be wholly bad. Hence it is possible that the sexual act might be conducive of some virtue. Indeed, it is meritorious when performed by married persons who are in a state of grace. Yet there is the intrinsic taint of evil by which every act of intercourse is contaminated. Following Aristotle, Aquinas found an element of evil in anything that impeded the exercise of the rational faculty. Like Aristotle, he saw in the intensity of sexual emotion, especially in its culminating orgasm, a potent hindrance to man's pursuit of the good life. This defect was attributable to the Fall. Aquinas argued that the effect of the first sin was a weakening of the will, strikingly demonstrated in man's impotence to bring his sexual emotions and actions under rational control. Hence, coitus is not possible without the ardent desire and rational disturbance which marks the rebellion of lust against volition. This, in turn, was a defect for which husband and wife could not be held morally responsible. It was simply a punishment in consequence of the race's initial rebellion against the Creator.

Although in the final determination of the medieval doctors, the pleasure of coitus was not sinful per se, it could not be pursued for its own sake without sin. If such pleasure was sought within marriage, the offense was venial; if outside marriage, it was mortal. If the sensual enjoyment was merely incidental to the desire for generation, or to the payment of the nuptial debt to the partner, or to the recollection of the sacramental blessing of marriage, then—but only then—there was attendant grace and the sin was only venial. Nonetheless, a mind-set prevailed that was akin to that of Jerome in earlier times who had said, "He who loves his own wife too ardently is an adulterer." The old emotional antipathy is still present! This, of course, is only a rational distinction, and completely oversimplifies the nature of the marital union. Aquinas simply could not separate his thought from Patristic beginnings. He justified his own acceptance of clerical celibacy on the ground that continence encourages the devotion of the mind toward divine things, and also ensures the bodily purity of those who serve the altar. Sexual taboos had become entrenched.

Catholic writers such as Ernest Messenger, admit that during the Middle Ages the church itself went to great extremes in attempting to derogate the sexual side of marriage. Complete abstinence from sex relations had to be maintained on no less than five days out of seven: on Thursdays in memory of the arrest of our Lord, on Fridays in commemoration of His death, on Saturdays in honor of the Blessed Virgin, on Sundays in honor of the Resurrection, and on Mondays in honor of the faithful departed. And can one imagine the negative implication conveyed to newly married couples who were enjoined to remain continent on their wedding night out of respect for the church's blessing—a blessing granted by a celibate priest invoked to the ever-virgin Mary![1]

It is easy to see how the religious sentiment of these times shrank from the thought that Mary, the mother of Jesus, had ever given herself to the contamination of conjugal intercourse. Since the beginning of the fifth century, it was inevitable that the perpetual virginity of Mary would be a part of popular piety, only to become in time a dogma of the church. The marriage of Mary and Joseph, conceived as completely continent, became the pattern to which all Christian marriage ought to conform. Was it not inevitable, too, that consent should be regarded as essential, and consummation incidental, to the formation of marriage?

The tenth century saw the beginning of a campaign to conform a reluctant clergy to obedient continence. Clerics were ordered to separate from their wives or concubines. Pope Nicholas II forbade Christians to attend mass celebrated by any priest known to keep a concubine in his dwelling. This edict aroused such fierce resistance as to produce an antipope in the person of Cadalus, Bishop of Parma, who claimed the title of Honorius II, and to whose cause the city of Milan rallied. The Milanese clergy had enjoyed the privilege of marriage from of old, and now papal attempts to suppress it were regarded as offensive to civic prestige and independence.

The papal victory in this matter was due largely to the efforts of

Gregory VII who made clerical celibacy a major program in his reform of the church. Any marriage contracted in defiance of the canons was declared to be no marriage. Two centuries of unremitting effort saw the eventual success of Gregory's reform. From the Fourth Lateran Council in 1215, little more is heard of clerical marriage in the Western church. The final stage in this development was to come with the Council of Trent about 1570. In the Eastern church the struggle was more prolonged. There the asceticism of the West never did take such a strong hold. The Eastern orthodox churches have never embraced clerical celibacy, and even in the Roman church to this day the Uniate Greek clergy is permitted to marry.

One cannot escape the political ramifications in forbidding marriage to the clergy. The popes were bent upon the dominance of ecclesiastical power in the West, and an effective instrument was the creation of a body of men set apart from the world and its life, bound entirely to the church, subservient to the will of its rulers, and owning no secular ties or obligations. Furthermore, the rule of celibacy successfully prevented the transferring of benefices and property from father to son. It also served to check ecclesiastical alliances founded upon intermarriage and family interest. Thus was the concept of clerical celibacy exploited for the aggrandizement of papal power. An additional corruption of papal policy was inevitable when the yoke of celibacy was laid upon many lesser clerics (one in every twelve adult males was to be found somewhere in the clerical heirarchy in the thirteenth century), men who had no true vocation and who succumbed all too easily to sexual temptation. This was turned to financial advantage through papal taxation of those who had concubines and children born to them.

Because the church was compelled to work out a theory of marriage adapted to the business of the ecclesiastical courts, the personal aspects of the husband-wife relationship were neglected. Concentrating upon the formal and legal aspects, the church failed to construct a true theology of marriage. The personal, relational aspects of marriage were regarded as outside any legitimate theological concern. Was this not reflective of the clergy's inexperience as celibates? It is not surprising that matrimony was little more than a social institution. And to students of the development of love, such as Denis de Rougemont, it is significant that the eleventh century not only marked the church's debate as to the efficient cause of marriage, but saw the emergence of the concept of romantic love as a cultural force destined to affect almost every facet of life in Western society from that time on. The culture of the Middle Ages simply left no scope for such a development as romantic love before that time.[2]

The status accorded to women in any age is the touchstone for evaluating the sexual thought of that age. Aquinas, representing the thinking of the Schoolmen, held that woman's origin from the rib of Adam destined her neither to exercise authority over man, nor to exist in a servile condition under him. Still, he limited the scope of her being man's helpmate to that collaboration for which she is biologically suited—procreation. Her subjection to him as her "head" was ontological, because in him "the discretion of reason predominates." Thus was Aristotle's view still prevalent, namely that the male was the perfect human being and the female was a defective man. Aquinas argued that man's superiority was demonstrated, furthermore, by the very act of intercourse wherein he takes the more active and therefore nobler part, while the woman is passive and submissive. It was left to Sanchez, several centuries later, to carry this thinking to its more extreme conclusion, that this is the one natural mode of copulation since it signifies the superordinate status of the male. Any deviation from this position was considered to be against nature and hence punishable.

The whole question of culpability in sexual offenses became a major concern in medieval times. The fullest treatment of all is found in Aquinas's *Summa Theologica*. Sin, he argues, is that which contravenes reason by which everything is directed to its proper end. Lust, being chiefly concerned with sexual pleasure, above all other sins debauches the mind and contravenes reason. There follows a minute classification of venereal transgressions and their appropriate penances. For example, kissing and caressing are innocent acts per se and can occur without inciting lust. But when they are done for the purpose of enjoying forbidden pleasure, then they become mortally sinful by reason of their motive. Another extreme example concerns male nocturnal emission (appallingly termed "nocturnal pollution"), which is not deemed sinful in itself, though it might result from a previous sin such as the entertainment of lascivious thoughts. (Aquinas was quick to point out that nocturnal emissions brought about by the thoughts which necessarily engage the moral theologian from time to time are not sinful!) His view of masturbation was that it is a vice against nature, an act contrary to right reason. Since sexual activity was designed for but one purpose, procreation, any act or motive contrary to procreation was a vice. The very word *masturbation* means "self-abuse," and does not describe the act itself, but is a value judgment upon it. By a curious reasoning, masturbation was deemed an offense more serious than incest, adultery, or seduction by use of violence. And the reason? Because it was an ejaculation of semen furthest removed from the possibility of procreation!

Another anomaly is the church's uneasy acquiesence to prostitution. The argument ran like this: the present conditions of human society made prostitution a necessary evil. From Augustine to Aquinas the church did not admit prostitutes into its fellowship, yet maintained that they filled a useful purpose to the well-being of the body politic. Aquinas calls Augustine to witness on the point that the toleration of necessary evils makes prostitution like a sewer in a palace; take away the sewer and you fill the palace with pollution. Take away prostitution and you fill the world with sodomy. Thus the use of harlots is a "lawful immorality," and is to be tolerated as the price of social "purity" and the preservation of feminine "virtue." As Bailey notes, "Nothing could demonstrate more clearly the strange and often perplexing ambivalence and confusion of medieval sexual thought."[3]

The free sexuality of the Middle Ages is traceable in court records and in the complaints of church moralists. Pope Boniface despaired that the English "utterly refuse to have legitimate wives, and continue to live in lechery and adultery." A century later Alcuin declared that "the land has been absolutely submerged under a flood of fornication, adultery and incest; so that the very semblance of modesty is entirely absent." Aphrodisiacs were much sought after. The root of the orchis, thought to resemble male testicles, was eaten to induce fertility. The famed restorative powers of the mandrake were similarly derived from its phallic appearance. In the same fashion, nuns ate the root of the lily, or the nauseus *agnus castus*, to ensure chastity. Clothing also betrayed the frank sexuality in the fourteenth century. Women wore low-necked dresses, tightly lacing them to elevate their breasts so that, it was said, "a candle could be stood upon them." Men wore short coats revealing their private parts in a glovelike container called a braguette. Public baths, introduced to Europe by the Crusades, became houses of ill fame, regulated from the time of Henry II and remaining until the seventeenth century. Many of these "stews" belonged to the Bishopric of Westchester. At least one English cardinal purchased a brothel as an investment for church funds, arguing that the church was entitled to 10 percent (a tithe?) of the girls' earnings. It was nothing for men and women to go naked through the streets on their way to the baths, while at the court of Charles V the daughters of nobility thought it an honor to parade naked in his Majesty's presence. Men were free to seduce all women of lower rank, while they might hope to win the favors of women of higher rank through deeds of valiance. So, too, women were free to take lovers both before and after marriage. Chrestien de Troyes explains: "The usage and rules at that time were that if a knight found a damsel or wench alone he would, if he wished to preserve his good name, sooner think of cutting his throat than of offering her dishonour; if he forced her against her will he would have been scorned in every court. But, on the other hand, if the damsel were accompanied by another knight, and if it pleased him to give combat to that knight and win the lady by arms, then he might do his will with her just as he pleased, and no shame or blame whatsoever would be held to attach to him." Traill and Mann say, "To judge from contemporary poems and romances, the first thought of every knight on finding a lady unprotected was to do her violence."[4]

This was an age when nudity was no cause for shame, when marriage was often temporary, when women exposed themselves to men to show them honor. To be called a bastard was a mark of distinction—the implication being that some especially valiant knight had slept with one's mother. William the Conqueror was shamelessly known as "William the Bastard." The tenth-century ordinances of Howel the Good allowed for seven years of trial marriage, and one year's trial marriage existed in Scotland up to the Reformation. The legal age for marriage was fourteen for males, twelve for females. In feudal times it was not uncommon for the feudal lord to deflower the new bride before releasing her to her husband. Monks who were at the same time feudal lords also held this right.

Henry C. Lea, in *History of Sacerdotal Celibacy*, recounts the failure of the church to impose a life of celibacy on the clergy and the extent to which the clergy defied its efforts by marriage, concubinage, fornication, and homosexuality. In some areas, such as Spain and Switzerland, the populace insisted that the priest have a concubine as a measure of protection for their wives. The danger of incest was deemed sufficiently serious for the Papal Legate in France, Cardinal Guala, to rule in 1208 that mothers and other female relatives must not live in the houses of clerics, a regulation repeated up to the end of the fourteenth century. Although clerical sins were often overlooked unless they became a public scandal, and exceptionally light penalties were imposed, and frequent absolutions granted by the Curia, still the courts of the day record more infractions for clergy than laymen. This situation was rendered even more deplorable when some priests used their supposed power of granting or withholding absolution for sin as a means of forcing a woman's compliance. It was this abuse that brought about the official requirement for confessional boxes, on order of the Council of Valencia in 1565—an order that was still being ignored in many places two centuries later.

The following is cited by G. Rattray Taylor:

"Sergius III contrived, with the aid of his vicious mother, that his bastard should become Pope after him. The notorious John XII (deposed 963) turned St. John Lataran into a brothel: at his trial he was accused of sacrilege, simony, perjury, murder, adultery and incest. Leo VIII, while still a layman, replaced him: he died stricken by paralysis in the act of adultery. Benedict IX, elected Pope at the age of ten, grew up 'in unrestrained licence, and shocked the sensibilities even of a dull and barbarous age.' While the popes were resident in Avignon, 'the vilest issues were the pastime of pontifical ease. Chastity was a reproach and licentiousness a virtue.' Balthasar Cossa, elected Pope to end the Great Schism, confessed before the Council of Constance to 'notorious incest, adultery, defilement, homicide and atheism.' Earlier, when Chamberlain to Boniface IX, he had kept his brother's wife as mistress: promoted to Cardinal as a result, he was sent to Bologna 'where two hundred maids, matrons and widows, including a few nuns, fell victims to his brutal lust.' "[5]

Religious erotomania was common, the mystical Christ being the object for cloistered nuns, the mystical Virgin being the object for celibate priests. One cannot read the devotions of Bernard of Clairvaux or St. Theresa without noting this erotomania. The medieval ceremony for the consecration of nuns was in several respects like a wedding. A ring was put on the candidate's finger and a wedding crown on her head. One of the responses which she had to make was: "I love Christ into whose bed I have entered." After the kiss of peace had been bestowed, she was urged to "forget there all the world, and there be entirely out of the body; there in glowing love embrace your beloved (Saviour) who is come down from heaven into your breast's bower, and hold Him fast until He shall have granted whatsoever you wish for."[6] Taylor then notes that the church received the sum of money which had been put aside by the parents for their daughter's dowry if and when she married.

By a strange confluence of ideas, virgins thus dedicated were considered the brides of Christ—which fully ignored what the Scriptures teach about His holy bride, the church of the redeemed. Hence it followed that anyone who seduced a virgin was not simply committing fornication but the more serious crime of adultery. What is more, it was adultery at the expense of Christ Himself! In earlier times, Cyprian had expressed this idea: "If a husband come and see his wife lying with another man, is he not indignant and maddened? . . . How indignant and angered then must Christ our Lord and Judge be, when He sees a virgin, dedicated to Himself, and consecrated to His holiness, lying with a man. . . . She who has been guilty of this crime is an adulteress, not against a husband, but Christ."[7]

The Penitential of Theodore imposed penance in varying degrees, according to the age of the sexually misbehaving person, the frequency of the sin, etc. The seducer of a nun was denied burial in consecrated ground. Even confessed sexual fantasies merited penance. Most curious of all, involuntary nocturnal emissions ("pollutions") were a sin for which the offender must rise at once and sing seven penitential psalms, with a further thirty in the morning! If that were not enough, it was required that if the "pollution" occurred when one had fallen asleep in church, he must sing the whole psalter! As in earlier times, the sin of all sins, and upon which the greatest attention was devoted, was masturbation. To anyone living in the twentieth century, the shadow of such thinking has not seemed far removed.

Sexual repression by the church reached into the marital relationship to specify all the possible variants to the one accepted mode of intercourse and other sexual contacts as subject to penance—up to seven years' penance for those deemed the most horrible. Confessors were supplied with detailed manuals descriptive of every imaginable sexual act and supplied with questions they were required to ask. One can imagine what it meant for confessors thus to dwell upon such possibilities and the fantasies inevitably generated!

In its effort to reduce intercourse to a minimum within marriage, the church also specified the number of days each year when the sexual act could be legitimately performed. It was illegal on Sundays, Wednesdays and Fridays (that would take care of five months of the year!), then was added the Lenten period of forty days, the forty days before Christmas, three days before attending communion (and one must remember how often attendance at communion was required!), from conception to forty days after parturition, and during any period of penance. Newly married couples must refrain for three nights after their marriage—the so-called Tobias nights. A most likely possibility! Having once performed the sexual act, the couple must not enter a church for thirty days, and then only after doing forty days' penance and bringing an offering.

One of the most incredible devices of the church courts to derogate both marriage and sexuality was the attempt to use marriage as a punishment for fornication. Taylor tells of the procedure evolved in 1308 by Archbishop Winchelsey whereby a contract drawn up on the first offense stated that, in the event of a third offence, the parties were to be considered as having been man and wife as from the time of the first offense.

Taylor cites Lea for the following: "For a priest to marry was a worse crime than to keep a mistress, and to keep a mistress was worse than to engage in random fornication—a judgment which completely reverses secular conceptions of morality, which attach importance to the quality and durability of personal relationships. When accused of being married, it was always a good defence to reply that one was simply engaged in indiscriminate seduction, for this carried only a light penalty, while the former might involve total suspension. The simple clergy found it difficult to accept this scale of values, and frequently settled down to permanent relationships or entered into spousals and claimed to be married. For this they were periodically expelled from their livings and the women driven out or seized by the church."[8]

One summary judgment of the Middle Ages would be that the church lay under the pall of dark superstition. We've touched upon the element of magic, and two remarkable phenomena call for brief attention before we leave this dismal period of the church's history.

One of the most remarkable phenomena is the reality which came to be attached to sexual fantasy. Wherever it began, the specific form which such fantasizing took was the claim that one was visited in the night by a supernatural being with whom one then had sexual congress. In the case of women, this being was known as an Incubus, and in the case of men, a Succubus. Pictorial descriptions detailed their appearance, invariably accentuating the sexual organs. Virgins, widows, and most frequently of all, nuns, confessed to such visitants. The church accepted their existence as real, explaining that they were devils in human shape.

Such beliefs were only a step away from witchcraft, which the church located in the Old Testament Scriptures. How common this had become by the end of the Middle Ages is witnessed to by the Papal Bull, *Summa Desiderantes*, issued by Innocent VIII. In part it reads: "It has indeed lately come to Our ears . . . that in some parts of Northern Germany . . . many persons of both sexes . . . have abandoned themselves to devils, incubi and succubi, and by their incantations, spells, and conjurations . . . have slain infants yet in their mother's womb . . . hinder men from performing the sexual act and women from conceiving. . . ."

Strikingly apparent, the Bull is concerned almost altogether with sexual pathologies, and not a few have speculated on the psychological consequences of sexual repression such as the church was guilty of creating. During the Inquisition, two men commissioned for this task, Sprenger and Kramer, began accusing persons of witchcraft in certain German cities. They prepared the famous *Malleus Malleficarum*, which, like the Papal Bull, is preoccupied with sexual pathology. The largest group of accused were girls fourteen and up. Every case of reported sexual fantasy, or even of sexual impotence, was pursued by the Inquisitors and inevitably led to a burning. Concerning the purely sexual character of the phenomena which came under the Inquisitor's "witchcraft" category, the *Malleus* explicitly states: "All witchcraft comes from carnal lust." And if that isn't enough, it adds, "which in women is insatiable." Because a witch supposedly had had intercourse with the devil, it was assumed that evil, the devil, sexuality, and women belonged together. And by a strange parallelism of ideas, as the Virgin was representative of the pure and compassionate, the witch symbolized the impure and destructive. It followed, too, that if the Virgin was the patroness of fertility, the witch must be against fertility. Hence her activity was marked by the phenomenon of impotence. These figures were so real to the medieval mentality that in 1400 the civil courts consented to recognize copulation with the devil as a capital crime. Witch burnings followed. The Senate of Savoy condemned no less than eight hundred witches at one sitting. Paramo, in his *History of the Inquisition*, boasts that in the two centuries following 1400 the Holy Office burned at least thirty thousand witches. In Spain, Torquemada personally sent 10,220 such persons to the stake and 97,371 to the galleys. The Protestant Reformers also persecuted witches, so that this pattern of thought is not to be attributed only to the Holy Office. It extended, as we know only too well, to the witch burnings in the New World. Morton Hunt writes that sexual repression "undoubtedly played a part in the two outbreaks of witchcraft hysteria in New England; the earlier one began in 1647 and resulted in the execution of fourteen witches in Massachusetts and Connecticut while the Salem frenzy of 1692 brought about the execution of twenty persons and two dogs."[9]

The common reference to the medieval period as the Dark Ages must surely apply to the sexuality of that age, both as to the ethics and behavior in the Western world, and especially as to the understanding and teaching of the church. The distortions of the Patristic Age were carried to further extremes in the Medieval Period. How long it took to come to a positive and personalistic view is the subject of our next chapter.

4
Sexuality as Personal Relation

The Reformation, that formidable theological renewal that became Protestantism, was a spiritual Renaissance. While it recovered a more biblical view of human sexuality, it was a small beginning. Many erroneous notions and attitudes continued. In his early writings, Martin Luther was of the opinion that polygamy was not clearly forbidden in Scripture, although later on he modified this view, regarding it as a special dispensation for great people during the patriarchal period. By the same reasoning, Luther thought this privilege extended to the great people of his own day. This included Philip of Hesse, evidently, for Luther acted as his confessor, secretly advising Philip to engage in bigamy. In 1531 he advised Henry VIII to take Anne Boleyn as a second wife in addition to Catherine of Aragon. Yet in 1536 he declared Henry's marriage to Catherine invalid because the Pope had set aside God's Word to make it possible. With equal inconsistency, Luther felt, in 1522, that a person who committed adultery deserved the death penalty, whereas in 1530 he was more moderate, pointing out that the adulterer was spiritually dead.[1] He felt no reluctance that the innocent party in a divorce for adultery was free to remarry, and extended the Pauline privilege to anyone who was deserted by a marital partner. Ulrich Zwingli declared that since God had ordained marriage and had nowhere forbidden it, it is lawful for all without exception. He denounced compulsory vows of chastity, asserting that it was sinful for clerics and monastics to refuse matrimony if they knew they had been denied the gift of continence. With this Luther agreed. He counseled any priest who had succumbed to the weakness of the flesh to cohabit with the woman if she were willing, disregarding with a clear conscience the Pope's displeasure, the canon law or whatever—for in God's sight they were married. To live in continence, in Luther's opinion, was to presume the impossible, and such temptation of God only brings its own reward of uncleanness of thought and life. John Calvin argued in much the same vein; in the matter of virginity, however, Luther regarded it as something to be shunned in every case, whereas Calvin held virginity to be superior to marriage, provided it was given by God as a gift. However, Calvin more than Luther shows a more profound conception of the relational values of marriage, and here we see the dawning vision of sexuality as a personal relation. This concept was not to be developed much further for another two centuries, yet it was resident in the views of Luther and Calvin.

In his attitude toward sexual acts, Luther agreed with Augustine and Aquinas, ascribing our present sexual impulse to the Fall and its all-pervasive effects. He saw coitus as no longer performed in the knowledge and worship of God, as in Paradise, hence it is accompanied with shame and is somehow always unclean. Luther was quite negative about the relation of coitus to marriage, seeing intercourse only as an effective remedy for the incontinence that troubles every man.

When Luther, in 1521, defended the breaking of monastic vows and marriage for priests, he wrote that the sexual impulse was both natural and irrepressible. In 1525, some four years later, Luther, then forty-two, recommended to a group of nuns that they leave their convent. He helped them find husbands, but when it came to the last of the group, Katharina von Bora, a woman of twenty-six, his attempt to pair her off failed and she was forced to go to work as a domestic. Meanwhile the Peasant's War was raging, threatening the entire Reformation. It occurred to Luther that the war was the devil's attack on him, and to spite the devil—and only incidentally to solve Katharina's problem—he married her. By no means in love with her when he married, Luther was plagued with misgivings. Happily, he saw his misgivings as the work of the devil, and then accepted his marriage cheerfully. He did, we are happy to report, come to love his wife dearly. And Morton Hunt adds, in his recounting of it, that Luther evidently found the sexual side of marriage satisfactory. He continued to hold the medieval view that it was somehow sinful, but felt that within marriage "God covers the sin." But if he had less reluctance about married sex, he was hardly ecstatic. "Had God consulted me about it," he said in one of his table talks, "I should have advised Him to continue the generation of the species by fashioning human beings out of clay, as Adam was made." Luther was hardly the man to perpetuate the Renaissance idealization of woman or the romantic ideal of courtly love.[2]

John Calvin was so censorious and moralistic as a boy—and so excellent in Latin—that fellow students called him "the accusative case." By age twenty-six he had written his great and enduring theological work, *The Institutes of the Christian Religion.* Famous for his preaching in the city of Geneva, Calvin was made head of the Consistory, a governing body of five pastors and twelve elders, which held dictatorial powers over the religious observances and morality of the citizenry. Thus Calvin's views on sex, as on other pleasures, became the code by which Genevans lived for the next century. It was Puritanism in its beginnings. To sing or dance at weddings, to serve too many dishes at dinner, or to wear clothes of too extravagant a cut, were all punishable. Plays were banned, jewelry discouraged. But it was in the realm of sexual transgressions that punishments were most severe. Fornication was cause for exile, and adultery deserved death, sometimes by drowning, sometimes by beheading. Even legitimate love, as Hunt tells us, was stringently regulated. Engagements were limited to six weeks' duration, for one did not dally at romance. But let Hunt tell the story:

"Calvin had been a bachelor, and almost certainly celibate, until the age of thirty-one; he left no word as to whether he suffered temptations and lusts in all this period of youth, and perhaps in itself that is a valuable clue. During a brief period of exile from Geneva (1538–41), he lived in Strasbourg, was minister to a small church, and took in boarders. Finding this burdensome, he asked friends to find him a wife, and provided us with one clue to his nature when he specified: 'I am none of those insane lovers who, when once smitten with the fine figure of a woman, embrace also her faults. This only is the beauty which allures me, if she be chaste, obliging, not fastidious, economical, patient, and careful for my health.' A poor widow named Idelette de Bure filled this bill of particulars, and he married her in 1540. She served him faithfully until her death nine years later. Calvin wrote kindly words about her after she was gone, but remained a widower thereafter."[3]

Calvin was a stern and severe man albeit a giant theological mind. Like the Catholics before him, Calvin spoke of marriage as having two main functions: the production of offspring and the remedying of incontinence. He strongly repudiated Jerome's all-embracing recourse to Paul's words in 1 Corinthians 7:1, "It is well for a man not to touch a woman," affirming that coitus is undefiled, honorable, and holy since it is a pure institution of God. Yet Calvin never overcame his own uneasiness with the old problem that coitus was attended by sensual pleasure, an immoderate desire resulting from the corruption of human nature by the Fall. If Luther was a pessimist in sexual matters, Calvin could be quite prudish. He advised a husband to approach his wife "with delicacy and propriety," and held that it was inexcusable for a wife to touch or even look at her husband's genitals.[4] Despite all this, Calvin affirmed marriage as a high calling of God, which was indeed a radical reversal of medieval thought. He did envision woman as man's companion in the whole of his life, emphasizing her equality as against Luther's view that she was subordinate. This, too, was a step in the right direction.

Summarizing the Reformation attitudes, Andrew Eickhoff writes: "The Reformation brought changes of great consequence to the teachings about sex in Christianity. . . . This reemphasis on marriage as the highest Christian ideal laid the foundation for a new estimate of coitus and sex in general. . . . Although little new was said about the nature of sex by the Reformers, the open and forceful denunciation of celibacy as the religious ideal, and the marriage and establishment of families by the professional clergy, raised the status of coitus and of marriage as much as any formal teachings could have done."[5]

Sherwin Bailey also is correct in his assessment: "Although he [Calvin] allowed that the propagation of the species is a special and characteristic end of matrimony, he taught also that its primary purpose is rather social than generative."[6] Now, lest we read too much into such statements, the author of *The Reformational Understanding of Family and Marriage* makes this important admission: "The tragedy is that in this vital sphere of human life . . . later Reformed theologians fall back into a synthesis with pagan Graeco-Roman ideas."[7]

Let it be said to their credit that both Luther and Calvin rejected the medieval idea that wedlock was a sacramental rite with a special grace-bearing function. This ancient error had been given partial credence by Augustine's misinterpretation of the Greek word *mysterion* in Ephesians 5:32. The Latin Vulgate perpetuated this error in translating the word as *sacramentum*, leading to the false notion of marriage as a sacrament and hence indissoluble, voided only by the death of a partner.

The English Reformers, rejecting the medieval concept of marriage as a rite instituted by Christ and conveying sanctifying grace, nonetheless continued to use the term *sacrament*. But the word was used in the sense that the rite is sacramental in that its outward and visible sign is the exchange of consent, while its inward and spiritual grace is the sanctification of coitus. The sacrament itself consists in the union of man and woman as one flesh to signify Christ and the church. While there is a certain legitimacy about this interpretation of the term, its use must be guarded.

John Tyndale went so far as to feel that clerical marriage should be compulsory, not only as a moral safeguard, but because practical experience in ruling a household is the best preparation for the exercise of pastoral oversight. Furthermore, the union of the priest and his wife stand as the foremost exemplification of the marriage of Christ and the church. It is evident that as early as 1521 at least a few of the clergy had taken wives on their own authority. But the issue was confused for some time. A royal proclamation in 1521 deprived clergy who had married, threatening severe penalties upon any who henceforth infringed the canon law. But within a dozen years, Thomas Cranmer, on the eve of his elevation to Canterbury, married a second time and lived in defiance of the royal legislation. In the Convocation of 1547, following the accession of Edward VI, all canons forbidding the marriage of priests and monastics were abolished. But the new day was short; the reaction of Queen Mary brought a repeal of the legislation, and the liberty was not restored during Elizabeth's reign. Finally, the Edwardian statutes were reinstituted under James I.

The Anglican Prayer Book of 1549 introduced the three "causes for which matrimony was ordained": procreation, remedy for lust, and mutual society in that order. The testimony of seventeenth-century divines, however, suggests that this was merely an enumeration of causes without an intentional order.

One hundred years after Calvin, the English divine and chaplain to Charles II, Jeremy Taylor, defined mutual society, not procreation, as the first purpose of matrimony. The union of husband and wife in one flesh, he declared, was blessed by the mutual society, help, and comfort they enjoyed in the common life. Their marriage was also blessed by intercourse in which the sexual impulses were expended creatively in relational acts. These relational acts were to have the effect of preserving fidelity, and might lead to the blessing of children. Taylor's famous sermon, "The Marriage Ring," spoke of marriage as the queen of friendships, in which "everything is common." The love which binds husband and wife together is "a union of all things excellent." This changing definition of the marital relationship was undoubtedly responsible for the emergence in the seventeenth century of a higher view of the purposes of matrimony than had hitherto expressed itself in Christian thought. No post-Reformation divine shows so deep an understanding as Taylor's of the biblical teaching of marriage as a personal relationship of sexual love. For in fairness to the facts, it must be conceded with Hebden Taylor, "One of the tragedies of the Reformation was the failure of the great Reformers to provide a truly biblical basis for marriage. Instead they sought to explain it in terms of Natural Law."[8]

Careful attention must now be devoted to Puritanism, because "the culture of Puritan New England had more to do with the shaping of our national culture than did that of any other colonial region or that of any subsequent immigrant group."[9] We still tend to malign the Puritans, as though all present-day repression of sex is a carry-over from their times and attitudes. Not so. They were a stern and severe brand of Calvinists, to be sure, but we must distinguish their concern for a biblically sound sexual morality from their easy acceptance of sex as natural and necessary—yes, as a God-given blessing. They did indeed hold the law of the Old Testament in high regard and used it as the basis of their ethical legalism. This did lead them to a more rigidly prescribed code of moral behavior than that of the Lutherans, who tended to allow whatever the Bible did not expressly forbid.

The Puritans in England were a conservative party within the Church of England who disagreed with certain forms and doctrines and sought to "purify" the church of them. As the tensions increased between the aristocracy and the common people, and between the Renaissance tradition and the Reformation zeal, the Puritans grew increasingly severe. Elizabeth's successor, James I, moved to quiet them by persecuting them, but succeeded only in uniting them and driving some to emigrate to New England, beginning in 1620, and thus making them the inheritors of the New World. Like Calvin, the extremists closed the theaters, passed strict laws against the elegance of apparel, and made fornication punishable by three months' imprisonment, and adultery by death. While these measures did not prevail in England, they fared much better in New England. Nonetheless, so long as it lasted, the Puritan dominance was dreaded by sexual deviants. G. Rattray Taylor describes it:

"The Puritans, however, could not rely on confession and a system of ecclesiastical courts to make sure that private penances would be observed, and perhaps hesitated to use flagellation except for the most serious offenses. They therefore made extensive use of the pillory, the stocks and the jougs. In Scotland, even more feared than the pillory was the punishment of having to appear in church every Sunday for a given number of weeks, usually twenty-six or fifty-two, to be harangued for half an hour in front of the congregation by the minister—for which purpose, in some churches, offenders were fastened to the wall in iron collars, or jougs. This was the penalty for adulterers and fornicators of both sexes, and was greatly feared. So much so, that it caused a sharp rise in the infanticide rate, for women who had illegitimately become pregnant preferred to risk the capital penalty for infanticide rather than admit the facts and suffer such extreme public humiliation."[10]

Puritan values prevailed for almost three quarters of a century in New England and were, in effect, the laws of the land. Far from episcopal interference, these New England Puritans were able to regulate marital proceedings so as to leave no doubt as to the validity of every marriage. No couple could be joined in marriage before publishing their intention by an announcement made at three successive public meetings, or by a written notice attached to the meetinghouse door for fourteen days. Connecticut required these "espousals" by law. A couple espoused were set apart; they were married, as far as other persons were concerned, even though the final ceremony had not taken place. If they could not restrain their sexual impulses, they were forgiven more readily than couples not espoused. However, if after becoming espoused a man or woman had sexual intercourse with someone other than the espoused partner, the act was considered adultery rather than fornication.

Sexual union constituted the first obligation of married persons to each other. Without it, the couple were not considered married, regardless of consent. Massachusetts records show cases in which marriages were annulled on account of the husband's impotence or a wife's reluctance. Puritan Edward Taylor stated that "the Use of the Marriage Bed" is "founded in man's nature," and that consequently any withdrawal from sexual intercourse upon the part of either husband or wife "denies all reliefe in Wedlock vnto Human necessity: and sends it for supply unto Bestiality when God gives not the gift of Continence." In other words, sexual intercourse was a human necessity and marriage was the proper place for it. The members of First Church, Boston, expelled James Mattock, it is recorded, because "he denied Conjugal fellowship vnto his wife for the space of 2 years together vpon pretense of taking Revenge upon himself for his abusing her before Marryage."

There was just one limitation placed upon sexual relations in marriage:

sex must not interfere with religion. Man's chief end was to glorify God, and all earthly delights must promote, not hinder, that end. On a day of fast, when all comforts were to be foregone in behalf of spiritual contemplation, not only were tasty food and drink to be abandoned, but sexual intercourse as well. While the Puritans never wished to prevent the enjoyment of earthly delights, they insisted that the pleasures of the flesh be subordinated to the greater glory of God.[11]

Puritan love was a rational love, in which the passions were disciplined by the will under the guidance of reason. However, if we are to glean anything from the works of Thomas Hooker, the eminent divine, it is that Puritan marriage knew the warmth of conjugal love. The husband-wife relation furnished the usual metaphor of the relation of Christ and the believer, and Puritans knew well the command for husbands to love their wives as Christ loved the church and gave Himself up for it. They placed such love only second to their love for God Himself. Thus it is a mistake to charge the Puritans with asceticism. They never thought of marriage as a purely spiritual partnership, although they did envision that, too. As Morgan points out, they were a much earthier lot than their modern critics have imagined. This is humorously illustrated by the following anecdote: A letter sent by John Haynes to Fitz-John Winthrop in 1660 indicates that Haynes had been commissioned to buy a pair of garters for Winthrop to present to his fiancée. Gently suggesting that Winthrop not forget payment, Haynes wrote: "I do not say I am fond of the happyness to kiss her hands, but her feet, having interest in her legs til my Garters be payd, which I adjure you to be carefull of as you would be glad to have a Lady leggs and all." This in itself would have shocked the generation in England instructed in the notion that ladies have limbs, not legs!

The Puritans were exceedingly practical in their recognition of life's realities. As marriage was the way to prevent fornication, successful marriage was the way to prevent adultery. So every attempt was made to encourage happy marriages. One of the more extreme measures was for the county court to order a deserting husband or wife to return home. The record tells of one John Smith of Medfield who left his wife and went to live with Patience Rawlins. He was sent home poorer by ten pounds and richer by thirty stripes! Similarly, Mary Drury, who deserted her husband on the pretense that he was impotent, failed to convince the court, and had to return to him as well as pay a fine of five pounds.

In their attempt to prevent sexual activity outside of marriage, the court ordered that all single persons who took journeys merely for their pleasure, especially in mixed company, "shall be reputed and accounted riotous and unsober persons, and of ill behavior . . . and shall be committed to prison for ten days, or pay a fine of forty shillings for each offense." The "seven months rule" was aimed at couples who had committed fornication after precontract but before marriage, then married before the birth of their child. The couple had to humble themselves before the congregation, confessing that they had had sexual intercourse prior to marriage. Added to the public humiliation of public confession was the trial before the county court and the penalty imposed. Fear for the welfare of their off-spring evidently drove many couples to confess. Under the "seven months rule" children born within less than seven months after marriage were refused baptism and were thereby put in peril of eternal damnation, unless the parents made public confession of their premarital sexual intercourse.

Casual and illicit behavior involving unmarried young people led to laws governing mate selection. Massachusetts law specified that: ". . . whatsoever persons from hence forth shall endeavor, directly or indirectly, to draw away the affection of any Mayd in this jurisdiction, under pretense of marriage, before he hath obtained liberty and allowance from her parents or Governors or in absence of such of the nearest magistrate, he shall forfeit for the first offense five pounds, for the second toward the partie ten pounds, and be bound to forbeare any further attempt and proceedings in that unlawful design, without or against the allowance aforesayd. And for the third offense upon information or complaint by such parents or Governors or any Magistrate, giving bond to prosecute the partie he shall be committed in prison . . . *until the Court of Assistants shall see cause to release him.*"[12] (Italics added by author.)

Despite the severity of the law, Puritan proscriptions on sexual behavior were difficult if not impossible to enforce. Lord Dartmouth, secretary for the Colonies, referred to the commonness of illegitimate children among the young people of New England as a thing of accepted notoriety. Howard reports that it was "common practice in diverse places for young men irregularly and disorderly to watch all advantages for their evil purposes, to insinuate into the affections of young maidens by coming to them in places and seasons unknown to their parents for such ends, whereby such evil hath grown amongst us to the dishonour of God and damage of parties," according to a Massachusetts law of 1749. Arthur Schlesinger says that "town records show that Puritan ministers cheerfully married an astonishing number of New England maidens already well along with their first babies. After all, if the Puritans put people into stocks, they also bundled. No doubt this was because houses were small and winters cold, and young men and women could find privacy and warmth only in bed. 'Why it should be thought incredible,' wrote the Reverend Samuel Peters 'for a young man and young woman innocently and virtuously to lie down together in a bed with a great part of their clothes on, I cannot conceive.' If the Reverend Peters could not conceive, some of the young bundlers evidently did. One thing sometimes led to another, then as now; and still the practice continued in Puritan New England for nearly two centuries."[14]

Confession before the congregation was followed by a congregational vote either to accept the confession, with due penalty, or to reject it and proceed to excommunication or suspension from membership for a period of repentance. Dr. Emil Oberholzer, a diligent historian, recently read all of the 1,242 confessions of fornication, or reports of such confessions, that exist in church records between 1620 and 1839, concluding that what is most remarkable about them is how unremarkable they seemed to the Puritans, recorded as though they were nothing but routine business. Tabulating all disciplinary cases of every sort, Dr. Oberholzer discovered that a majority of them concerned fornication. As Morton Hunt concludes, "It was, in other words, the most prevalent and most popular sin in Puritan New England."[15]

Laws were passed to punish adultery with death, and fornication with whipping. Capital punishment apparently was carried out only three times. The usual punishment for adultery was a whipping or a fine, or both. Fornication met with a lighter whipping or lighter fine, while rape was treated the same as adultery. There was greater possibility that rape would invoke capital punishment. Sodomy was usually punished with death, not being regarded as a forgivable sin. The most humiliating practice was the sentencing of an adulterer to wear the letter "A" and the symbolical executions in the form of having the offender stand on the gallows with a rope about the neck.

In the matter of divorce, the Puritans sought to adopt the rules of the New Testament, yet they were somewhat liberal in their interpretation. If a partner were to fail in a major marital obligation, divorce could be obtained. Arthur W. Calhoun summarizes the situation: "By following what they construed to be the spirit of the book, rather than the letter, they spread out from adultery and desertion as the only causes of divorce.

Dissolution of the marriage bond was freely granted for a variety of causes, such as desertion, cruelty, or breach of a vow. Generally, though not always, husband and wife received equal treatment at the hands of the law."[16] This last statement is significant, as a thoughtful assessment indicates that woman's status continued to improve under Puritanism. In Puritan New England a woman whose husband beat her, for example, could win a legal separation, and sometimes divorce. A husband could be fined for treating his wife with disrespect.

How does all this equate with the stereotype of Puritanism that prevails in our own day? Unquestionably, the picture of early Puritanism has been distorted by the Neopuritanism that emerged in the Victorian period in the nineteenth century. Hunt expresses a balanced view: "Seventeenth century Puritanism was tight-lipped, severe, and pious, but it was simultaneously frank, strongly sexed, and somewhat romantic. Except for the extreme forms of Calvinism, it was as much an offshoot of the Renaissance as a reaction against it. The frigidity and neuroses associated with Puritanism belong to a much later date."[17]

Eighteenth-century Europe was disillusioned with the several traditions of the Middle Ages, the Reformation and the Renaissance. It sought a humane philosophy that would substitute reason for authority, tradition and emotion. The emphasis was upon the ultimate worth of the individual. In particular people chose to see love and sex as a matter of natural, personal desire—a normal hunger to be gratified whenever convenient and without any nonsense about moral values or scruples. Human behavior was to be natural, with cool, dispassionate purpose. Deism confidently taught that the universe, including man the rational animal, was an excellent mechanism made by a Master Mechanic who started it going in accordance with scientific laws and thereafter did not presume to interfere with its operation. Gladly He had handed it over to man, His little likeness, who was capable of governing all things in rational, utilitarian ways. Although the great philosopher of Utilitarianism, John Stuart Mill, was not yet on the scene, his precursors were. Aristocracy readily accepted the rationale of the Enlightenment inasmuch as it expressed their attitudes toward sexual ethics precisely. As a result, the emotional life of human beings all but disappeared behind the repressive facade of reason and stylized manners. Anything was permissible if only emotions were concealed and rules of etiquette observed. Rationalist love was nonetheless lustful and lecherous, but the game was gallantly played by the rules.

This was the age intrigued with the story of Don Juan, the master seducer. Edmond and Jules de Goncourt, as reported by Hunt, said that love in the Age of Reason had been reduced to mere animal sensuality, and to seduce and desert had become its most intriguing and malicious sport. Aristocratic marriage more than ever was characterized—and openly—by its economic base, parties on both sides bargaining over property. And in the age when Don Juan was the fictional ideal, there arose Jean Jacques Rousseau, the most important of the political philosophers. Rousseau's greatest work, *Social Contract*, begins with the statement that in its broadest sense epitomizes the philosophy of the time: "Man is born free, but everywhere he is in chains." (It sounds like the Communist battle cry of a later time, "Man has nothing to lose but his chains.") This notion of liberty extended to the idea of man's sexual bondage under the legalisms of Christian tradition and authority.

Rousseau's novel, *Julie or the New Heloise,* started the Romantic movement in French literature. As to be expected, it was a book the church regarded as dangerous. Within a few years after Rousseau's death, the practice of romantic love which he idealized was fast becoming fashionable. Here was individualism in the realm of emotional life—a reliance upon one's own inner feelings rather than on some external authority. How readily it was to fit the upward-striving individualism of the coming Industrial Age, and how central to the philosophy and morals from that time onward! As Hunt so aptly puts it: ". . . where the rationalists had repressed their emotion and acted out their sexuality, the romantics restrained their sexuality and poured forth their emotion."[18] In all of this, the woman's role was passive, quiescent, subject. True womanhood was actually put down by the process of elevating woman to a false pedestal. Men took on a new patriarchalism in the face of feminine retreat—a retreat the men themselves had manipulated.

In the Age of Reason, men like Voltaire joined Rousseau in the parade of those who brilliantly attacked the religious institutions of the times and helped diminish the church's authority in matters of morals. But back to Victorian morals and manners. Behind the mask of rationalism an excessive sensualism prevailed. Morality was served by an obsessive concern for women's chastity—married women's, that is, since it was lawful to have intercourse with girls over the age of twelve, a privilege not neglected by the middle-class factory owners who employed large numbers of girls, and others who in that society were able to take advantage of their economic and social dependency. Pornography and prostitution flourished in Victorian England. By a strange mode of reasoning—partly due to the lack of physiological and psychological understanding—sexual desire was presumably limited to males (recalling Lord Acton's remark that it was a "vile aspersion" to attribute sexual desire to females!). Women accordingly were instructed to ignore the "need" for men to obey the "beast in human nature." Only prostitutes were thought to enjoy sexual intercourse, a provision apparently of the Creator who looked after men's needs. Wives were to endure, without interest or pleasure, the necessary though admittedly distasteful coitus. With such conditioning, many wives never experienced female orgasm or even knew that such an experience was possible, settling it that there was indeed no pleasure for them.

As women's chaste mind and innocent behavior were cherished virtues, they were allowed little access to reading that would in any way be sexually enlightening, let alone titillating. Prudery was the mark of the time, both in public discourse and in available reading matter. Books were censored in ludicrous ways, even Shakespeare considered by some as being too coarse for female eyes. The subjects of sex and procreation were hidden away in an aura of shame. Pregnant women remained inside their homes so as not to put on public display any reminders of the sexual side of life. As Rollo May sums it up:

"In Victorian times, when the denial of sexual impulses, feelings and drives was the mode and one would not talk about sex in polite company, an aura of sanctifying repulsiveness surrounded the whole topic. Males and females dealt with each other as though neither possessed sexual organs. William James, that redoubtable crusader who was far ahead of his time on every other topic, treated sex with the polite aversion characteristic of the turn of the century. In the whole two volumes of his epoch-making *Principles of Psychology*, only one page is devoted to sex, at the end of which he adds, 'These details are a little unpleasant to discuss. . . .' "[19]

As for the New World, men absorbed in building a new land in the wilderness had little time or energy left for the cultivation of romantic passions. Alexandre de Tocqueville, visiting the United States in 1831-32, noted that few American men were "ever known to give way to those idle and solitary meditations which commonly precede and produce the great emotions of the heart." And if American men were becoming too preoccupied for passion, American women were becoming too rational. Scarcity gave women in those times a bargaining power they could never have enjoyed in Europe, and they happily seized every opportunity for self-

assertion and a measure of independence. Tocqueville was impressed that
the result of all this was "to make cold and virtuous women instead of
affectionate wives and agreeable companions to men." Passion and marriage were being sundered in the nineteenth century, and sex once again
became a matter of physical pursuit, which man pursued largely on his own.
Marriage was separated away from the sensual, idealized as a union of souls,
with sexual emotion strictly confined to its procreative goals. The American
husband elevated his wife on a pedestal of virtue, above the temptations
of physical passion by which he was ever drawn downwards. The shadow
of Queen Victoria fell more extensively upon America than upon her own
land. Quite understandably, this became the heyday of the double standard
and flamboyant prostitution. And little did "affairs" seem to affect the
nation either politically or religiously. Grover Cleveland, governor of New
York, was elected the Republican President despite his admission to having
had an affair with Maria Halpin and fathering her child. Even more notorious was the case involving the most popular preacher of the day, the
Reverend Henry Ward Beecher, who seduced Elizabeth Tilton, a Sunday-
school teacher at his church. In time the story reached Victoria Woodhill,
a leading feminist of the day, who published it in her weekly magazine.
Elizabeth, who had earlier confessed her relations with Beecher to her
husband, rushed to his defense and denied the charge. Theodore Tilton
sued Beecher for alienation of affections. While the whole nation waited
with prurient curiosity, the case ended with a hung jury. It was only later
that Elizabeth publicly acknowledged that the charge was true. But this
failed to diminish Beecher's following.

Arthur Schlesinger makes this final comment on the Victorian Age:
"By barring the joy of sex from wedlock, the Victorian code at once
degraded the sexual impulse and weakened the marital tie. By transferring
romantic love to the fantasy world of the sentimental novel and emptying
serious literature of adult sexual content, it misled the national sensibility.
The Victorians' unsatisfactory pursuit of happiness thus ended half on
Main Street and half on Back Street, with marriage denied passion and
passion denied legitimacy."[20]

Within Christendom it was to be expected that reform and Puritan
movements would reassert themselves. The protest against formalism in the
churches and immorality in society is associated with the name "Pietism."
This movement is connected with Philip Spener and August Francke in the
late seventeenth century, and its chief center was the University of Halle.

It was an attempt to rally within the Lutheran body a type of life consistent with piety. It was marked by austerity and only those who avoided the practices and pleasures of the world were regarded as giving proof that they were regenerate. Rather than looking to the Scriptures as a source of doctrine for the proof of impeccable orthodoxy, the Pietists looked upon them primarily as a mirror of holiness. Count Zinzendorf, the noted Moravian Pietist, taught that there should be no more enjoyment of sex in marriage than of wine in the sacrament—and that was precious little. Speaking of the entire Puritan-Pietistic period—for they had close ties— Seward Hiltner observes: "The prudishness that made several generations of Protestant theologians discuss marriage with practically no direct reference to sex supports the notion that some aspects of later Protestantism distorted the Biblical and Reformation views of sex."[21] The church in the mid-twentieth century was only beginning to extricate itself from the prudish views and practices rooted in the Pietistic reaction.

While other philosophers of the Age of Reason were positioning themselves against the Christian faith and against the traditional Christian views on sex, David Hume and Immanuel Kant argued for such views. They both revised the course of human thought, and argued their case directly, not by appeals to Scripture or to reason that is in the end based upon it.

To understand contemporary Christian thought with reference to sex ethics, it is important to reflect briefly on the contribution which Kant made. His argument that the proper sexual relationship must be one in which the two persons approach each other as subjects and neither is made an object is a view that is at the heart of much contemporary thought about sex.[22]

The following excerpts are taken from Kant's *Lectures on Ethics:*

"Man can, of course, use another human being as an instrument for his service . . . he can use him for his own purposes with the other's consent. But there is no way in which a human being can be made an Object of indulgence for another except through sexual impulse . . . a love that springs merely from sexual impulse cannot be love at all, but only appetite. Human love is good-will, affection, promoting the happiness of others and finding joy in their happiness. But it is clear that, when a person loves another purely from sexual desire, none of these factors enter into the love. Far from there being any concern for the happiness of the loved one, the lover, in order to satisfy his desire and still his appetite, may even plunge the loved one into the depths of misery. Sexual love makes of the loved person an

Object of appetite; as soon as that appetite has been stilled, the person is cast aside as one casts away a lemon which has been sucked dry. Sexual love can, of course, be combined with human love and so carry with it the characteristics of the latter, but taken by itself and for itself, it is nothing more than appetite. Taken by itself it is a degradation of human nature; for as soon as a person becomes an Object of appetite for another, all motives of moral relationship cease to function, because as an Object of appetite for another a person becomes a thing and can be treated and used as such by every one. This is the only case in which a human being is designed by nature as the Object of another's enjoyment. Sexual desire is at the root of it; and that is why we are ashamed of it. . . .

"Because sexuality is not an inclination which one human being has for another as such, but is an inclination for the sex of another, it is a principle of the degradation of human nature, in that it gives rise to the preference of one sex to the other, and to the dishonoring of that sex through the satisfaction of desire. The desire which a man has for a woman is not directed towards her because she is a human being, but because she is a woman; that she is a human being is of no concern to the man; only her sex is the object of his desires. Human nature is thus subordinated. Hence it comes that all men and women do their best to make not their human nature but their sex more alluring and direct their activities and lusts entirely towards sex. Human nature is thereby sacrificed to sex. If then a man wishes to satisfy his desire, and a woman hers, they stimulate each other's desire; their inclinations meet, but their object is not human nature but sex, and each of them dishonors the human nature of the other. They make of humanity an instrument for the satisfaction of their lusts and inclinations, and dishonor it by placing it on a level with animal nature. Sexuality, therefore, exposes mankind to the danger of equality with the beasts."

How clear and contemporary Kant sounds! Strange that Christian theologians took so long to adapt his insights to their own understanding! Yet a century and a half would elapse from Kant's time (1724-1804) until the important work of Martin Buber (*I and Thou*, published in 1923). Note the mature reasoning as Kant, a century before modern psychology, writes of sexuality in relation to marriage:

"If I have the right over the whole person, I have also the right over the part and so I have the right to use that person's *organa sexualia* for the satisfaction of sexual desire. But how am I to obtain these rights over the whole person? Only by giving that person the same rights over the whole of myself. This happens only in marriage. Matrimony is an agreement between two persons by which they grant each other equal reciprocal rights, each of them undertaking to surrender the whole of their person to the other with a complete right of disposal over it. . . . If one devotes one's person to another, one devotes not only sex but the whole person; the two cannot be separated. . . . Thus sexuality leads to a union of human beings, and in that union alone its exercise is possible."[23]

The twentieth century opened with a new interest in the nature of human sexuality. Havelock Ellis began to collect the medical, historical, psychological and anthropological data, publishing his research in the monumental *Studies in the Psychology of Sex*. Cultural variations in sex attitudes and practice were beginning to be researched by cultural anthropologists, leading to the work of George Murdock and Margaret Mead in our own generation. Sociology was born, as was psychology. Sigmund Freud labored before the turn of the century and after, giving the role of sex in life a fresh legitimacy and influencing psychological theory to the present time. In 1923 Martin Buber, the Jewish philosopher, expounded his philosophy of personal relation in the important work *I and Thou*. About the same time Karl Barth and Emil Brunner, two towering theological minds, gave impetus to a whole new interest in the relational aspects of the man-woman dualism. Further penetration into the subject matter was undertaken by such men as Sherwin Bailey in England and Helmut Thielicke in Germany, and Otto Piper in this country. The study of theological ethics assumed independent stature, a notable contributor in America being Paul Ramsey. The views of the theologian Rudolph Bultmann, for whom the central motif in ethics is "radical obedience," by which he means "to listen for and respond to the Word of God speaking through the situation in which one exists," set the stage for other proponents of "situation ethics." Famous in this camp is John A.T. Robinson, Bishop of Woolwich, whose book *Honest to God*, published in 1963, had a bombshell effect on both sides of the Atlantic. The duo was joined by Joseph Fletcher. Today there is a galaxy of lesser lights in the debate over what is known as "Contextualism." An evaluation of situation ethics will be presented in a later chapter, so mere mention must suffice at this point.

In mid-twentieth century the term "Sexual Revolution" became the subject of many observers. The sex research of Alfred Kinsey led to that of William Masters and Virginia Johnson and their many interpreters.

Victorian attitudes were swept away forever as the prosperity of the twenties began to free the American people from the acquisitive compulsion that Tocqueville had observed a century before. And as the new psychology and the new leisure encouraged romantic love, so the new technology simplified life for the romantic lovers. The automobile made them mobile, removing them from parental and community surveillance, giving them privacy just at the time that contraceptives promised them security and antibiotics promised freedom from infection. The media celebrated the cult of sex, and today X-rated movies provide the explicit portrayal of sex as a way of life. Hugh Hefner has built an empire on sexploitation in his *Playboy* world. But if sexual repression in the nineteenth century failed to produce happiness, sexual liberation appears to have done little better in the twentieth century. If sexual repression accounted for neurosis in the nineteenth century, who is to say that sexual liberation is producing less in the twentieth? More than that, while repression at least preserved the family intact and made for a stable society, the pursuit of individual happiness through sexual freedom is evidently weakening the family structure and threatening the stability of society as we have known it.[24]

Will the church of Jesus Christ have a response to the confusion and pluralism of our day? Will evangelical Christianity have a viable rationale for its sex ethic? Only if it understands its history and traditions in the light of a fresh study of God's Word, readily confessing the errors of the past and relinquishing them entirely. Only if ethics are structured upon a sound theology of sexuality.

It would be easy to moralize at this point, or perhaps, with more sophistication than that, to proceed directly to Christian ethics. But for the Christian the heart of the matter is theology. He must ask such fundamental questions as these: What is the mind and purpose of God in the creation of man as a sexual duality? What order has God given to the relation between man and woman, especially in the unique bond of marriage? How has God related sex to marriage? Is it sex with love, or is it sex with love in marriage? Does sexual intercourse have its justification in and of itself, or as an integral component of the marital union only? What rationale does Scripture give in support of the absolute commands of God regarding sexual behavior?

We have concerned ourselves to this point in the book with the long history of the church's distorted and inadequate views. We have noted the challenge to Christian conviction arising from present-day alternatives to traditional Christian sex ethics. From here on we shall engage ourselves with the biblical theology itself. To do so is to embark upon something far more thorough than assembling a daisy chain of Bible verses from which to derive sexual moralisms. By theology we mean the systematic and coherent treatment of biblical themes. Because the separate themes of the Scriptures cohere in a unified whole, it is proper that we begin with the theology of man as a creature of God. From this base we shall seek to deduce the nature of man's sexuality and its proper functioning.

Part Two

A CHRISTIAN THEOLOGY OF SEX

5
Modeling the Image of God

Any theological discussion of human sexuality must begin with the creation of male and female. For the theology of man takes precedence over the theology of sexuality, even as theology itself takes precedence over the ethics of sexuality. Before we can determine the meaning of human sexuality in God's design, we must seriously wrestle with the nature of man himself in God's design. Happily, it is a fascinating study in its own right.

Curiously, the most popular modern paraphrase of the Scriptures, The Living Bible, shares the reticence of the King James Version in translating a crucial passage in Psalms 8. The important phrase correctly reads—in the *Revised Standard Version,* and similarly in the *New American Standard Bible*—as follows: ". . . what is man that thou art mindful of him, and the son of man that thou dost care for him? Yet thou hast made him *little less than God,* and dost crown him with glory and honor. Thou hast given him dominion over the works of thy hands; thou hast put all things under his feet" (Psalms 8:4-6, italics added).

Our first task is to determine the ontological basis of human nature. Since the word *ontology* refers to the study of "essential being, or reality," the ontology of man concerns the nature of his existence as a living being. Traditionally, this has referred only to certain aspects of his personality. For example, Aristotelian thought viewed man as a rational animal. To be sure, human nature does have unique ontological aspects, and we shall survey these further on, for they are highly significant to our understanding of human sexuality. Of even higher significance, however, are these aspects of human personality in dynamic relation to God and to other human beings—especially a sexual partner. So the larger question which draws our attention is that of man's true existence in relation to God. As Scripture puts it, ". . . in him we live and move and have our being" (Acts 17:28). (In Him we live and move and have our *sexual* being, too!)

Psalm 8 provides an ontological clue in that stupendous phrase, "little less than God." Man is the crown of all creation. He himself has been crowned, says the psalmist, with glory and honor. Hence he is to be regarded as having infinite worth and dignity in every aspect of his being, including his bodily, sexual being. To him God gave dominion over all His earthly creation. One implication of this is man's intellectual superiority which enables him to make nature serve higher ends. This is true of his own personal nature as well, for he is able to make sexuality serve higher ends than those of mere physical function. So man could not stand in closer proximity to God.

While no passage of Scripture is more appropriate than Psalm 8 from which to begin our study, second to it is the Creation narrative which describes man as created in the image of God. And surely, if man is a "little less than God," can we not expect him to have been endowed with supremely unique and God-like attributes? Of this we are left in no doubt when Scripture records that man was created in the very image of God.

In the opening pages of his book *The Image of God in Man,* David Cairns says, "The subject of the image of God in man is really the great subject of the Christian doctrine of man; for there is no part of man's nature which was not created to serve that image, and no part which has no relation to the image, even in man's state of sin." A few pages further on he adds, "It is worth while to pause and reflect here that the Bible, which exalts the otherness and the glory of God, which emphasizes as no other ancient book the twofold barrier of creation and sin that separates man from Him, yet speaks of man as created in the divine image."[1]

It is the image of God in man that marks man as God's peculiar possession, uniquely sacred as is no other created being, and in consequence of which man is fitted to fulfill holy purposes. As Cairns clearly perceives, the image of God in man "indicates, first, a purpose of God for man, and secondly, a quality of man's existence." Purpose is something that must be actively fulfilled. If man has a true purpose in his sexuality, it is because he is distinctly a creature made in God's image and functioning in that image. He has the potential for sharing the glory of God and expressing it in all his life, including life's sexual dimension. As the glory of God is His Self-Revelation in the splendor of His holy Person, so the intent of man's creation is that through the functioning image of God the very glory of God would be revealed on the plane of human creaturehood in all its relationships. This, too, is why the New Testament can speak of Jesus

Christ, God incarnate as Man, as bearing the image of God when all other men no longer reflected that image because of sin's disablement. And, again, it is a New Testament disclosure that all who are redeemed by Jesus Christ are renewed in the image of God, can participate in His resurrection life, share in the glory of God, and live out this image in their sexual being. Therefore, the starting point of any theology of sexuality necessarily includes the mystery of the two sexes created in God's image, uniquely capable of reflecting that image within a full personal commitment in marriage.

Now, there is a certain ambiguity in this expression, "the image of God" as it stands. By itself, this phrase might easily be construed as descriptive of man's essential being *in and of himself.* Only recently have theologians concluded that the image of God points beyond mere human attributes to a living, dynamic relation between man and God. The *analogy of relation* supplants the older *analogy of being.*

Karl Barth, who perhaps more than any other theologian has wrestled with this problem, says that man's nature "must from the very beginning be understood as a nature standing in some kind of relation to God."[2] G. Berkouwer quotes Gogarten as saying of theological anthropology, "When it discusses man, it does not speak of man alone, man in and by himself; it always speaks equally of God." To this, Berkouwer himself adds: "Every view of man which sees him as an isolated unity is incorrect. We are concerned with a nature that is not self-enclosed. If man's relation to God is not merely something added to man's nature, then it is clear enough that any view which abstracts man from this relation can never penetrate the mystery of man."[3] The words of Helmut Thielicke come to mind: "Luther declared that if we were to see the *imago Dei* in ontic qualities, we should have to describe the devil as the most perfect image, since he possesses all these qualities in superlative form. *The real being of man therefore does not consist in a sum of attributes, but rather in a relationship.*"[4]

This term "image of God" usually refers to a concrete representation, but when man is the subject, it incorporates the idea of interpersonal relationship. Thus the image of God in man has more to do with verbs than nouns; an image is an image only as and when it images! In the New Testament the meaning is clearer still. For the pinnacle of New Testament truth is its depiction of Jesus Christ as the ultimate expression of the image of God in humanity. He embodies all that the image of God is and can be.

To the statement of Nikolai Berdyaev, "The problem of man is the basic theme of philosophy," we reply, "The problem of man is the basic theme of the Bible." And certainly the problem of man is inseparable from the problem of his sexuality and its design. Man is a sexual being; sexuality is essential to any definition of man. Implicit in theological ethics is the notion that man cannot be studied as an abstraction, as a being in and of himself. Man and his sexuality has his existence in God, and can be fully understood only in the light of God's purposes.

If modern psychology and sociology have demonstrated anything, it is that personhood can exist only as individuals interact with other individuals in a social context. It also perceives sexuality as a dimension of one's nature as either male or female. The nature of maleness is understandable only in reference to femaleness; similarly, the nature of femaleness is understandable only in reference to maleness. But this is still only a precondition, for sexuality is perceived in the experienced relationship between man and woman. Sexuality has its reality in social expression, and there alone.

It is true that the phrase "the image of God" does not play a prominent part in the Scriptures. The term itself is rarely found. Nor do the Scriptures give us any systematic theory about man in the image of God. But Carl F. H. Henry wisely notes, "The importance of a proper understanding of the *imago Dei* can hardly be overstated. The answer given to the imago inquiry soon becomes determinative for the entire gamut of doctrinal affirmation."[5] This includes a doctrinal affirmation of human sexuality.

This initial inquiry would not be necessary—indeed it must seem totally irrelevant to humanistic ethics—were the nature of man isolated from God, if man were an autonomous creature.

But the image of God has its fundamental reference in the communion between God and man; it is defined by that communion. The effective result is a dignity conferred on man which makes him somehow *like* God as well as a *little less* than God, while at the same time uniquely different from all other creatures. One would have to say that the biblical picture of man in completeness is actually both ontological and relational. As Helmut Thielicke verifies, the image of God expresses man's original, unmediated relationship with God.

The Fall indicates that the image of God is nonexistent apart from man's living encounter with God in love and obedient faith. On the other hand, the New Testament equates new life in Christ with a renewed image of God. And not without dramatic effect upon his sexuality does man live in the renewed image of God in Christ. For Christian couples, the man-woman relation is meant to be reflective of the God-man relation through Jesus Christ.

The image of God is explicitly stated in only three Old Testament passages. The first is the divine announcement in the Creation narrative, (Genesis 1:26,27): "Then God said, 'Let us make man in our image, after our likeness. . . .' So God created man in his own image, in the image of God he created him; male and female he created them."

At this point the whole cosmos has been brought into existence. In each creative act, the divine imperative was, "And God said, 'Let there be' . . . and there was. . . ." But now a new kind of creative act is coupled with a new kind of creation—man. In this singular instance in all creation, the Creator does not speak man into existence. He does not say, "Let there be man." Rather, as so magnificently represented by Michelangelo in the Sistine Chapel fresco, God stooped down to take the dust of earth and breathe into it the breath of divine life. What a peculiarly apt correspondence between the new kind of creative act and the new creature! As David Hubbard commented in a recent article, God "brings about human life by fusing earthly dust and divine breath. Man is material and spiritual, tied to the earth while related to God in the mysterious synthesis of human personality." Emil Brunner elaborates: "Man, in contrast from all the rest of creation, has not merely been created by and through God, but in and for God. . . . Hence he can and should understand himself in God alone."[6]

Today it is generally agreed that both words, *image* and *likeness* in Genesis 1:26 convey one and the same meaning, the second word used to clarify the first. The words are in fact used interchangeably. In the second of our three passages from Genesis, only the word *likeness* is used in reference to man's creation, while in the third passage, the word *image* is used alone for the same purpose.

The next Old Testament passage also comes early in Genesis, immediately preceding an enumeration of the generations of Adam. Genesis 5:1, 2 reads: "When God created man, he made him in the likeness of God. Male and female he created them, and he blessed them and named them Man when they were created."

One thing that shall occupy our attention when we turn directly to man's sexuality is the dualism represented in this passage. An almost paradoxical declaration follows to the effect that "they" (male and female) were named "Man." This, too, shall prove instructive with respect to the nature of sexuality, for man (unity) exists as man (duality).

The third passage, also located within the earliest narratives of the Bible story, is found in Genesis 9:6. Here God is found making a covenant with Noah which establishes the ultimate value of human life in the society of earth. It is God who enjoins: "Whoever sheds the blood of man, by man shall his blood be shed; for God made man in his own image."

To some commentators the divine rationale supporting capital punishment for the taking of human life is this: man exists in God's image; to take his life is to sin against the divine image in man. But one may also contend that this construes too much in assuming that all men presently bear the image. In all likelihood this passage refers to the fact that because God created man in His image in the beginning, conferring this dignity upon him and clothing him with unparalleled worth, it is an incomparable affront to God Himself to take such a life. The author inclines toward this view.

The problem which theology has not solved with unanimity, and which remains crucial to biblical anthropology—and thus to the theological ethic of sexuality—concerns just what it is that the image of God does and does not incorporate. What is lost through sin and what is retained, and what is renewed in salvation and henceforth operative in Christian life? The Old Testament discloses nothing of the idea that after the Fall the image has been lost. The New Testament offers two divergent viewpoints, the implications of which determine one's perspective on the nature of sexuality. We shall look at these two viewpoints in order.

Recall that of the three Old Testament passages where the image is mentioned, the third, Genesis 9:6, seemed to intimate fallen man's retention of the image. But reasons were given suggesting that this is not the proper interpretation. Two New Testament passages are usually included to prove the same point, the first of which is 1 Corinthians 11:7: "For a man ought not to cover his head, since he is the image and glory of God."

Our present concern is simply to point out that Paul is speaking of man in the present, intimating that he does bear the image and glory of God. Those contending for this position insist that it can speak only of man now, and this is true. But their argument is readily disposed of by the obvious fact that Paul is addressing Christians only. This verse is consistent with other New Testament passages that clearly indicate that the image of God is restored to man in redemption. It is not speaking of all men of the present time.

The second New Testament verse to consider is James 3:9. Here the

Apostle tells how difficult it is to tame the tongue; what an evil it can be! "With it we bless the Lord and Father, and with it we curse men, who are made in the likeness of God."

No distinction is drawn between Christian and non-Christian men. It appears simply that men in general are the objects of the sinning tongue. Does this not make it implicit then that unregenerate men bear the likeness of God? With the same tongue God is praised and His image cursed—it is just that plain. But, plausible as this may sound, it reads too much into the passage. The verse says only that the sin is against a class of persons who have their origin in the image of God—not who presently bear that likeness. We may regard this as an incidental reference pointing to man's unique origin and the worth which this gives him in God's sight.

Looking back over the three passages which occasionally have been construed to teach that fallen man retains the image of God, what general conclusion can we reach? Klaas Schilder sees them as references to man's lofty origin, and also says that God from the beginning intends something glorious for him. Thus is an original reality alluded to in anticipation of its renewal, and this in spite of man's present fallen condition in which the image is lost. Here is an intimation of God's remaining faithful to His intent and covenant with man. These passages also refer to man's glorious position as the object of God's grace and as potential subjects for whom God intends the restoration of the image. Is this not, indeed, the very basis on which God continued after the Fall to act as the covenant-keeping God? And is it not "like" God to speak in terms of what shall be, of the potential yet to be realized? Brunner holds that although there is nothing which now relates man to God, nonetheless in the covenant of grace there is that which continues to relate God to man.

Just what has been lost through sin? What, if anything, of the image has been retained, and how? What is restored by grace in salvation? Is there, paradoxically, an ontological aspect which has been retained while a relational aspect has been lost? These questions have been answered in two different ways, which can be referred to as the broader and the narrower sense. Briefly, in the broader sense, which we consider to be incorrect, the image is regarded as not having been altogether lost. Specifically, reference is made to man's unique humanness, to the God-like qualities which cannot be denied. Usually the ontological description has included rationality, affectionality, volition, moral consciousness and judgment, self- and other consciousness, and either God-consciousness or the conception of personal relation with some divine Other. In retaining these elements of his being, man to that extent is said to retain the image of God.

To be sure, man retains these human faculties. What is in question is that these faculties in themselves represent a retention of the image, even in part. Does man, as the Reformers maintained, retain a "relic" of the image? No Scripture directly supports such an idea.

In the narrower sense, which we consider correct, the image of God stresses the idea that because of the Fall man lost his communion with God. With that relationship broken and inoperative, man's God-like capabilities are lost upon himself; they no longer function as God purposed. A radical reversal occurred in man's nature, a nature originally oriented toward God and now oriented away from Him. Uprightness of heart, originally derived from God and possessed in relationship with God, is man's no longer. The image is completely inoperable, although the potential for its reactivation is still present.

Consistent with the narrower view, the presumption of the New Testament doctrine of sin and redemption is that the image has been lost in the Fall, that man is totally alienated from the life of God, and that only the redemptive work of Jesus Christ brings about a radical reversal of his lost condition. This reversal includes the renewal of the divine image. Although man retains the uniquely human characteristics designed for dynamic relationship with God (still potentially possible), these characteristics in themselves do not comprise the image; that image exists only as man is in proper relation to God.

Paul teaches, in Ephesians 4:24, that life in Christ has been "created after the likeness of God in true righteousness and holiness." Here the fruits of redemption are equated with the renewed image of God. In Colossians 3:10 Paul speaks of the redeemed person as one who has put off the old nature with its practices, and has put on "the new nature, which is being renewed in knowledge after the image of its creator." The dynamic, ongoing nature of the renewed image is plainly indicated. In Romans 8:29 Paul sees the destiny of the redeemed person as the consummation of the renewal of the image: "For those whom he foreknew he also predestined to be conformed to the image of his Son. . . ."

For the Christian who is living out his new life, the divine image is modeled for him in the Person of Jesus Christ who Himself is the perfect image of God. This is exactly what Brunner had in mind when he says of the phrase *in His image:* "The whole Christian doctrine of man hangs upon the interpretation of this expression—but on the interpretation which is drawn from the New Testament, from the point of view of Jesus Christ."[7] In Jesus Christ the image of God in humanity has become knowable. As Hebrews 1:3 declares, "He reflects the glory of God and bears the very stamp of his nature." Phillips's paraphrase reads, "flawless expression of the nature of God." He is God incarnate in human flesh, the very embodiment of the personal attributes of God. Paul instructed the Colossians, "He is the image of the invisible God. . . . For in him all the fulness of God was pleased to dwell" (Colossians 1:15-19). In His daily life on earth, Jesus was known to His disciples as expressing the very nature of God. In fact, Jesus dared to say to them, "He who has seen me has seen the Father" (John 14:9).

The further we proceed, the more evident it becomes that the nature of man is nothing in itself alone. Its ground of existence is in God, not only in origin but in continuance. Though man is a thinking, feeling, willing being in himself, these capabilities do not equate with the image. Instead, we think of them as preconditions.[8] "Hence," says Brunner of the image, "it cannot be understood by looking at man, but only by looking at God, or, more exactly by looking at the Word of God."[9] He is speaking here of the Logos, Jesus Christ.

Another way of stating it is to say that man in his total being, is made to answer to God. Created to stand over against God in a relationship at once dynamic and reciprocal, man's selfhood is defined in its living encounter with God's Selfhood. Only as man answers to God through the totality of his uniquely human attributes can he manifest the purpose of his creation. As Klaas Schilder remarks, "Only in dynamic discharge of his calling can man reflect God in His world here below."

Central to the meaning of the word *image* is the idea of *making visible*. God at creation gave man the task of representing Him on earth through being His image. Man, in answering to God by means of his complementary responses, was to make the invisible God visible. To adopt a phrase of Gerhard Kittel, the man in Christ now "bears the comprehensible and visible image of Christ in him." This flow of life from God downward to the human creature, man, is reciprocal in the return of love, trust, and obedience. These are all living qualities. Concisely put, love is as love does; man is as man does; the image of God is as the image of God does.

In terms of what happened to the image as a result of man's fall, Scripture itself makes no reference to a lost or corrupted image. The consequence of man's sinful rupture from God is conveyed under various terms. A minor sampling shows that his life is characterized by "ungodliness" (Romans 1:18). He is said to be "dead through the trespasses and sins" (Ephesians 2:1), "alienated from the life of God" (Ephesians 4:18). He has "exchanged the truth about God for a lie" (Romans 1:25). Paul says that God gave man up to "dishonorable passions" and to "a base mind" (Romans 1:26, 28). His human creature is now under the "dominion of darkness" (Colossians 1:13), "estranged" (Colossians 1:21). He is "lawless" and a slave to sin; his inclination is "enmity against God" (Romans 8:7 KJV). The human heart neither is nor can be obedient to the law of God (Romans 8:7). Sinful man is out of relationship with God, not partially but entirely. There is no New Testament evidence whatever to suggest that man retains any vestige or relic of the divine image. It is completely inoperative, and in that sense lost to man.

Sin, however, is itself a reflection of the image of God man once knew. For only he who has been created in the image of God can sin, inasmuch as sin is personal transgression. Even when he commits sin, man demonstrates his creaturely superiority; no animal is able to rebel against the form in which it was created. But man shows the very power of decision against God which was given him in creation. So even as a sinner, man can be understood only in the light of the original image of God, namely, as one who is living in opposition to it.

Man, with his unique God-like endowments, chooses a life inimical to God. His God-like endowments are a necessary means through which his fallen nature expresses itself. Thus the image is corrupted. Today, as always, man does not cease to be man, or to be responsible to God. What has changed is that his responsibility has been altered from a state of *being-in-the-love-of-God* to a state of *being-in-the-love-of-self*, while remaining accountable to God's law. This deeply affects man as a sexual being, inasmuch as love is directly related to sexuality.

Sin means a broken relationship but not a dissolved one. This is quite different from supposing that man is autonomous. No, he remains responsible to God, but that responsibility is now operative in a negative and indirect manner. He who was destined to say yes has said no; he who was destined for love has fallen away from love; he who was destined for community-in-love both with God and humanity, has broken community. And so it is for the totality of man's existence. God has been effectively removed from the center of man's existence, and self has arrogated to itself that place. Here is the problem, too, in sexual ethics: self is at the center seeking its own satisfactions.

In summary, there is nothing human which does not suggest the once-present image of God, nothing human which does not at the same time indicate the total perversion of that image. At best, responsibility can be known only as response to the demand of God's law, nevermore as a relation of love and trust—nevermore, that is, except as individuals are transformed by saving grace.

Further inquiry shows that human personality is no longer an integrated unity, but a contradiction. It is still "I think," "I feel," and "I will," in what appears to be an integrated personality. But apart from God there can be no wholeness, no integration of the human endowments, for they integrate only in active relation to Him. And if there is to be a union of two persons in their sexual totality, these contradictions must be resolved. It is redemption that can affect every aspect of life, including the sexual.

Even in the perversion of the divine image we've seen that traces of it are present in the ontic structure of human personality. The potential for wholeness and personal relation continues as a human longing. His God-like endowments remain intact as something more than the means through which the corrupted image manifests itself. They are truly the precondition for the renewal of the divine image. This carries the promise of a renewed sexuality and marital union.[10]

Now, if all human relationships, including the sexual, are indirectly affected by the corruption of the divine image, how is it that many non-Christian couples express their sexual partnership in what appears to be a highly satisfying unity of persons? The question is important because in the course of things we must clearly see the difference between the limited sexual fulfillment experienced by non-Christian couples over against the greater fulfillment which is possible to Christ's own. Within the corruption of man's nature through sin there is still room for the operation of some kind of divine grace—not the grace that will eliminate this corruption or even reduce it, but that will hold it in check. This is what reformed theology terms *common grace*, which means that the living God concerns Himself with the life of fallen man, not leaving him utterly to his own destruction. This does not mean, however, that there is a remnant of goodness in man's nature; man is still corrupt in his total orientation to the Source of goodness, God. But the gracious God is still active in men's hearts, active both in restraining evil and in providing means for some ethical insight and direction. How beautifully this bears witness to the covenant faithfulness of God![11]

One major problem is that Scripture nowhere addresses itself to the question of common grace directly. An intimation can be gleaned from Paul's declaration in Romans 2:14, 15: "When Gentiles who have not the law do by nature what the law requires. . . . They show that what the law requires is written on their hearts. . . ." We are to understand by this that for the Christian the insights and principles of ethical humanism are not enough. Neither is a personalistic philosophy adequate. Sexuality, as God designed it, can be understood and fulfilled only by those existentially in Christ, actually experiencing the renewed image in Him.

Now we must focus attention on the way in which the human creature employs his unique God-given endowments to reflect the divine image. This requires compartmentalizing man for the purpose of analyzing some separate and distinct functions of personality.

Scripture teaches that God designed man with the capacity for personal intimacy with God Himself. Through sharing personality likeness, man can share a common life with God and with a mate.

Contrary to expectation, Scripture nowhere attempts to analyze the features of human personality as separate components. Man is treated as an integrated whole. For our purpose, however, six features of human personality exhibit how this sharing of life with God is possible. Each in turn opens up a window on the dynamics of the man-woman relation.

1) *God made man a rational being, a creature sharing His intelligence.*

Here the presupposition is that God Himself is a cognitive being, a creative intelligence. Intelligence in man is grounded in the intelligence of God. All the themes of Scripture support this presupposition. Man can both know and reason, having been given the capacity to contemplate his world, himself, and God's own Self-Revelation. By means of rational interaction, it was possible for God and man to enter understandingly into the very being of one another. No creaturely privilege could be greater. This is the Creator's gracious gift to man. Personal intimacy is an intelligent relationship.[12]

The application to the man-woman relation could not be more evident. Men and women, if they are to gain a knowledge of themselves as *persons-in-relation*, must possess rationality. This is also the first requisite for human community. Unity of mind is prerequisite to unity of persons and to a workable life-partnership.

We know that relationships between men and women are built as they grow in knowledge of each other. This, by its very nature, is a mutual undertaking. In the very nature of their differentiation, each sex has a unique contribution to make to the other, and these relationships become mutually supportive as each grows in the knowledge of the other's needs and special capabilities. This kind of knowledge might be categorized as knowledge *about* the other person. But along with this cognition there is another kind of knowledge which is existential in nature. This is alluded to somewhat frequently in the Old Testament, especially in the early chapters, which speak of sexual intercourse under the term "to know." In a couple's sexual union an existential knowledge is gained which is essential to the establishment and nurture of a truly intimate personal union. To this existential knowledge, each sex makes a uniquely necessary and valuable contribution.

2) *God made man a creature of affect, a creature sharing His emotionality.*

It is one thing to think and to know, another thing to have feelings about what one thinks and knows. A person responds to the people and events around him, as well as to his own inner thoughts and choices, with feelings. Some feelings are pleasurable, hence positive; other feelings are painful, hence negative. Implicit in why a person feels as he does in any given situation or about any given individual, is his own developed system of values—values emotionally as well as rationally meaningful. Most highly accentuated of all are feelings which people have about themselves, about other persons, and especially about the relationships between themselves and others. And so we perceive that personal intimacy is indeed an emotional relationship.

Here our presupposition is that God also responds to personal events with appropriately positive or negative emotion. According to the biblical witness, God is not indifferent to what happens in the world of persons. He, too, experiences pleasure and pain, joy and sadness, sympathy and indignation, etc. God is also truly empathic, entering into man's feelings as well as having His own. Man, for his part, was not created to be an emotionally autonomous being, but to image God's own felt responses, to share His emotionality. In sharing a common life, he would comprehend that he and God had similar feelings. They could fully experience one another.

On the human plane, personal intimacy is fulfilled as two people reciprocate such feelings as love, compassion, sympathy, etc. Along with the positive emotions come tenderness, kindness, and a sense of responsible caring for each other. The most ennobling, most positive and other-affirming emotion, is love. A higher emotion than this, man does not know. Must it not remain incredible to sinful creatures that God made man to receive His love and to reciprocate it? Yet through this means man enters into God's very purposes, sharing something of His loving concerns.

No deeper need exists in human personality than to be loved and to love. God placed that need in man's constitution from the beginning, at the same time giving him the capacity to fulfill love through another. Love creates its own response, its own returning love. And as love is life's most positive, other-affirming emotion, so anything antithetic to love induces an aversive emotion in response. Thus God made man to stand with Him in the same continuum of emotionality. The human person is made, in other words, to image the divine Person in emotional response.

Now, the Scriptures teach that God loves. In fact, in the analogy of being, Scripture declares, "God is love." The wonder of wonders is that God, as Subject, chose man as love's object. And when God chose to love us, He thereby chose to need us. The Almighty Sovereign of heaven chose to place Himself in need of us! Not that it is "I need you, therefore I love you," but rather, "I love you, therefore I need you." His is an unconditional love that gives itself without putting demands upon the beloved. And the gift worthy of divine love was God's gift of Himself, consummated in the sacrifice of His Son. Such love cannot be merited by goodness nor diminished for lack of it. Love wills to love, and love creates worth in its object. This is the glory of love!

In the man-woman relation, love is indeed more than emotion, although it is that, too. Men and women, powerfully drawn by love, commit themselves to one another. But human love does not have the quality of God's love, nor is it adequate to the full commitment of life. Only when that love takes its nature from the divine love is it capable of binding a sexually differentiated pair into an enduring unity.

3) *God made man a creature of choice.*

The biblical witness discloses God to be not only infinite in wisdom, but sovereign in will. His is that perfect freedom of choice inherent in the Creator of the universe. This attribute of volition is imaged in man, though limited by man's finitude and disabled by the corruption of the image of

God. Still it is the basis for responsibility and the values following upon responsible choice.

What possible significance could attach to personal communion between God and man were it not freely willed on man's part? Within the limits of human freedom, man chooses between the various options before him. His personal choices reflect his knowledge, feelings, and values. Created for responsible choices, his will originally was to be in conformity with the will of God. The terrifying possibility attending freedom of choice was that man could answer to God with a human yes or a human no. To choose God's will is to choose the possibility of glorifying God through the right use of His gift. To obey God's will is to render back to the Creator the highest creaturely response. In choosing existence within the love and will of God, man could assure for himself the highest of all possible relationships.

Freedom of will, operating as the power of choice, distinguished man at first as a responsible being with power to enact the image of God. Now, even in the fallen state, the volition of man combines knowledge, feelings, values, and desires—and acts upon them. The consequences that follow upon an act of will affect not only the one making the choice, but the lives and destiny of all who are related to him in the community of man.[13]

If it is anything, personal intimacy is a relationship of choice—an initial choice, yes, but something more. Involved in choice is a specific degree of commitment and fidelity. Only thus is choice a responsible personal act. And as long as the man-woman relation is subject to changing conditions and emotions, and as long as options exist in terms of other partners, some degree of commitment to the choice is important. Choice always renders its maker responsible. In a partnership of the sexes, it must be borne in mind that the will is an aspect of the divine image. Whether or not a couple is united in their submission of will to Jesus Christ is reflective of whether or not they belong to Him and are experiencing the renewal of the divine image in their life together. The will of God is the ultimate criterion. For the Christian it takes precedence over any considerations that humanistic psychology or ethics might pose.

4) *God made man a moral being, a creature with values.*

Wherever man is found and at whatever time, his life is characterized by value systems. A value system may be of one's own devising, or derived from outside oneself. Inasmuch as life is comprised of countless options and the choices they require, it is necessary to attach values to these separate options if choices are to be made intelligently and responsibly.

In relationships between persons there is an awareness of moral and ethical implications. Attitudes and actions alike reflect one's personal value system. Each person attaches a moral quality to his free acts. His very vocabulary implies his moral and ethical judgments. Common to speech are such words as "ought, should, right, wrong, good, bad," etc. No human society would be possible were it not for man's ability to make those judgments. Life thus is characterized by codes and laws, and by each individual's internalized value structure.

Implicit in the image of God is the presupposition that God is the sovereign source from which the good, the right, and the beautiful are derived. What God purposes for the life of this world is good and right; man's participation as the image of God was to be his response. Man's volition was free to the extent that he could choose either the good and the right or repudiate it.

Implications of the volitional aspect of the divine image, corrupted through sin but renewed in Jesus Christ, are apparent for the man-woman relation. Two persons sharing a common life and marital identity are mutually responsible to each other as well. Of all that they share together, highest importance may be assigned to their value system. While individual value structures must be brought into congruence, the main question is whether or not their congruence is established in the will of God. As a couple, are they in harmony with God? Do they see their relationship— including their sexuality—as fulfilling God's explicit design? Are they morally and ethically in tune with Him? Are they finding for themselves the good, the right, and the beautiful within the divine plan for marital sexuality? For the Christian couple, the final answer is not what seems best to them, not what appears to be the most acceptable norm from the standpoint of their own reasoning. Neither is it the adoption of ethical values of humanistic psychology. It is solely a matter of God's declared purpose. The same faith that responded to the call of Jesus Christ, is now to pattern the sexual relationship in all of its dimensions on the biblical design. It is faith believing implicitly that what God orders is both right and good. Intimacy is built upon the values which two people hold in common.

5) *God made man a self-conscious being.*

Consciousness of one's own self—as a being different from other selves —is an awareness peculiar to man. Only man can stand outside himself and look at himself objectively. He alone can stand in judgment upon himself and his own acts. He perceives himself to be finite and dependent. He is not autonomous and he knows it.[14]

Self-consciousness equips a person to discern the values of interpersonal relationship. He is able to ask the question of himself: What makes a relationship meaningful in personal terms? What is it that can alienate and quite possibly destroy a personal relationship? This awareness of self makes possible the understanding of the unity of persons in sexual partnership. In such a union, the sense of individuality is not lost, even though there is a profound sense of two having become one. Without having suffered the loss of one's individual identity, there is nonetheless a larger, more encompassing identity of two united selves. The *I* is still *I* although it has become a *we*. Just as one who is subject can stand apart and view himself as object also, so one can unite with another who is object, but view that other as subject also. This is the nature of self-perception that makes possible man's union and communion with God, and makes possible his union and communion with a partner of the opposite sex.

Parallel to this is the New Testament concept of the believer's spiritual union with Jesus Christ. That union forms a new entity called "the body," of which believers are the members and Christ is the Head. Of the five metaphors employed in the New Testament to portray this union, the one which most emphasizes communion of spirit is that of Christ the Bridegroom with His bride the church. Here, too, the nature of the union is such as to retain the sense of individual self while forming a new identity of two in one. This is a mystery which finds its highest expression in the Godhead as Three in One. The highest earthly expression is the union of two persons in marriage. And when it is Christian marriage—marriage in Christ—He is present in the union, making it an earthly three in one.

Inasmuch as a new identity is formed in Christian marriage, sexual union must be viewed as sacred. More than being merely a new identity in the eyes of man, it is a new identity in the eyes of God. Through His presence, purpose, and power, He Himself is part of that union. He is central to all that it represents, even its sexual dimension. That union, established now for the accomplishing of His purpose, carries with it the intent of indissolubility. Although sin may intrude and failure result, involving in extreme instances the tragic moral choice of divorce, marriage—by the very nature of its design and purpose—is intended to be a permanent union.

The thrust of biblical teaching is that self-identity and self-growth take place in relation with other persons of both sexes—and uniquely with one other person of the opposite sex. It is a mature person who sees other persons as the source of his own personal being and growth. First and foremost, man as a finite being was created in the image of God to be in intimate relation with the Creator. And in the earthly community, God's greatest gift to men and women is a life-partner to complement and complete their lives. The relationship between God and man was meant to be prototypical. As each *I* needs the divine *Thou* to be a complete person in the divine image, so each *I* needs an earthly *thou* to be complete as a person-in-relation. Marriage is the most intimate and fulfilling possibility of all.

Personal intimacy is a conscious relation of self with self, in which there is *I* and *we*. This paradox of the loss of self in another—which is the finding of self in another—is expressed by the apostle in Galatians 2:20: "I have been crucified with Christ; it is no longer I who live, but Christ who lives in me; and the life I now live in the flesh I live by faith in the Son of God, who loved me and gave himself for me." This is self-in-Christ consciousness.

Applying this to the Christian marital union, it would read: "We have been crucified with Christ; it is no longer we who live, but Christ who lives in us; and the life we now live in the flesh we live by faith in the Son of God, who loved us and gave Himself for us." Here is an entirely new consciousness—that of a union-of-selves-in-Christ.

6) *God made man self-transcendent, a creature with an immortal spirit.*

Man derives a sense of dignity and ultimate worth from his consciousness of spiritual selfhood. He is physical, tied to earth, and earthy; he is also spiritual, with aspirations which transcend his mortality. How beautifully this was expressed in Augustine's words, "God has made us for Himself, and we are restless until we rest in Him."

Not all men would identify their awareness of a spiritual self with a clear sense of a personal God, much less the God revealed in Jesus Christ. But men and women everywhere and in all times have experienced an inner longing for the completion of self through spiritual identity with a transcendent, infinite, and perfect deity. They aspire toward the knowledge of such a deity with whom they might have an abiding relation. On scriptural grounds, we might call this "God-consciousness." The biblical witness is of the "true light that enlightens every man." In the midst of man's flight from God, he ever turns to catch sight of Him. And though man with the divine image corrupted is far from God, God Himself is "not far from any one of us." Paul is even more definite in Romans 1:19, 20: "For what can be known about God is plain to them, because God has shown it to them. Ever since the creation of the world his invisible nature, namely, his eternal power and deity, has been clearly perceived in the things that have been made. So that they are without excuse." Man is unable to settle for dust and drudgery, for a life of mortality. Aware of his spiritual being, spirit crying out for Spirit, he longs for light and personal relatedness to a transcendent, infinite, and perfect Other.[15]

And what of the man-woman relation in light of this spiritual dimension of human personality? No person can expect to find completion of his being in another finite human person, be it beloved wife or husband. To attempt this, moreover, is idolatry. Man is a spiritual being and his ultimate fulfillment is in God through Jesus Christ. It is only then that he is given eyes to see the true spiritual dimensions of his earthly relationships. Those relationships he learns to develop in the light of God's presence, purpose, and power. Especially is this God's gift in Jesus Christ to married couples. In Him, the relationships of earth are formed with the blessing of heaven upon them.

We've outlined the nature of six major features of human personality which distinguish man from all other creatures and enable him to live in the image of God. Through these "relational bridges" an intimate union with God is made possible. This intimacy was God's intent in His creation of man. At the time of the Fall the divine image was corrupted, and all six attributes of human personality were cut off from God and disabled. Not that they were rendered inoperative in themselves; rather, they were made dysfunctional so far as any continuing relation with God was concerned. In brief outline, the following consequences ensued:

1) Man could no longer know God and understand His way. Intellectual intimacy with Him ceased.

2) Man could no longer receive and reciprocate divine love. Emotional intimacy with God ceased.

3) Man could no longer choose the will of God for his life. Volitional intimacy with God ceased.

4) Man no longer had moral guidance and motivation from God. Moral intimacy with God ceased.

5) Man no longer perceived his own intrinsic worth as deriving from God. His consciousness of self was alienated because intimacy with God ceased.

6) Man no longer perceived his spiritual worth and destiny because his personal intimacy with God ceased.

Man chose an independent existence in separation from God, electing to violate the very purposes for which he was made. In consequence he suffers the loss of personal intimacy with God and the problem of alienation from other human beings. How profoundly is this accentuated in the close relationships between husbands and wives. Man has lost the prototypical relationship from which to model every earthly relationship. Still he longs for the experience of personal intimacy, often with the expectation that marriage will satisfy what only God can satisfy.

For Christians, all this is meant to be radically different. Reconciliation through Jesus Christ paves the way for restoration of the divine image in its fullest functioning. Personal intimacy with God is experienced once more. The existential loneliness ceases. Once again there is a prototypical relationship from which a husband and wife can model their own intimate partnership. With Jesus Christ as the unifying center, a Christian couple can experience the fulfillment of the purposes for which they were called into union.

With the restoration of communion with God through Jesus Christ there begins for every Christian the process of growth into His likeness. This is the progressive work of God's Spirit which we call *sanctification.* And the end result, as noted earlier in Romans 8:29, is that we are "predestined to be conformed to the image of his Son." John adds,sofar ". . . we know that when he appears we shall be like him" (I John 3:2). So the goal of the Christian life is likeness to Jesus Christ, bearing once again the image of God. And for Christian couples, the goal is a union which reflects their mutual growth in His likeness. Because both husband and wife seek life and growth in the same Lord, they grow closer to each other as their lives grow closer to His. Through the power of the Holy Spirit, He becomes the unifying life-center which draws them into a spiritual union. A living out of the purposes of God is mutually undertaken as a couple commit themselves to a life of love, trust, and obedience to His calling. Their marriage is under His call, and sexual intimacy is received as His gift within that calling. In response to His will, husband and wife seek to complement and complete one another in an exclusive union representative of God's union with His people.

Is there a model for their personal relation? Each attribute of human personality which functions in the image of God also functions in the couple's intimate relationship. Their union is one of mind, affections, and will. It is oriented to moral and spiritual values. The value they accord to each other is the value which Jesus Christ has given. There is communion between two total persons. In Christ they find unity and wholeness, and this pervades their relationship together. With every faculty renewed toward God through Jesus Christ, a couple develops and matures in a life that is truly spiritual at heart. The presence of the Holy Spirit will enhance the entire relationship. Thus the image of God will be reflected in everything that the marital union comprises. Insofar as their marriage represents God's original intent, His blessing can attend them and they may find the hoped-for fulfillment. But quite beyond even the satisfaction of their own needs and their sense of spiritually fulfilling their calling, a couple may know that God Himself is glorified. His design for sexuality is fully validated in human experience.

Inasmuch as sexuality is expressive of our total personhood, it too is multidimensional. A sexual relationship is, first and foremost, a personal relationship, expressive of this total union of persons. Human history, however, points to the frequent parody of this intention. A purely physical relationship, whatever else it may be, is less than personal and hence less than sexual. If there is no communion of minds, hearts, and wills, the relationship is neither personal nor, in the truest sense, sexual. If the union is to express two whole persons, minds must engage in a sense of purpose under God. Hearts must fuse in the uniqueness and permanence of God's agape love. The relationship must be freely chosen and sustained in a willful commitment, not coerced nor impelled by passion. The Creator's intent of a chaste and holy union must be a couple's moral intent in coming together sexually. They must experience the spiritual dimensions of a Godward relation. And not only temporal but eternal values must ever be present. Sexuality, in other words, is meant to reflect something more than our mere humanity in its physical and psychic interactions, however meaningful they may be in themselves. Sexuality must reflect our being in the image of God. In Him we do indeed live and move and have our sexual being.[16]

When thinking theologically about human sexuality, it is important for us to realize that the facets of relationship between a man and his wife are not less nor fewer than those which comprise the image of God in man. But to bond a marriage relationship in an exclusive and profoundly intimate way, there is added to these facets a seventh—*the physical*. The physical facet, however, is integral with the other dimensions in the total personal union of a man and wife. The physical cannot stand alone and apart from the rest. It has no purpose in doing so, and becomes merely an erotic expression. But the Scriptures clearly teach that not only is the sexual relationship intended to be a personal relationship, but a full marital relationship as well. The biblical theology of sexuality is the theology of marriage.

Whenever man in his disordered state seeks to separate physical sex from the other dimensions of interpersonal relation, he distorts and diminishes its meaning, robbing it of its intended ends. Or whenever man seeks to align the physical expression of sex only partially with the other dimensions of personal relation, he suffers incompletion. We were made man and woman for full personal relation, including sexual intercourse, and in its most intimate and ultimate form, that personal relation is union through marriage. Sexual intercourse is the most significant symbol of a relationship meant to encompass two people whose marital bonds are a modeling of the image of God. Every aspect of personal interaction that describes the image of God in man must reappear in the Christian husband-wife relation if it is to fulfill His design for marital sexuality.

6

One Plus One Equals One

The literature of Christian sexual thought discloses that theologian Karl Barth did the most profound and advanced thinking upon the man-woman relation in our time. One does not have to be Barthian in theology, of course, to appreciate the genius of his mind or to cull the evangelical insights from his landmark work. Any contemporary theology of sexuality must necessarily take its direction from the heights he scaled. Our present task is to abstract from Barth those concepts which evidence their truth in Scripture, and to build upon them. What follows in this chapter, then, is substantially an interpretation of several key features of Barth's development. Upon this foundation the author has advanced his own theological thought.[1]

Franklin Sherman summarizes three of Barth's contributions to an understanding of the sexual: "First, it 'demythologizes' sex, which is to say, it views the sexual as a realm of genuine joy, but not of ultimate fulfillment. Secondly, it 'de-demonizes' sex by placing it in the context of man's total physical and psychic life, thus preventing it from becoming an independent and perhaps tyrannical element." This reminds us of the statement that sex is a good servant but a poor master. Thirdly, "it 'decentralizes' the question of man-woman relations, insofar as it affirms that not only marriage but also celibacy is a possible and valid form of existence and of Christian obedience."[2] Marriage or singlehood—either one—thus arises out of the freedom of individual decision, and equally as vocations under God. Quite realistically, with the rise of a Singles' Culture in the past decade in the United States, and with the sociological forecast that this is a permanent direction of the future, the ancient question of a celibate life is relevant once again.

Helmut Thielicke says, "The differentiation of the sexes is so constitutive of humanity that, first, it appears as a primeval order (Genesis 1:27;

2:18ff.) and endures as a constant despite its depravation in the Fall (Genesis 3:16), and, second, that to it is attributed symbolic value for the fundamental structure of all human existence, that is to say, for the existence of man in his relationship to his fellow man, for the fact that he is defined by his being as a *Thou* in relationship to a *Thou.* "[3] So it is natural that we ask how it is that the constitutive sexuality of man relates to his being in the image of God? How does this sexual differentiation also figure in the unitive view of man which is basic to Christian doctrine?

Both the origin and object of human sexuality are found in God. He relates to sexuality in three roles: Creator, Redeemer, and Lord. First, sexuality is given to fulfill the purposes of God the Creator. But because sexuality is integrally involved in man's sinfulness, it necessarily comes within the work of God as Redeemer. For the Christian to whom redemption reaches every dimension of his being, sexuality is to be governed by Jesus Christ the Lord. So then, no aspect of sexuality lies outside the design and purpose of a holy and loving God.[4] Understandably, the ends for which He gave mankind the gift of sexuality are obscured to the eyes of sinful man. Ultimately, human sexuality is a mystery not subject to analysis by psychologists or to researchers such as Masters and Johnson. Rather, it is revealed by the Creator whose purposes are known only to Himself and those to whom He reveals them. Thus human sexuality is comprehended first by turning to the earliest Creation accounts, then to the Old Testament passages dealing with God's covenant marriage with His people. Next we turn to the New Testament disclosure of the redemption in Jesus Christ, and finally to the passages portraying the final union of Christ the heavenly Bridegroom with the church, His bride. So our beginning point is the Creation narratives.

The basis for understanding human sexuality is found in a single verse in the very first chapter of the first book of the Bible. Genesis 1:27 reads, "So God created man in his own image, in the image of God he created him; male and female he created them." In the space of a single sentence, and in the context of the Creation of man in the image of God, sexuality is established as intrinsic to the image of God in human nature. Sexuality then, is somehow included in whatever is distinctive of the image of God in man. In a comparison of the two Creation accounts this clearly becomes the case. These so-called "orders of Creation" have a special claim to our attention because they lay down basic principles having to do with man's place in the earthly purpose of God.

Genesis 1 is the foundation upon which the succeeding chapter builds. In Genesis 1:1-2:4, the majesty of the Creation corresponds to the greatness of the One who brings all things into being by the Word of His mouth. But even the tremendous acts of creation turn out to be but the setting for the human drama which unfolds once man is created. For quickly we see that man is the crown of Creation. Yet it is important to note that it is man generically—mankind, not man the male—that is the object of God's crowning work. This is brought out in the language itself. On the same sixth day, God created both the animals and man. The animals were created first and then man, but there is a significant contrast between "let the earth bring forth," which heralds the appearance of the animals, and "let us make" man. This announces a new departure, a more direct and personally involved process upon which God embarks. Yet, by creating mankind on the same day as the animals, He classes man in some sense with them; man belongs to earth, to the space-time creation. But this is not all, for man is created in God's image and likeness.

The words, "And let them have dominion" anticipates the mention of male and female in verse 27. Dominion was not given to man alone, which surely argues for equality of the sexes, equality of responsibility, and equality in the capacity to fulfill it. The commission in Genesis 1:28 is given to both the man and the woman; neither sex could fulfill the given tasks without the other.

Then follows, "So God created man in his own image, in the image of God he created him; male and female he created them." Note the change from "him" to "them," and all within the space of a single verse. The bisexual nature of humanity is now explicitly stated in such a way as to make it clear that both man and woman are in the image of God, just as both were created by His Word and together given control over all creation. Both sexes are, by inference, directly accountable to God in the exercise of this God-given responsibility. With due emphasis, here in Genesis 1 the man and woman are seen in relation to their Creator; in Genesis 2 they will be seen in relation to one another.

If there were any doubt about the meaning of Genesis 1:27, its supplement in Genesis 5:1, 2 is plain: "When God created man, he made him in the likeness of God. Male and female he created them, and he blessed them and named them Man." That is, he named them "the adam" which means "man." Our confusion rises over the common usage of Adam as the name of the male parent of our species, not as the generic name for humanity. The problem lies with the English language where there is only one word to mean both the male human being and humanity itself, whereas Hebrew makes the distinction abundantly clear by saying literally, "In the male and female genders he created them, and called their name Man."

Genesis 2:4-25 does not attempt to restate what the first chapter has already established, but neither does it contradict it. Interest now centers on man the individual. Made from the dust of the ground, man's continuity with the rest of creation is accentuated. The same Godward aspect of his nature is expressed this time, not in a direct statement that he was made in the image of God, but actually in the kiss-like breath of life which God gives newly formed man—a personal self-giving on God's part in full correspondence with the declaration of Genesis 1 that man is made in God's image. Up to this point we can say that the man is first among equals, for only his equal was worthy to be his helpmate and worthy to share dominion over all the earthly creation.

Turning now to the image of God in the man-woman relation—a new thought to many—recall that we previously related the image of God to the individual only. Naturally we think of men and women individually bearing the image of God without considering that their sexual differentiation and union might enter into it. Yet reasonably it must be asked, as Barth did, "Is the image of God to be located only in individual men or women as such, without regard to the existence of the sexual duality? Or is the image of God somehow to be found also in the man-woman relational unity? In other words, is there more to bearing the divine image than is traceable to the individual man or woman?"

When God created Adam He said, "It is not good that the man should be alone" (Genesis 2:18). Milton reminds us that this is the first occasion where God declares something to be "not good." Yet, had not God already said of His creation that it was good? With reference to man, God could say "good" in the sense of his individual perfection as a creature, "not good" in the sense that he was incomplete because of his unfulfilled potential for human relationship. The paradox of man's sexual duality begins with the recognition of the individual as incomplete in terms of the image of God and his destiny as a human being. So we ask in what sense the male or female is an individual bearer of the image of God, yet personally incomplete? What is required for completion? Up to this point we've concentrated upon the manner in which the individual interacts with God and thus images Him. This corresponds with the Old Testament reiteration that God is one. In this model we have man as one and God as one. Man images God in a one-to-one relation. Now we are about to see that the image of God is more complex; man is more than one and God is more than one.

Christian orthodoxy views God as a Trinity. He is self-related as three persons in a triunity of being. Dynamically, the one God exists as three persons-in-community. The Reformers referred to this mystery as "one substance, three distinct persons." The mode of God's Self-Revelation is clearly that of three persons who confront each other, each distinct and separate from the other. Here we face a paradox, a divine mystery. It is a concept above reason, something that is beyond human analogy. God is a *Being-in-relation.* How do we relate this to the image of God in man? Implicit in the image of God concept is God representing a triunity of persons, and man representing a biunity of persons. This biunity of the husband and wife is analogous to the triunity of Father-Son-Holy Spirit. Man and woman represent relational poles within the one humanity, and between them a certain real union is possible. So all-embracing is this union that Scripture speaks of it as "one flesh." God's triune being is thus the original, the model over against which man is the image. This is why Scripture says that men and women together are made in the image of *Elohim,* which is the plural name of God, and why God says, "Let us make man in our own image. . . ." God and man have this in common, that they are both *beings-in-relation.* There is nothing in human personality, nothing in human sexual differentiation, nothing in the unity of the man-woman relation which does not image a corresponding reality in God.[5]

Marriage as a life partnership inclusive of sexual union represents man the completed being, man imaging God most perfectly. A unity is established, comprised of two equal and complementary halves. Furthermore, sexual self-identity is intrinsically a part of an individual's self-understanding. Sexual self-identity cannot develop except in relation to its sexual opposite. Thus maleness is experienced only as it stands over against femaleness, and vice versa. Man is not man without woman; woman is not woman without man. Sexual interdependency is necessary for establishing self-identity, and this argues for the unity which is possible in marriage.

So the question reduces to this: What is it in God that is represented by sexual differentiation in man the image? It is Barth's contention that there is a very special correspondence between the community of persons in the Godhead and the community of persons formed by the union of a particular man and woman. He further contends that the relationship itself has a reality all its own, beyond the reality of each person in the union. Two sexually differentiated persons in a marital union form a new being, as it were. They are indeed two complementary halves making up a new whole. What they form together as husband and wife is greater than what they represent as individuals. This is the compounded value of marriage as God intended it to be. Even as God the triune Being experiences Himself as unity and completeness, so husband and wife the biune being can experience themselves as unity and completeness. Thus do they share, in this added sense, the image of God in their union.

Barth maintains that there is no such thing as a self-contained male or female life, saying that the life of man is ordered, related, and directed to that of the woman, and woman to man. This is summed up in 1 Corinthians 11:11 KJV: "Nevertheless neither is the man without the woman, neither the woman without the man, in the Lord." Barth insists that there cannot be such a thing as an abstract masculinity and corresponding femininity which it is our task to cherish and preserve as such, but that "man is directed to woman and woman to man, each being for the other a horizon and focus . . . that man proceeds from woman and woman from man, each being for the other a centre and source. This mutual orientation constitutes the being of each. It is always in relationship to their opposite that man and woman are what they are in themselves."[6] Barth has so fully and brilliantly set forth this concept that in summary of it he is best read in his own words:

"God created him in His own image in the fact that He did not create him alone but in this connexion and fellowship. For in God's action as the Creator of a reality distinct from Himself, it is proved that God Himself is not solitary, that although He is one in essence He is not alone, but that primarily and properly He is in connexion and fellowship. It is inevitable that we should recall the triune being of God at this point. God exists in relationship and fellowship. As the Father of the Son and the Son of the Father, He is Himself I and Thou, confronting Himself and yet always one and the same in the Holy Ghost. God created man in His own image, in correspondence with His own being and essence. He created him in the image which emerges even in His work as the Creator and Lord of the covenant. Because He is not solitary in Himself, and therefore does not will to be so *ad extra*, it is not good for man to be alone, and God created him in His own image, as male and female. This is what is emphatically stated in Genesis 1:27 . . . God is in relationship, and so too is the man created by Him."[7]

With Barth we see that in its basic, most essential form, humanity is fellow humanity. Everything properly described as human nature stands under this sign. Fellow humanity is not something that a person can accept or discard at will, something he can practice or not practice. It is an inviolable constant of human existence, affecting every part of life and at all times. Man is nothing if not fellow humanity; he exists in the encounter of the *I* and *Thou*. This is true even when he may seek to contradict it in thought or in act, even though he may pretend to be a person in splendid isolation. For in doing so, he proves rather that he is contradicting himself, not that he can divest himself of this basic form of humanity. As there is no such thing as abstract man or woman, so there is only man and woman in relation. As Barth would say, man *or* woman implies man *and* woman. This is the fundamental clue to man's being. There can be no question, furthermore, that man is to woman, and woman to man, supremely *the other*, that is, fellow man. So whether in fellowship or in conflict, every form of human life in the image of God is fellow humanity. The highest form of all is the union of the sexes in marriage, because it is the most inclusive form possible within the conditions of God's Creation.

This sexual antithesis is experienced variously, of course. Sometimes it is experienced as attraction, sometimes as estrangement. It always contains the potential for unity or disunity, for completion or contradiction. Such is the potential in a sinful context. Nevertheless, the simple truth is that the power of relatedness is imperative in human life, and especially the basic man-woman relatedness. This is so whether the consequence is positive or negative. And this counterplay of the two sexes encompasses a much larger circle than that more narrowly defined as sexual love. Besides, it should be obvious that the encounter is fully achieved only where there is one man lovingly committed to one woman, and one woman lovingly committed to one man, in the choice of full life-partnership. This is the divinely appointed center from which the couple, as individual man and woman, continually go out and return.

This, then, is the primary form of humanity to which no person can be wholly indifferent. No one can escape the fact that he is man or woman, and therefore in some sense man and woman. In the husband-wife relation, fellow humanity is most concretely, incontestedly, and ultimately a fact. It is basically with this antithesis and connection of the two sexes that we have to do.

The Old Testament magna charta of humanity is the Creation narratives which describe how God completed the Creation of man by giving him woman as a companion (Genesis 2:18-25). The account of the Creation of man as male and female is the climax of the whole history of creation. As in Genesis 1:27, the theme is here introduced by a special reflection on the part of the Creator: "It is not good that the man should be alone; I will make him a helper fit for him." In this saying there is rejection of any conception of man in isolation. When God created man as male and female, He did not make two independent, self-subsistent beings, bound together by no closer tie than their common humanity and the need to cooperate in social life and in the propagation of the species. On the contrary, He created one dual being, an "adam" consisting of two distinct personal components, one male and the other female. Each is naturally oriented toward the other, so that together they are compelled to realize their mutual belongingness as the two constituent elements of mankind. Fulfillment can be achieved through many forms of relationship, but supremely through the one-flesh union in marriage.

The business of theology, as Sherwin Bailey reminds us, is to a large extent concerned with two primary obligations created by man's constitution as a dual being: the preservation of sexual integrity, and the acceptance of sexual partnership. Or as Barth expresses it somewhat differently, the double duty to live as man or woman, hence as man and woman. The first of these obligations, the preservation of sexual integrity, means simply the affirmation of one's own sex as God's good gift which one may neither reject nor somehow seek to transcend. The second obligation, acceptance of sexual partnership, does not pertain only to marriage, although quite evidently the common life of one-flesh is the central form, the prototype of such partnership. The necessities and opportunities of a community of persons involve the sexes in an ever-widening range of associations. God demands of both those who marry and those who do not a willing acceptance of their relational responsibilities, acceptance of the fundamental nature of sexual interdependence in all the human enterprise. Truly, no man can function optimally in the way of God except as his self-identity is formed in relation to woman; no woman can function optimally in the image of God except as her self-identity is formed in relation to man. While this is true of the entire human community, it is especially fulfilled in the one-flesh union of husbands and wives. And we can say with firm biblical support that it was primarily for this one-flesh relation that God differentiated the sexes. Yet for those who by vocation or circumstances do not marry, His design for them involves personal association and a degree of real interdependence. Although not expressed necessarily in the physical dimension of sexual intercourse, nonetheless this interdependence has its own highly satisfying fulfillment.

In Genesis 2:18-25, the second Creation account is brought to its climax and conclusion. Remarkably, it has only one theme—the completion of man's creation by the addition of the woman. Thus the original unity, Adam, was deliberately made into a duality, Adam and Eve. God's purpose is the man-woman duality, so that a unique unity might be formed by way of an intimate, enduring relation. Everything points to one fact—that God did not create man to be a single human being in isolation, or even a society without sexual differentiation. Rather, He created man as male and female to exist in this unique duality for the ultimate purpose of making possible a union of persons unique in all the created universe. That union of persons would lift the human creation closest to God Himself, for it would be a community of persons in love similar to the community of persons in the Godhead. What was formerly stated in one short sentence in Genesis 1:27 ("male and female He created them"), is developed here with instructive detail.

The question is posed for our consideration: What is the deficiency in man's essential nature that God perceives as existential loneliness? What divine provision will alter this condition? Implicit in the scriptural answer is the deep truth that man needs more than a companion—though he does need this. He needs more than society—though he needs this, too. He needs more than a mere multiplication of his exact self. He needs a complement—a companion with a unique contribution to make to humanity's fullness. Man in his incompleteness cannot fully relate to God. What is necessary for his complete humanity is also necessary for his relation to God. So the deficiency is fundamental to man's most fundamental relationship. For God's primary intention in man's creation has to do with having a partner for Himself, an earthly creature in His very likeness, one to share with Him the meaning and purpose of history. To this end God enters into covenant-partnership with man. However, without experiencing himself as man-woman duality, or that duality as it becomes a unity through marriage, man could never be the whole person with whom God could enter into covenant-partnership. No solitary, unisex form of humanity could fit this divine bill of particulars. Man as a solitary individual could not be the image of God, for God is not solitary. God is a *Being-in-community*, a triune Community of Persons. Thus the Creator reflects in His soliloquy upon man's need for a special creation suited for his completion. In God's mind this is woman.[8]

In God's plan for humanity, His covenant relation with man was an established reality. Before the foundation of the world He determined the covenant bond to be the mode of all His dealings with His human creature. In turn, the nature of this covenant relation between God and man is prototypical of the man-woman covenant. This determines the form the one-flesh marriage relationship takes. In other words, *to have* a partner, man's first requisite is *to be* God's partner. What God purposes, you see, is a helpmate resembling man yet different from him. If man's partner were an exact replica, a multiplication of his exact kind, incompleteness and solitariness would remain. Man would have no alter ego, no true complement, no life-enhancing companion. Yet—and this is the other possibility —if his helpmate were so different as to be not at all like him, they together could never form a true unity, a new single identity. Such a partner could not complete his humanity. Neither could they form the unique community of persons God had in mind. Moreover, man's relation with his helpmate must image God's covenant relation with His people. The union of the two sexes is more than mere addition; it is a complementary union in which the whole is greater than the sum of its constituent parts. Both the man and the woman contribute something uniquely their own to this new entity, the couple. As for unredeemed men and women, they will never so much as discover this configuration with its own distinct goal and values. It will be forever outside their experience.

With the creation of woman and her subsequent acceptance by Adam, the completion of humanity is effected at last. Humanity is not achieved merely by the creation of two sexes, but by their union in a marital partnership. In recognition of this, Adam triumphantly cried, "This at last is bone of my bones and flesh of my flesh" (Genesis 2:23). Here he expresses immediate, certain recognition of his perfect counterpart and complement. He also proclaims his decision and choice. Thus the first recorded saying of man in Scripture is more than an epilogue to Creation; it is man himself acknowledging—though undoubtedly without full awareness of its significance—that the woman's creation completes his creation. The goal of creation has been reached and the Sabbath rest of God follows. Appropriately, man's recognition of the true nature of his helpmate is announced in his naming her "woman" "because she was taken out of Man" (Genesis 2:23).

Can we not see added glory for woman in Adam's recognition and choice of her as the gift worthy of his majestic position on earth? With perfect freedom and the wisdom of his unfallen state, he acknowledged the woman to be the perfect partner and companion to share his life and divide his labor. He chose this helpmate not for this or that particular end, but for his very existence as man. At last the image of God is complete, the type fully formed!

What is further attested is God's unwillingness to be alone with respect to His human creature. He wills to be with and for man! Nothing less than covenant marriage, if you will, shall suffice. The grand type of this union of God and man shall be the union of sexually differentiated humanity. Human marriage is modeled after that of God and His people. As God wills to be with and for man, so man wills to be with and for woman, and woman in turn wills to be with and for man. The idea of a unique, exclusive, intimate, and enduring covenant rules in both cases.

Who and what is woman? According to this account, she is not man's creation. Like himself, she is the thought and work of God. As Helmut Thielicke puts it, both man and woman are equally immediate to the Creator and His act. As God created both man and woman, He also created the relational form that binds them together, a unity of persons like Himself. It is He who brings them together, this too being part of the completing of man's creation. But such a relationship, which is not just any kind of association or contract, is the distinctive relation which Scripture from the very start calls "one flesh." This God in His infinite wisdom appointed, but left man to recognize and choose in the integrity of his own mind, heart, and will. Man affirms for himself this distinctive provision, thereby attesting God's purpose for his life. This affirmation did in fact take place when Adam triumphantly cried, "This at last is bone of my bones and flesh of my flesh." Adam at that moment fulfilled the one part God gave him to play in the drama of his own creation.

We now perceive man in his completion as a "being-in-encounter." He exists only as a "being-in-relation." The woman, although created for man, has her own equal and independent honor and worth. This she has by virtue of her own act of choosing what God had designed her to be, namely, man's helpmate. Hers is a conferred honor, conferred by Him who fulfilled His own design and purpose in her creation. No honor or worth, of course, belongs to the creature in and of itself; in every case it is conferred by the Creator. Woman, in her special creation and function, shares an equal glory with man, equal because conferred by Him whose will and purpose she serves.

The whole of Genesis 2:18-25 speaks of the coexistence of man and woman as the original hence basic form of fellow humanity. It singles out the man-woman relationship of "one flesh" from among all other possible relationships and gives it precedence. The man-woman relationship of one flesh is the center to which all other relationships of fellow humanity are the circumference. The marital pair is the basic model of men and women in a community of love. Significantly, in the whole creation account no reference is made to fatherhood, motherhood, or the establishment of family. The entire concern is focused upon man and woman and their relationship to one another. Prior to the institution of the family comes the institution of marriage. This is noteworthy since the accent on progeny is all but total throughout the Old Testament. (There is but one other clear exception—the little book known as the *Song of Solomon.*) Barth rightly insists that Genesis 2 is imperious in this respect, that man is first of all *man-and-his-wife.* Only then is man all kinds of other things, including perhaps father and mother, even neighbor.

The emphasis of the second Creation narrative falls upon God's act of placing before man the choice of selecting his own mate, a choice which he must consciously and responsibly make. This is man's first decision so far as we are told—and what a decision it is! Not only is he offered a partner of God's making, but he must freely accept her for himself, doing so within the conditions of marriage God sets. What she was created by God to be, she now shall become through man's choice. The union they form, should man choose it, shall become the prototype of all the marriage unions to follow in the course of human history. Not only that, but this union will represent (1) the basic form of fellow humanity, and (2) the type of God's covenant marriage with His people.

In order that Adam might make this discovery for himself and come to a personal choice in the matter, God first brings the animals to him. By this means it is demonstrated that Adam cannot find in any of them his true counterpart and complement, the helpmate who can fulfill his life needs. Not one of them can he address as *thou.* They are living beings, lovable and useful, but not in any sense fitted to be his mate. So we read in its majestic simplicity, "but for the man there was not found a helper fit for him" (Genesis 2:20). Barth's comment is that this whole transaction was not a divine experiment that failed; no, God had to act in this manner if the gift which He had in store for man was not to be man's undoing. That is, man must recognize, choose, and hence confirm woman as the helpmate ordained and specially created for him. There could be no compulsion to accept her merely in the absence of other possible alternatives. Nor must he discover her without having first sought elsewhere and exhausted every possibility. He had to reject all other possibilities, eliminate all alternatives. As man, he was free to prefer otherwise. He could choose solitude. He was free to remain unsatisfied and alone in the condition which God had earlier pronounced "not good." But in that same freedom he decides in favor of the one whom God had already chosen but kept unannounced. So in the very first exercise of man's freedom of choice, he gained the blessing God had for him, demonstrating his original integrity of perception and will. Gladly did he choose to conform to the Creator's purpose. And in making this choice, he at the same time confirmed his own completed humanity. Thus we are brought to the very climax of creation.

Now, the details of the second Creation account are not many, but neither are they superfluous. They are fraught with profound meaning. In the truest sense, they are prophetic enactments. Upon such details we confidently build our theology of man and his sexuality. Our justification rests in the fact that there is no other source for thus theologizing, and our confidence rests in the integrity of the account and the ends for which it is constructed. So our attention is drawn to this detail, that the Lord God caused a deep sleep to fall upon man at the time the rib was removed from him. Man was thereby effectively removed from active participation in the creation of the woman, that is, from active participation in the completion of his own creation. Indeed, in all likelihood he did not know precisely what he lacked and looked for, nor in what manner God was going to provide for his need. It was not his to know that God was about to take away part of his essential being, only to remove that deficiency in the form of a separate living being with whom he could unite.

It was not Adam who thought up woman as his helpmate; she was exclusively the thought and plan of the Creator. He alone knew man's need and what would fully meet it. Adam could not know this, nor can man know it today apart from God's disclosure. Without some word from God, man remains with the mystery of his own existence as a man-woman duality. He approaches the solution to his enigma in various ways, some of which he calls marriage. But he never quite reaches the full satisfaction of his needs in the union God devised. It is possible only as he and his relationships are restored in Christ.

In the mystery of man's creation as man-woman in relation, we are face to face with God's great secret in Christ. This mystery is alluded to by Paul in Ephesians 5:21-33. It is a secret no creature, not even man, could understand apart from divine revelation. Dimly that secret is opened to us in the orders of Creation in the Genesis narratives. Limited as they are, they nonetheless incorporate details which are highly instructive, and it is to four of these details that we now turn.

First, Adam found in the woman another human being whose origin was not the same as his own. She is neither wholly like nor unlike himself. She is, however, of and from himself. She is related to him as member is related to body, so close is she to him. She satisfies a need, fills a place that not even he himself could adequately anticipate. This is what the narrative implies in depicting the removal of the rib from which God fashioned woman and gave her back to complete his creation and make possible his humanity.

Second, the man recognizes in the woman something of himself, but at the same time someone who, even in her intimate relationship with him, retains her autonomous nature. While he identifies this human nature as unmistakably his, it is also unmistakably hers. For she was fashioned out of that which was taken from him and still remains recognizable in her. Here is a paradox: two human beings, one man and the other woman, seem to be complete in themselves, yet are not; seem so much alike, yet are not; seem so different, yet are not. They are made for one another yet can only experience this in marriage. They are equal halves making up the whole, yet have unequal functions. They stand in an unequal order; still, they are equal in honor and value. Although both seem complete in themselves alone, yet neither can be what he is meant to be without the other. What a paradox this is!

Third, man suffered something, experienced a loss, with the removal of a part of his own body and the consequent formation of woman from that part. He is no longer wholly himself, though he seems to be. He has had to surrender a part of himself, though he does not know why. Tellingly, the narrative recounts how God covered with flesh the wound where the rib was taken, thus sustaining man even in the time of his loss. Man bears no evident wound, nor has he ceased to function exactly as he had at the beginning. But even greater now is the determination that he is not fully completed humanity. Nor shall he be wholly man until he is reunited with that part taken from him and restored in the form of his helpmate. This is a deficit in his realization of full humanity which cannot be filled by any other than the woman God has made for him.

Fourth, he cannot divest himself of that part of himself which now is returned. He cannot alienate or isolate himself from that which is still a part of his own being. He cannot do this anymore than he could have participated in the fashioning of his own helpmate. He cannot disinterestedly separate himself from her without depriving himself of a very part of himself. She, too, can exist disinterestedly and in separation from him only by denying her origin and place in God's design. There is therefore an interdependence established between the two sexes which they cannot escape; it is God's own doing. It may be denied—they are free to do this —but not without irreparable loss.

These four considerations are implicit in the Creation story. They represent the basis of the man-woman relation in the covenant typology. This complex consideration must be regarded with all seriousness in any adequate theology of sexuality. Herein is God's secret, concealed in its Old Testament context, but culminating in the New Covenant in Jesus Christ. The New Testament focuses attention upon the climactic aspect of God's covenant undertaking with man, namely, the church as it becomes the bride of Christ the heavenly Bridegroom.

The non-Christian husband and wife reach out to humanistic ideologies to provide a basic concept for marriage, but all of these prove to be inadequate. Such an approach which may at times lead to a relatively high degree of love and oneness is still short of God's ideal. For though they experience much, there is far more. Because a Christian marriage is a type of the covenant marriage between Christ and the church, Paul speaks of it as a "great mystery" (Ephesians 5:32). Because it is a sacred mystery with profound spiritual implications, it lies wholly outside the range of secular thinking. Just how far removed the secular view is from the sacred is illustrated by the remark of Pierre Dommergues, "The sexual revolution . . . has freed America from her traditional puritanism with its accompanying guilt. But it has also turned love into a physical performance . . . *from which mystery is excluded.*"[9] When sexuality is secularized, one of the greatest losses is that of its mystery.

The second Creation narrative clarifies another theological matter. Man in the very first exercise of his autonomy, in his very first decision as man, says yes to the Creator in the act of saying yes to the woman who is offered him. Adam might have said no—as indeed he said no to the animals previously brought before him. So the question was whether man in his existential loneliness, in his need for a helpmate, would recognize and

choose the one God provided? Or would he reject this sexually differentiated human being, perhaps in further hope of something different still?

When Adam awoke from his sleep and fixed his eyes upon the woman
for the first time, what might have been his response? He might have said,
"O Lord, not *this!*" Or, "Surely, Lord God, you could have done better
than this!" Perhaps he might have said, "Lord, why didn't you put *me* on
the committee; *we* could have really come up with something great!" Or
he might just have taken a look and said, "Lord, just put me back to sleep."
But no! Adam needed just one look, and in his unfallen state he perceived
perfectly that only the Lord God could have supplied him with so perfect
a mate.

This recognition and choice, by the way, is the question facing men
and women at all times, and especially every professed Christian homosexual. Scripture spells out a specific design in providing woman for man,
creating this singular sexual basis for an intimate, exclusive, and enduring
union between human persons. Whatever other considerations might be
introduced, the ultimate appeal is to God's creative purposes. Beyond this
the Christian speculates at the risk of contradicting God's appointed plan
for sex, marriage, and society.

Since the woman is the completion of man's humanity, she herself has
no need of further completion for herself. She, too, is completed in union
with him. And although the Creator brought her to Adam, offering her to
him, her autonomy as well as his remains intact. Upon their meeting, she,
too, makes a decision. She also must choose that for which God has chosen
her. She, too, must say yes to man, and in so doing say yes to God.

Can we not read in all of this that the Creator has an intention for
each couple which is far more extensive than mere association? He created
woman to be the complement of man, capable of the most intimate union
in body, mind, and spirit. In view of this, can Adam choose to associate
himself with the woman while at the same time disassociating himself from
God's plan for their union together? The choice established the first possibility for man's exploitation of woman, and quite evidently he resisted it.
Man in the image of God did not treat this person as a thing. He looked
upon her in terms of unity, not utility. In making the decision to accept
God's plan for their union, man resolved the issue, thereby joining in the
completion of his humanity. What a suspenseful moment, this dawning of
human decision! But how necessary it was to the establishing of God's order
in the world! It is this very decision which continues to be man's foremost

responsibility to God's social order. It is the decision of every man and every woman to whom God comes with His offer of sexual union and life partnership in marriage.

With man's yes to the woman as his helpmate, he gains the knowledge of his own maleness. Seeing the woman as feminine in her total being, the man awakens to the recognition of his own distinctive male being. Until then maleness had no meaning for him, for maleness—like femaleness—is known only as it is experienced over against its opposite. To this new revelation man also said yes, accepting it as God's gift and purpose. We dare say that his words, "This at last is bone of my bones and flesh of my flesh" was Adam's celebration of sexuality.

A further implication is that Adam's deficiency as man alone was not greater than Eve's capacity to fulfill it. One woman was sufficient to complete his humanity and to fulfill his every need. It is important to remember that this is the prototype for every marital union that follows. Only because of man's sinfulness is he unable to appropriate God's provision of a single woman and be satisfied with her alone. Quite clearly, then, the purpose in creation as it concerns the two sexes is the establishment of marriage as a unique, exclusive, lifetime partnership of one man with one woman, a partnership in body and spirit.

It would be blindness on our part not to see the height to which God's second sex has been exalted by the order of Creation. It is she who is God's special gift, the noblest God could conceive for His highest creature, man. It is she who caused man to say an unequivocal yes to God's plan for them both. It is she who completed man's humanity, opening to him the possibility of a full human existence. It is she who unites with him to form the mystical union of persons, the one-flesh union, the type of God's ultimate relation with His people in redemption. It is she who orients man to the order of Creation and his place in it. Her glory and honor come not one bit behind that of the first sex! And now together they share a heavenly *Thou* to whom they can address themselves as *we*. And each has an earthly *thou* to address as *I*. The man is only first among equals; the man-woman relationship is not that of sameness, but equality.

The very naming of woman by Adam recalls the fact that she is of him. She is not his property—an insight lost for many centuries when male strength and aggressiveness were dominant. She is a full human person—again, a fact lost to male perspective for aeons of time. She belongs with and for man, even as man belongs with and for her. Ordained to be his helpmate, she is part of a relationship entirely consonant with her true autonomy as a human person. That the man stands first in the order of being, the woman second, and that she belongs to him in a primary sense whereas he belongs to her only secondarily, must not be misunderstood. It is not a question of value, dignity, or honor, but simply of order. Nor does it denote a higher and lower humanity. The acknowledgement of God's order brings a singular glory to the man and a singular glory to the woman.

It is only now that we can speak of love and marriage—the love between a particular man and woman, and the marriage built upon it. Love and marriage are God's appointed means for fulfilling His creative purpose. Spoken to the first couple by way of anticipation, the words fittingly look ahead to all the coming generations: "Therefore a man leaves his father and his mother and cleaves to his wife, and they become one flesh" (Genesis 2:24). Here a new emphasis comes before us. The man must make a decisive move, not just in the direction of the woman, but away from his family ties. He is to enact the decision to follow her who follows him. The one-flesh relation awaits this aspect of male initiative, too.

Love is more than a feeling; it is also a power of will. It is an intention which has its greatest force in the ability to care. The very nature of love may be seen in this one-flesh relationship of the first man and his wife. Bound by love and its commitment to enduring marriage, the first couple realize the goal of unity. It is the comprehensive unity of two total persons, expressed most uniquely by the exclusiveness of their sexual union. It is to this arrangement that every man and woman is called to say yes. This climax of the Creation account enables us to say that in the marriage of the man and his wife the crown of Creation has been displayed.

Another way of expressing what God did is to say that He created a "woman-sized void" in man, a void that none of the animals nor even another man could fill. It was a deficit imposed by the Creator in anticipation of its restoration in another form. The concept of one-flesh is comprehensive of all that the man and the woman bring to their total union. The intimate and exclusive sexual union is representative of this fusing of total persons. There is a dissimilarity of the two sexes of which sexual differentiation is a single part. In his total being, man is man; in her total being, woman is woman. This forms the basis for an important aspect of relationship: the mutual attraction between two persons who are mysteriously alike yet unlike. This attraction serves to bring a particular man and woman together in a mutual desire and subsequent commitment more profound and far-reaching than that between intimate friends. The attraction of unlike qualities serves to excite the anticipation of complementary need fulfillment. The success of any marriage, as we know, has a lot to do with need satisfaction. The helpmate, by the very nature of the term, is one who can respond to the other's needs. She does more than divide the labor of life; she shares his life, doubling the joys and the strengths. She draws man out of his isolation and into the partnership of life, expanding the scope of his selfhood. What she does for him, he does for her; it is complete mutuality. (It recalls the quip: "Although God took woman out of the side of man, in no way does this make her a side issue.")

Already it has been indicated that the establishment of a unique, exclusive, and enduring union requires a fundamental commitment on the part of the couple. To make such a commitment, a couple must have the reinforcement of conviction not only that this is desirable to them, but also that it is the will and favor of God. Two people must believe that this is the order of Creation and that fulfillment is made possible by redemption. As a couple they must be committed to this truth in order to be committed to each other and to their relationship. This is why the man is commanded to "leave his father and his mother and cleave to his wife." To do this demands more than a mere social relation which people may enter and leave at will. This demands a commitment from each one to a deeply personal union.

When a man and a woman unite in marriage, humanity experiences a restoration to wholeness. This is beautifully expressed in a rabbinical commentary: "The man is restless while he misses the rib that was taken out of his side, and the woman is restless until she gets under the arm from whence she was taken." Paradoxically, this means equal glory and equal humility for both man and woman. The glory of the man is the acknowledgement that woman was created for him; the glory of the woman is the acknowledgment that man is incomplete without her. The humility of the woman is the acknowledgment that she was made for man; the humility of the man is the acknowledgment that he is incomplete without her. Both share an equal dignity, honor, and worth. Yes, and each shares a humility before the other, also. Each is necessarily the completion of the other; each is necessarily dependent upon the other. This basic equality of persons was beautifully expressed by Augustine centuries before the women's liberation movement:

"If God meant woman to rule over man, He would have taken her out of Adam's head. Had He designed her to be his slave, He would have taken her out of his feet. But God took woman out of man's side, for He made her to be a helpmeet and an equal to him."

This early commentary has inspired many others similar to it, one of which reads as follows:

> "Creation of woman from the rib of man:
>   Not made of his head to top him;
>   Nor out of his feet to be trampled upon;
>   But out of his side to be equal to him;
>   Under his arm to be protected;
>   Near to his heart to be beloved."

The concluding remark in the second Creation account reads: "And they were both naked, the man and his wife, and were not ashamed" (Genesis 2:25 KJV). This has peculiar significance inasmuch as the immediate consequence of the transgression will be an awareness of their nakedness as something shameful to them. First we note that man now exists in the plural and God addresses him in the plural. Furthermore, man no longer has sole responsibilities; both the man and his wife together are the acting and responsible subjects of God's address. The striking expression "the man and his wife" already points to the definite order of relationship between the two sexes, the norm which God established at the beginning for all time.

Our interest next turns to the declaration that the man and his wife were naked and unashamed. Barth goes to the heart of it:

"They are now a pair . . . and in this divinely ordained relationship they . . . had no cause for mutual reproach. They had no need to envy their respective advantages. . . . Nor had they anything to conceal from each other. They were together without embarrassment or disquiet. They were not against one another but with one another, the man being the husband to the woman, and the woman the wife to the man. There is shame only when there is cause for envy, complaint and therefore disgrace. No shame can cling to the nature of the man as created by God, to male and female as He created them, to the due sequence and order of their relationship. This can never be an object of shame. In spite of the incomparability of the partners, the sex relationship in this respect, too, is a similitude of the covenant of grace, in the fulfillment of which God will prove Himself to

be the One who is not ashamed to be the Brother of wretched man, nor
will man need to be ashamed in the presence of the transcendent God, but
both will be together, true God and true man. On this basis, the command
of God the Creator in the sex relationship has always the dimension that
man and woman must both of them be what they are, the man accepting
his sex and the woman hers."[10]

There is no shame where there is no inner need for the justification
of life or some aspect of it. To be the creature of God, and in relation with
a life partner whom God Himself has given, carries its own self-justification,
and needs no other. For what had this first pair to hide or to blame?
Humanity was not for them some ideal which lay beyond masculinity and
femininity. They both perfectly accepted their sexuality, each his own and
each the other's. Their innocence was part and parcel of their full acceptance of creaturehood as God had given it. Nakedness and shamelessness
were thus the correlate and expression of innocence. When because of their
transgression their relationship with God was disturbed, then their relationship with one another was also disturbed. Now as we might expect, the
disruption and disorder strikes at the very heart of fellow humanity, going
directly and at once to the man-woman union, alienating it on all levels of
their common existence. Everything in its created order and with its own
justification becomes confused. Sin brings with it an evil eroticism formerly
unknown; this evil eroticism intruded directly and immediately into the life
partnership of the sinning couple. The awful genius of sin, as Barth reminds
us, is nowhere more plainly evident than in the fact that it shames man
before God and his fellows at the very center of his humanity, in the
man-woman relation of sexual union. Now, every self-justification—or even
the denial or suppression of sexuality—can only confirm and increase this
shame. Where, from God's standpoint, everything was created in purity
and holiness, there the impure eyes of disobedient man sees impurity,
unholiness, and temptation. In so doing, man defiles, dishonors, and often
destroys the good gifts of God. The resultant shame is now indigenous to
sinful man—a hallmark of his disoriented nature—and is removed from a
couple's experience only as they stand redeemed in Jesus Christ, transformed by His Spirit, and committed to His purpose for their union.

We come to the heart of the matter in the biblical concept of the
covenant between God and His people. The covenant is the center of the
Old Testament. God's eternal purpose is to have a people for His own
possession. Before the foundation of the world God appointed His own Son

to be the Mediator of the everlasting covenant. In His foreknowledge and foreordination, God knew that the people created to be His covenant possession would be unfaithful to that covenant. In His gracious plan He would send His Son to give Himself for the sins of the world, redeeming to Himself all who would believe on His name. In the secret purpose of God, a people would be called out of the kingdom of this world into the kingdom of His dear Son. The redeemed would be as the bride of the heavenly Bridegroom, so intimately related to Him would they be. This covenant relation between God and His people, so binding and intimate, is the original of which the man-woman relation in marriage is the earthly model. That union becomes a type in which the man is properly representative of the Lord God, while the woman is properly representative of God's people.

The Old Testament speaks of the covenant made with Israel and in time broken by Israel, who is spoken of as the unfaithful wife. In contrast, it also speaks of the faithfulness and mercy of the Husband, the covenant-making and covenant-keeping God. Despite the failure of His people, His love remains constant; the betrothal continues in force as well, giving an indestructible continuity and reality to the covenant from God's side. The end and goal of Israel's history will demonstrate before all angels and principalities the covenant continuity in the face of Israel's unbelief, disobedience, and separation. It is to this end that the second Creation account in Genesis points. As God did not will to be alone in relation to the created order but to have His helpmate—His people as counterpart and complement—so man was not to be alone either, but to have his helpmate. Hence it is not at all impossible or even inappropriate to find outlines of the covenant union of God and His people in the unique one-flesh relation given to man and to his wife at the very start.

Now it is true, the New Testament reaches back beyond the Old, telling us that the covenant between Jesus Christ and His redeemed community was in existence in the beginning, yes, in the mind and purpose of God before ever the world or man was brought forth. This was the first object of the divine will in election, and thus the basis of the Creation with its man-woman model. The New Testament tells us that the covenant between Jesus Christ and His community is the secret of creation, that despite the unfaithfulness of God's elect people, its adulterous sin is met in the atoning death of Jesus Christ. He, the risen Lord, now woos and wins them back to Himself and the covenant marriage between them. The history of the covenant culminates in the death and Resurrection of the Saviour and in the redemptive restoration of the covenant union between God and His people.

In a glorious passage, Ephesians 5:32 KJV, God's secret is finally disclosed in unambiguous terms. Paul, speaking about the relation between a Christian husband and wife, says, "This is a great mystery, but I speak concerning Christ and the church." Here the relationship of Christ to the church becomes the great model of that between husband and wife. One thing Paul is careful to do is to spell out the terms of such a marriage union. At its heart, there is love, even as God loved His people, and despite their unfaithfulness sent His Son to die for their sins. There is fidelity, also. The Christian couple is called to be as faithful to their marriage covenant as Jesus Christ is to His covenant with His redeemed community, despite whatever failure might occur on their part. This is the condition of an enduring relation, one that fulfills its every prospect. There is also intimate communion on every level of personal being. As the relationship between Christ and the Christian is intended to be the closest in all of life, so the communion between husband and wife is to be the closest known to purely human relationships.

Again and again the Old Testament prophets spoke of Israel as the chosen bride of God. ". . . I will betroth you to me for ever," Hosea hears God say. "I will betroth you to me in faithfulness . . ." (Hosea 2:19, 20). Isaiah says, ". . . your Maker is your husband; the Lord of hosts is his name" (Isaiah 54:5). Jeremiah hears God's appeal in these words, "Turn, O backsliding children, . . . for I am married unto you" (Jeremiah 3:14 KJV). The whole picture of the covenant as a marriage is worked out in detail in Ezekiel 16. Again and again we are reminded that the covenant which is the prototype of human love and marriage was appointed by God, broken by Israel. Yet the Lord God is always the Lover, Bridegroom, and Husband. His sinning, adulterous people are always His beloved, bride and wife. At the close of the Book of Revelation and with the final triumph of Christ, we read "Hallelujah! For the Lord our God the Almighty reigns. Let us rejoice and exult and give him the glory, for the marriage of the Lamb has come, and his Bride has made herself ready . . ." (Revelation 19:6, 7). The picture points to the full and final union between Jesus Christ and His church—that which God had in His mind and purpose from before the foundation of the world. R. H. Charles says that the marriage symbolism "denotes the intimate and indissoluble communion of Christ with the community which He has purchased with His own blood." Is it any wonder that God, who sees the end from the beginning, who before all time designed the covenant union between Himself and His people, should choose as the earthly model the intimate, unique relation between sexual opposites? Unmistakably, the union between Himself and His own redeemed people is represented as one of unchanging love and fidelity, of exclusive and enduring commitment. It is the full partnership and communion of Lover and beloved. Can the earthly model be anything less? Surely not when the pattern and purpose of God from the beginning are made known and accepted! Our theology of sexual relation thus finds its true center and model and goal in the covenant concept, the ultimate union of God and His own beloved.

It is on this presupposition that Paul addresses the Corinthians, "I feel a divine jealousy for you, for I betrothed you to Christ to present you as a pure bride to her one husband" (2 Corinthians 11:2). It is the jealousy of God that Paul makes his own as His apostle. It is the jealousy of the God who has brought the history of the covenant from Creation to its goal in Christ.

Another passage which becomes luminous in view of the covenant as typified by the marriage union, is Romans 7:1-6. The decisive verses are Romans 7:2-4: "Thus a married woman is bound by law to her husband as long as he lives; but if her husband dies she is discharged from the law concerning the husband. . . . Likewise, my brethren, you have died to the law through the body of Christ, so that you may belong to another, to him who has been raised from the dead." The first husband was the Mosaic law. But believers have been set free from the law through the death of Christ. They are now free to be married to Christ, and so they are as redeemed people. The covenant analogy, ever most appropriate, is that of marriage.

Over many centuries one of the sure signs of the inability of the church to understand the place of sexuality is seen in her many commentaries on the Song of Songs. In more biblical commentaries than one would care to cite, this unique Old Testament book of love songs has been allegorized— spiritualized—in a way that actually denies what the book says, or that it is to be interpreted literally as love songs, as the erotic history of two lovers. The Song of Songs has been an embarrassment to the church, and some have suggested its removal from the canon of Scripture. But there it stands, and it must be understood in the context of Old Testament teaching. Undoubtedly and unequivocally, it is an erotic history of two lovers. The love of the lover and his betrothed is expressed in long lyrical effusions in which all the various aspects of joyous love are blended frankly and with perfect freedom, from discreetly evoked sexual pleasure (1:1-3, 16; 2:6; 4:16-5:1; 7:8, 9; 8:3, 4), to the most delicate and heartfelt affection. Although it may be insisted that the primary interpretation is not an allegory, almost instinctively spiritual writers have recourse to the Song of Songs to find adequate expression of their intimate relationship with God. When read from this perspective, the Song of Songs, taking human love as its starting point, gives us a glimpse of the mystery of the divine covenant of love which is the theme of the prophets. The Song of Songs gives us this glimpse of the mystery, not in conceptual terms, but in its existential reality. This, we may be quite sure, is the twofold intention of the divine Author in incorporating the Song of Songs in the canon of Scripture.

Judaism, bound as it is by the limits of the Old Testament, could only provide bare outlines of such an interpretation of the Song of Songs. It is in the light of the New Testament that the fullness of the text's significance will be appreciated. What is remarkable, as Pierre Grolot reminds us, is the extent to which the Song of Songs is ideally suited by its divine Author for the purpose of New Testament reinterpretation. The experience of human love in its sexual connotations is the context in which the divine Author of the song cradled the truth of God's covenant love and coming marriage with His people.

Surely, any developed theology of sexuality has little difficulty finding a meaningful place in the Old Testament canon for an absolutely pure and holy erotic history, simply because its context is the spiritual history of God's covenant love. The covenant is the history of God's faithful love, of marriage with His people, of the covenant preserved from His side through the long period of their adulterous disobedience. Eschatologically, this covenant marriage is to be realized in that day when the Messiah is joined with His people—as the New Testament puts it, when the Lord Jesus Christ is revealed with His glorified church, following the marriage of the Lamb. On this basis it is comparatively easy to understand the message of the New Testament as the fulfillment of the Old.

According to the Song of Songs, the Old Testament expresses the proper meaning to be attached to the sexual relation as such. Genesis 2 and the Song of Songs are related components of the Old Testament, having a correspondence which is God's secret until revealed in the covenant between Jesus Christ and His church. But in Christ all becomes clear at last. The intimate husband-wife partnership throws light upon the covenant between Christ and His bride. Similarly, the faithfulness of God, the divine Husband, or of Christ the faithful Bridegroom, throws light upon what marriage can and should be. Jesus Christ is our ever-faithful Advocate, Intercessor, and Lover! His covenant love demonstrates that the marriage of men and women is appointed to be just as unique, enduring, and intimate in its own way as is the relation between Christ and His beloved. But, understandably, only the redeemed will ever appreciate this glorious truth, or seek to make it a reality in their own experience. In the midst of multiplied examples of unfulfilling marriages and sexual unions outside marriage, the present-day subculture of true Christians is called to bear witness. The Christian has the conceptual framework from Creation on to understand Ephesians 5:28-30, that husbands are to "love their wives as their own bodies," and the biblical commentary that "He who loves his wife loves himself. For no man ever hates his own flesh, but nourishes and cherishes it, as Christ does the church, because we are members of his body." Do we not hear the echo of Genesis 2:24, ". . . and they become one flesh"? The New Testament commentary teaches us that one-flesh does not mean merely a physical joining through intercourse—although most certainly it does mean that as well—but the total life partnership of the united pair. One-flesh is established as a personal unity which includes sexual uniting. The aim of creation is the existence of man and woman in relation, the most significant form of which is marriage, including exclusive sexual coupling. This is what is fulfilled whenever love and marriage take place according to the will of God and among couples committed to Jesus Christ.

The biblical basis for monogamy is not presented in Scripture by way of a gross command. Monogamy has a spiritual model. The *one Christ* and His *one community* are *one-flesh* in the *one covenant* of love and redemption. An experience of the total fulfillment of sexual relation, including the spiritual, belongs to God's people. They alone are able to celebrate God's purposes in sexuality.

From the New Testament standpoint, the calling of the church of Jesus Christ, for whose sake He came into the world, was crucified and risen, is a matter of His own election on one hand, confirmed by the redeemed's choice on the other. This is left a mystery in the New Testament. It is not ours to deny either election or personal decision, but to accept the paradox. He calls and "My sheep hear my voice" (John 10:27).

In Ephesians, His own are called "the elect." Perhaps all we can say is that His own bride will be known by the reality of her response.

We might ask, why did God choose to put the first man into a deep sleep, open his side and take from him that which was then fashioned to make woman? From the New Testament standpoint, the church of Jesus Christ has its origin in His mortal sleep, when His pierced side gave up life to the spiritually dead. In His wounds the church was born. The church is now part of His own body, owned as such by Him. Of His life the church partakes. He came down, unlike man in His deity yet like man in human form. By His incarnation He has forever assumed man's nature. He identified Himself with His people, even to the extent of taking upon Himself their very flesh. In the redemptive union of Himself and His bride, He lifts man's nature into His own. In the consummation of all things we are told that we shall "be like him, for we shall see him as he is" (1 John 3:2). This is our blessed hope in Christ! The church partakes of His Resurrection life and is conformed into His very likeness. From henceforth the church is not without Him nor He without it!

Another question arises: Why is the husband called to leave father and mother and cleave to his wife? Did not Jesus leave His Father to come to earth in order to take His bride? Love drew Him to forsake all that had been His life. He did not look back. He took upon Himself the need of His own. The heart of it is echoed in Ephesians 5:25: "Husbands, love your wives, as Christ loved the church and gave himself up for her. . . ." There is no greater love in heaven or earth than the love of Jesus Christ for His own beloved. On earth there is no love so full and meaningful between human persons as that between husband and wife who are one in Jesus Christ. For them marriage is a divine calling, each partner the gift of God to the other. Sexual fulfillment and life partnership are all part of God's loving design. Its fullest reality is reserved for God's own people. As they gaze into each other's eyes they catch a glimpse of His smile upon them, and they celebrate their marriage in its sexual expression.

A fitting word to close this chapter comes from William Wylie: "Man was made male and female, eternally separated from one another yet eternally complementary, eternally divided yet eternally attracted, blessing one another and infuriating one another, but ever unable to be their real selves alone. God divided man so that out of the union of the two separated yet complementary halves there might come something greater. It was by sex that God divided man, so that each should yearn for the other and feel incomplete alone, and it is by 'sex-in-love' that humanity can be reunited into a greater whole. Sex is division, but sex plus love are the union."[11]

7

One Flesh, One Spirit, One Love

The beginning point of this chapter is the closing point of the last: ". . . and they become one flesh" (Genesis 2:24).

Four extraordinary men of the early to mid-twentieth century are helping us shape our theology of sexuality within these chapters. Emil Brunner pointed the way to our understanding of the image of God in man as relational. Karl Barth expanded that image to include the man-woman relation, the image as fellow humanity in community. Now Dietrich Bonhoeffer and Sherwin Bailey set the scene for our discussion of the one-flesh union as it comprises the essence of marriage.

Bonhoeffer was in the vanguard of theological thinkers who saw the one-flesh concept of Genesis 2:24 in terms of full personal relation, and sexuality as an expression of the whole person—not what a person *does*, but what he *is*. Since what we know of human sexuality by scriptural revelation is contained in the Creation accounts, we shall traverse this ground once more, this time with Bonhoeffer's enabling insights. We begin with his exposition of Genesis 1:27, "So God created man in his own image, in the image of God he created him; male and female he created them." Prior to the creation of man, says Bonhoeffer, "God loves his work, he loves it in its own being, for the creature honours the Creator. But still God does not recognize himself in his work; he sees his work but he does not see himself. 'To see oneself' means as it were . . . 'to see oneself in a likeness'. . . . How shall he find himself in his work? The work does not resemble the Creator, it is not his image."[1] To this question Bonhoeffer provides the answer. Creation is fixed, bound by law and not free. If the Creator wills to create His own image, He must create it as a person with freedom; only in freedom would this image fully praise Him and fulfill the will of the Creator. The Scriptures express the difference between God's act of creating His image and all previous creating by the way it is introduced: "Let us make man in our image . . ." (Genesis 1:26). God does not call forth man out of nonbeing as He called forth everything else, but man proceeds from God as a new and ultimate work. Essentially this means that man is like the Creator in that he, too, is free—but free to worship and serve God, not free for his own independent ends.

Bonhoeffer establishes an important point, namely, that freedom is not something man has for himself but something he has for others. God is the Other toward whose worship and service man's freedom is to direct itself. Now the woman becomes the earthly "other" to whom this freedom is most purposefully to direct itself. Being free means free for the service of the other. Man differs from the other creatures in that God Himself is in him; he is God's image in which the Creator views Himself. God views His image in man as wholly dependent, limited, and relative. Bonhoeffer, looking at man in his male-female duality, says that it is in the interdependence of the two that man's higher creatureliness consists. The man-woman relation images God as One who exists in and for Himself yet at the same time exists for His creatures. God incarnate in Jesus Christ bears witness to His being for man. It is only now that God can look upon His finished creation, including as it does the duality of the man and his wife, and the one-flesh relationship now established between them. He can say, "Behold, it was very good."

In our quest for an understanding of what God means by *one-flesh*, the term which essentially describes the man-woman union, our task will be to search out the scriptural meaning of two terms, *flesh* and *body*. Bonhoeffer starts us off well. Turning to Genesis 2:7 we read, ". . . then the Lord God formed man of dust from the ground, and breathed into his nostrils the breath of life; and man became a living being." Here everything takes place in a very earthly way. "It is God's earth out of which man is taken," says Bonhoeffer. "From it he has his *body*. His body belongs to his essential being. Man's body is not his prison, his shell, his exterior, but man himself. Man does not 'have' a body; he does not 'have' a soul; rather, he 'is' body and soul. Man in the beginning is really his body. He is one. He is his body, as Christ is completely his body, as the Church is the body of Christ."[2] Bonhoeffer takes a holistic view of man. He perceives his indivisible nature, and the fact that in the body man objectifies, or exteriorizes, himself.

Having established that man has his earthly being as body, Scripture hastens to say, ". . . then the Lord God . . . breathed into his nostrils the breath of life; and man became a living being." Here, as Bonhoeffer indicates, body and spirit enter into one another totally. Man indeed is indivisible. "God breathes his Spirit into the body of man. And this Spirit is life and makes man alive. God creates other life through his Word; where man is concerned he gives of his life, of his Spirit. Man as man does not live without God's Spirit. To live *as man* means to live as body in Spirit. . . . All this can be said only of man, for only in man do we know of body and spirit."[3]

Here Bonhoeffer insists that man is the image of God, not in spite of, but just because of, his bodiliness. "For in his bodiliness he is related . . . to other bodies, he is there for others." Thus it is Bonhoeffer's vision that because God is "for others," so must any man who images Him be "for others." The "other" who is to serve as the prototype is man's companion, his helpmate in the one-flesh union.

After God made woman and brought her to be received by Adam, Eve is seen by Adam not as a cause for self-glorification, but for gratitude toward God, as an incentive for new dependence upon God. For only as he is truly dependent upon God, can there be a corresponding interdependency between himself and his wife. He knows that he is connected in a completely new way to this Eve who derives her existence from him. He now belongs to her as she belongs to him; *this is their essential unity in one-flesh.* They are no longer without one another; they are two, yet one. They were one from their single origin, then distinctly two, and now as they become united in one-flesh they relate once again through their common origin. Bonhoeffer is careful to note that in becoming one there is not a fusion of the two, the abolition of their creatureliness as individuals. Becoming one is the utmost realization of belonging to one another, based directly upon the fact that they are different from one another and remain so. Thus the unity of one-flesh is seen as belongingness.

And now an important observation must be made. Freedom for the creature implies limitation—the limitation of God's purpose. Initially, the prohibited tree in the garden marked out that limitation; this was the boundary to the freedom God gave to man, a boundary that reminded man from whom he received his freedom and for what purpose it was granted. It is correct to say that man's limit was marked out by his relationship to God. Now, on earth, man's relational existence is also to have its limit, its specific purpose which freedom is to serve. Man is subject to freedom in responsibility. The woman who is given to be his helpmate, his counterpart and complement, is also to serve as man's limit. This is basic to his sexuality. If we go back and look at man's freedom with reference to God this will be clearer. Man is free to serve God's purpose, free to love and serve Him, free to worship and glorify God in both spirit and body. Now as Adam receives God's special gift of Eve, he is free to love, cherish, and serve her. He is not free to worship or use her or cast her away. Bonhoeffer did not develop this idea, but the initial suggestion is there in his concept of the limit. He does say that in His unfathomable mercy, the Creator knew that this creaturely life of man, lived according to God's limit—with freedom in responsibility—could be borne only if he is loved by the woman who represents God's limit upon him. Like Adam, Eve is also given personal freedom—freedom to love, cherish, and serve him. She is not given freedom to worship or use him. Thus they are a limit to each other, and are to live in joyful interdependence, never seeking independence from each other anymore than they would seek independence from their Creator-God.

In our last chapter we discussed God's covenant union with His people, and how this had its earthly prototype in the man-woman union. We also noted its eschatological fulfillment in the union of Christ and His bride, the church. Bonhoeffer, coming at it more obliquely, says that in bearing the limit which each is to the other, they share responsibility for one another as the first two human beings in the community of love. In this freedom in responsibility, in this mutual love and the union of complementary halves, the church is manifest in its first, prototypical form. It is fellow-humanity in the community of love, the basic polarity of mankind and the most intimate and perfect union of mankind. How splendid and far-reaching indeed is the connotation of one-flesh. Were it not for the blindness of our sin, how obvious this would be!

The shadow of the Fall is seen in Bonhoeffer's comment that where love toward the other is destroyed, man can only hate the limit which the other partner represents. "Then he only wants to possess or deny the other person . . . for now he is appealing to . . . his claim upon the other person, to the origin of the other person in him; what he hitherto received humbly now becomes the occasion for glorification and revolt."[4] What God put in order, man through sin brought into disorder. Now that order is obscured in the age-long mystery of God, and ultimately disclosed only in Jesus Christ in His relation to His redeemed community. But because of sin, says Bonhoeffer, the power of life becomes the power of destruction, the power of community becomes the power of isolation, and the power of love becomes the power of hate. The woman who was given to complete man now exists as his contradiction; she is with him, yet in a new and threatening way she is his rival. A one-flesh union will henceforth no longer develop naturally; it will be realized only as a couple experiences redemption in Jesus Christ, a redemption that affects every part of their life together.

The next declaration, Genesis 2:24, is the key to our present theme. Here one of two further passages from Bonhoeffer is worthy of full quotation. The verse in Genesis reads, "Therefore a man leaves his father and his mother and cleaves to his wife, and they become one flesh." Bonhoeffer writes:

"It is the profoundest way possible of describing the depth and seriousness of belonging to one another. This ultimate belonging to one another is undoubtedly seen here in connection with man's sexuality. Very clearly sexuality is the expression of the two-sidedness of being both an individual and being one with another person. Sexuality is nothing but the ultimate realization of our belonging to one another. Here sexuality has as yet no life of its own detached from this purpose. Here the community of man and woman is the community derived from God, the community of love glorifying and worshipping him as the Creator. It is therefore the Church in its original form. And because it is the Church it is a community eternally bound together."[5]

In anticipation of the Fall, we notice with Bonhoeffer that as the Adam-Eve union was established in terms of sexuality, so this first community of love and belongingness shall be torn to pieces and radically disoriented by sexuality. Pleasure shall be transformed into passion, love self-directed rather than other-directed. Self shall be affirmed, the other denied affirmation. But all this is by way of anticipation; we return now to the text to read, "And the man and his wife were both naked, and were not ashamed" (Genesis 2:25). Bonhoeffer does not deal directly with the question of what it means to be unashamed, but rather with what it is to be ashamed. If one understands this, then he will perceive more clearly the original state of shamelessness. Here one final quotation succinctly captures Bonhoeffer's thought:

"Shame is the expression of the fact that we no longer accept the other person as the gift of God. Shame expresses my passionate desire for the other person and the knowledge that belongs to it that the other person is no longer satisfied just to belong to me but desires something from me.

Shame covers me before the other because of my own evil and of his evil, because of the division that has come between us. Where the one accepts the other as the companion given him by God, where he is content with understanding himself as beginning from and ending in the other and in belonging to him, man is not ashamed. In the unity of unbroken obedience man is naked in the presence of man, uncovered, revealing both body and soul, and yet he is not ashamed. Shame only comes into existence in the world of division."[6]

The very first consequence of the Fall had to do with the man-woman relation, not with God's response to their sin nor even with the curse which was imposed upon them. Consistently with the Holy Record, this passage continues to point to man in his sexual relation, to the image of God as expressed in the man-woman relation. What, we ask, is happening to their one-flesh union to change it? What is happening to their belongingness in love, to their community as it reflects the intimate, enduring union of God and His people? Is it destroyed or radically disoriented? Does it remain, continuing in an altered mode, or is it discontinued, even replaced by another kind of relationship? The account provides some very instructive clues.

Bonhoeffer notes that it does not say that they knew and recognized good and evil. This we might have expected from the nature of Satan's promise prior to the Fall. But no. It says, ". . . the eyes of both were opened, and they knew that they were naked" (Genesis 3:7). This is surprising, because nakedness was not a matter of shame prior to the Fall. Once again the focus of Scripture is upon man in his sexuality, where the sin of man has its first consequence. A new duality is introduced into human existence, the duality of pleasure and pain inherent in the same experience. Here is self-giving love versus self-gaining passion. Man is now subject to a disruption in relationship resulting in a contradiction in his very being. This division which sin created expresses itself first of all in Adam's relation to Eve. She, his counterpart and complement given him by God, had represented the limit of God's gift to him. Adam had acknowledged her in undivided devotion. But now sin has caused division and contradiction, bringing a new and alien devotion to self. Adam no longer accepts Eve as his limit; in place of gratitude to God there is glorification of self. No longer does he look upon Eve through eyes of love alone but with eyes of passion and possession. Love turns inward and is there corrupted. Eve also changes. Unity gives way to discord and disunity, interdependence to independence, and completion to competition and contradiction. Each partner looks at the other in terms of his or her own claim. By way of anticipation, we note that it shall be only in Christ that such division and contradiction shall be healed, and the one-flesh unity restored. Even so, this will entail redemption from self-devotion, from divisive and destructive self-affirmation. Love, having turned inward upon oneself must once again become other-directed, transformed into the agape love which has its source in Jesus Christ.

Alienated from his helpmate in a most pervasive way, the man now covers his nakedness and she hers. Why? Their nakedness had been declarative of their unity of total self, or as Bonhoeffer says, of being *for* the other. Nakedness is innocence; innocence that is not even aware of nakedness. Shame thus is an acknowledgment of an original innocence; it bears witness to the lost blessedness of formerly sinless minds, hearts, and bodies. But the new condition which the tree of the knowledge of good and evil brought upon Adam and Eve is passion and possession in place of pure love, hence also shame in place of innocence. Sin's effect was most direct and profound at this very point of their relationship. The Fall, in other words, intruded its evil consequences at the point of intersecting sexuality. It is at least understandable that the early Christians confused original sin with its most immediate interpersonal consequence! Where mankind most sublimely images God—in the union of man and woman, there precisely is where sin's disruption first manifests itself. This is only to be expected, inasmuch as the man-woman relationship is typical of the God-man relationship which suffered total disruption with the entrance of sin. The disruption of the covenant union between God and His people is thus directly and immediately reflected in the disruption of the union covenanted between the man and his wife. This leads to the conjecture that when the God-man union is restored in Christ, the first sphere to reflect that restoration will be the Christian couple's one-flesh union. This indeed is the way it should be.

The woman's relationship to her husband is especially complicated by the Fall: ". . . your desire shall be for your husband . . ." (Genesis 3:16). This, quite understandably, refers not to her original, natural desire toward him, but to a new, inordinate, and enslaving passion. It is a passion in which pleasure and pain are inherently in tension. The full statement reads, ". . . your desire shall be for your husband, and he shall rule over you." That original equality which characterized their relationship has become inequality. And while the consequence of sin is equally distributed to both the man and his wife, it is the woman's relationship to her husband that is affected, not his relationship to her. The new burden falling upon him has to do rather with his coping with a resistant nature from which he must draw their common subsistence. But for him this raises no relational question as it does for his wife. His relationship to her, including roles and responsibilities newly accruing to him in the face of their division and contradiction, is simply a burdensome one.

What so evidently was an inadequate coping with their new state of sinful awareness, their seeking to cover their nakedness with fig leaves, is met by the grace of a faithful Creator who "made for Adam and for his wife garments of skins, and clothed them" (Genesis 3:21). God affirms them as fallen, as helpless in their division and contradiction; nonetheless, He is present in grace, for He does not leave them exposed before one another in their nakedness and shame. He covers them with covering of His own making. God acts to restrain their passion as well as to mitigate their shame, though not actually removing their passion or alienation. Continuing passion and its accompanying shame shall bear eloquent witness to man's originally sinless one-flesh relationship with his wife. The creation order is still discernible in God's gracious act, but restoration of the one-flesh union awaits man's redemption—body and soul together.

At this point we have another clue to the change which sin wrought in sexuality. Whereas Adam originally named his helpmate "woman" ("because she was taken out of man"), and in the process declaring her relation to himself, now he calls her "Eve" ("life"), because he thinks of her now as *the mother of all living.* Joyce Baldwin suggests that this change of name indicates, perhaps subtly, her demotion in status. No longer does she stand alongside him in equality, sharing Adam's full personhood; rather, she represents a means whereby certain ends will be achieved. Adam now looks upon her instrumentally, defining her not in terms of *being* but of *doing.* She is no longer *person,* but *performer.* She is *means,* not end, *supplement,* not complement, *inferior,* not equal. Here is the essence of the struggle that reaches down to our own time and the women's liberation movement! There is indeed a shadow over the place and role of women!

Adam and Eve shared equally in the sin of disobedience which gave sin its entrance into human existence. Mutual participation in sin signals their unity of personhood. And although chronologically Eve sinned first, Paul, in Romans 5:12-19, relates that "sin came into the world through one man," that "death reigned from Adam" and that "many died through one man's trespass." Paul continues, ". . . because of one man's trespass, death reigned through that one man. . . ." Not once is Eve mentioned, though an equal participant and chronologically first to sin. Why is this? It is because even in their sinning they are one-flesh, hence one in responsibility. Yet Adam is singled out to bear a particular role in that responsibility before God. He is regarded as the head of the race, and, in a representative sense, the accountable one. In verse 14 it reads, "Adam . . . a type of the one who was to come." Christ was the second Adam, the Head of the new race of the redeemed. All who share in His redemption share in His headship. Here, then, is the principle of solidarity, of unity expressed at the very beginning. As sin and condemnation came through one man, Adam, so now righteousness and salvation come through one Man, Jesus Christ (see also 1 Corinthians 15:22, 45-49).

What we have before us is that Eve is under the headship of Adam and counted one with him, rather than as an independent person. By the same principle, Adam, although the accountable one, is not considered independently of Eve. In no way does this suggest that Eve occupies an inferior place. Rather, she is present, really present; she is responsible, really responsible. But Eve is not mentioned for the reason that she is part of Adam, completely identified with him with whom she is one-flesh. Obviously, they are not one-flesh in physical joining alone, but in the totality of their persons. And here the headship of Adam is significant in assigning responsibility for the Fall. When this is grasped as an essential principle rooted deeply in the order of Creation, then the headship of the husband over the wife as a New Testament principle will be more readily comprehended. Here let it suffice simply to emphasize that the New Testament does not ignore or diminish the significance of Eve. Rather it assumes her identity as part of Adam in the one-flesh unity which in every respect counts them to be one.

The implications of the Fall for Adam and Eve as the first representatives of the man-woman relation are discussed by Helmut Thielicke: "Whereas originally its purpose, in conformity with the common origin of both man and woman, was to maintain this original unity and make them one flesh, Gen. 2:24, now it is promised that the sexes will be 'against' each other. . . . This antagonism between the sexes immediately becomes apparent in the fact that now one partner proceeds to denounce the other (3:12). But, all this is, of course, not in accord with the order of creation, but rather a disruption of the order of creation . . . the fact that one shall rule over the other is not an imperative order of creation, but rather the element of disorder that disturbs the original peace of creation; for the domination of the man spoken of here is the result of the desire (libido) of the woman. . . . This indicates that sexuality has lost its original form."[7]

When we recognize the universal implications of the Fall upon man, then we can more realistically determine our own place in the context of the redemption in Jesus Christ. The assertion of Emil Brunner is especially noteworthy here: "There are two facts which accompany all 'love' and especially all genuine human 'love'—in the sense of sex attraction: a shame which cannot be overcome, and a longing which cannot be satisfied. Sexual shame is . . . a genuine human feeling founded deeply in human nature. . . . It would appear that in sexuality there is something fundamentally and irreparably out of order, that is, out of divine order."[8]

When neither physical, mental, nor spiritual elements are lacking in the marriage union, still there is a division which no intimate communion can fully overcome. It requires the transcendent power of the unifying Christ and the enabling power of the Holy Spirit to overcome this contradiction.

As the most immediate consequence of the Fall, Adam and his wife felt shame in the presence of each other because of their sexual differentiation. New feelings selfishly generated within them. In sinning against God, becoming independent of Him and breaking the covenant, they discovered that their integrity toward one another was altered. They had become independent of one another; their own covenant unity of marriage was somehow changed. The sexuality which drew them together now serves to separate and isolate them from one another. The sexuality which formerly existed in the context of love now exists in the context of passion and possessiveness—selfish exploitation of the other as means to an end. To perceive this contradiction and to experience this sinful exploitation was the cause of a feeling never before known—the feeling of shame. In the fig leaf apron we see the attempted avoidance of shame, the anxious wish to preclude the guilt which focused upon them as individuals but more particularly as a couple.

A modern philosopher, Merleau-Ponty, expresses a similar idea: "Usually man does not show his body, and, when he does, it is either nervously or with an intention to fascinate. He has the impression that the alien gaze which runs over his body is stealing it from him, or else, on the other hand, that the display of his body will deliver the other person up to him, defenseless, and that in this case the other will be reduced to servitude

. . . in so far as I have a body, I may be reduced to the status of an object beneath the gaze of another person, and no longer count as a person for him, or else I may become his master and, in my turn, look at him. But this mastery is self-defeating, since precisely when my value is recognized through the other person's desire, he is no longer the person by whom I wished to be recognized, but a being fascinated, deprived of his freedom, and who therefore no longer counts in my eyes."[9]

Shame points to the separation between one's sex nature and one's personal life. How evident this is in our day when every attempt is made to expose anything sexual, to make it so utterly commonplace that shame no longer attaches to it! But such attempts are self-defeating, for they violate the very nature of human sexuality. Shame continues to express this separation, this contradiction. Emil Brunner noted this, adding that an inordinate curiosity now attaches to sexual life which readily accommodates itself to lust and shame. The attempt is nonetheless a very strong one in our day to so completely eliminate curiosity as to cancel the sense of shame at the same time. But sexual freedom has proved to have fostered nothing other than a new bondage, a new disgust—if you will, a new shame. Sexual desire, separated from personal destiny, is subject to longings that cannot be fulfilled. It also creates inordinate desires that lead invariably to a sense of disorder and shame. As Brunner says, "Man is tempted now to make a dualism between personal being and sexuality. Only the complete return to love, to existence in love, could banish that division, bridge that duality. Man's inability at this point causes him to treat sexuality in the only other way he knows—impersonally."[10]

Thus do we have impersonalizing secrecies and the shame that accompanies them. A comment of Reinhold Niebuhr is apropos, that "man, having lost the true centre of his life in God, falls into sensuality; and sex is the most obvious occasion for the expression of sensuality and the most vivid expression of it." What he is stressing is that sex is not sin per se, but "the most obvious occasion for the expression of sensuality and the most vivid expression of it."[11]

Returning to our consideration of the one-flesh concept, it is necessary for us to understand just what the Old and New Testaments mean by the term *flesh*. That it occurs first in a relational context is certain. In a remarkable disclosure of how God looks upon man, the Creation accounts show man almost exclusively as a relational being. By this we mean that neither his body nor his personality nor even his personal capabilities are described in those accounts. Rather, man's nature as a thinking, feeling, willing person is first displayed in the context of entering into his first human choice.

If we are to truly understand what God means by the one-flesh concept of union, we must determine the biblical use of the terms *flesh (basar, sarx)* and *body (soma)*.[12] The primary characteristic of Old Testament Hebrew thought with regard to man is his essential unity of being. It is a holistic view of man that dominates Old Testament thought and makes it compatible with modern psychology. In this view, physical and psychical functions are closely related. Linguistically, two common Hebrew practices must be considered. First, it is common to find the Old Testament referring to a particular part of the body as making a psychical response. For example, "Fill me with joy and gladness; let the bones which thou hast broken rejoice" (Psalms 51:8). Second, there is the use of synechdoche (the part for the whole) in referring to one part of the body as representing the whole, hence the vehicle for expressing the personality. This is the typical Hebrew way of expressing what we mean today by the self, or the personality. It is important to recognize that the Hebrews did not have a word for body as such, nor for personality, either. The word most frequently employed for the whole man is *basar* (flesh), often representing the whole of man organized in corporeal form. From its simple root meaning, *flesh* came to denote the whole body, as expressed, for example, in Proverbs 14:30, "A tranquil mind gives life to the flesh." By a natural extension, flesh means the whole man, as when the psalmist says, ". . . my flesh also shall rest in hope" (Psalms 16:9 KJV). The term *all flesh* refers to mankind, the totality of human existence. This led H. Wheeler Robinson to say that "the Hebrew ideal of personality is an animated body, and not an incarnated soul," and hence that "man does not *have* a body, he *is* a body."[13]

The Hebrew word for "flesh" *(basar)* appears sometimes in distinction from man's soul (*see* Isaiah 10:18), but these are not fundamentally different forms of existence. Indeed, soul is more than flesh, but flesh is nonetheless a perfectly proper manifestation of the soul in Hebrew thought (*see* Genesis 2:7). Therefore, in Psalms 16:9, heart, soul, and flesh all mean—though in different manifestations—the whole man. Ernest White notes that the Hebrew concept of personality is essentially social. Thus *basar* (flesh) was used to convey the idea of the Hebrews being God's people, God's peculiar possession. Personality, to the Hebrew mind, was conceived as man in his wholeness before God and in relation to fellow humanity.

How intriguing, then, that the prototypical expression of this is the union of two total persons in marriage called one-flesh.

A high view of the continuity of Scripture elicits the expectation that the Old and New Testaments will correspond in their concepts of one-flesh. With this in prospect, New Testament scholars look at the Greek terms *sarx* (flesh) and *soma* (body) not with the expectation of their expressing Greek dualistic philosophies, or their possible conflict or uneasy accommodation with Hebrew unitive or holistic views. Rather, they expect a close correlation. From the perspective of contemporary studies, it is remarkable that the varied meanings of the Hebrew and Greek words made it possible for the ancients to understand these terms within the limits of their restricted understanding of the whole man, whereas for moderns these same words permit a holistic understanding corresponding to today's more advanced concepts of psychological theory.

The Greek word *sarx* (flesh), like the Hebrew *basar*, has its elementary connotation in the fleshly substance of man and beast. Thus in classical writings it was always used in a purely physical sense, invariably referring to the substance out of which the body is made. But by the time of the New Testament, *sarx* had become a highly developed and sophisticated term. So when we read "one flesh" in the New Testament, its wider meaning is consonant with that of the Old. As we shall see shortly, the one-flesh unity is a merging of total persons. As Edmund Elbert has written, sex must be seen and lived within a context much wider and richer than the immediate good of personal satisfaction. It must take into account those deeper layers of personal existence where persons truly meet and where all relatedness, sex included, derives its genuinely human significance. In other words, sex is a human value proper to the whole person, a total expression that takes place between two people in their mutual effort to communicate their wish to love and be loved, to mutually belong to one another in an exclusive and enduring way. It is a covenant intended to answer for a lifetime the pain of incompleteness which is the lot of all who share in the condition called human. So human love and human sex will be only what man himself makes them. How he regards himself and his intimate other will govern the measure of dignity he accords to these values. As William Banowsky expresses it:

"Sex is not a biological appendage; it is an aspect of human existence by which every man, through his attitudes and actions, reveals something of his deepest convictions about life itself. . . . Most important of all, it is in the relationships of sex that men mirror their basic beliefs concerning their own nature, their origin and dignity as men. . . . The biological side of sex cannot be isolated and viewed as autonomous because it is but one aspect of the whole, indivisible man. Sexual intercourse is not merely one physical act among many; it is, instead, an act that engages and expresses the entire personality in such a way as to provide insight into the nature of man. . . . The significance of manhood and womanhood resides, not in what each is unto itself, but in what each can become along with the other. As radically different as they are, yet perfectly complementary, man and woman hunger innately to immerse their separate, prior selves into one complete self. Each yearns to know the other fully, to experience the mutual completeness possible only through communion with the other."[14]

The expression "one flesh" is found only once in the Old Testament, in the order of Creation, Genesis 2:24. But in the New Testament it is reiterated by Jesus (Mark 10:2-12; Matthew 19:3-11), and by Paul (1 Corinthians 6:16; Ephesians 5:22-31). These are affirmations of a principle which, although never precisely defined, was clearly of fundamental importance. The one-flesh emphasizes a union that takes in all of life as it is shared by the couple. It is no less than that union of one entire man and one entire woman. As Otto Piper says, the attainment of oneness of the flesh creates a mutual dependence and reciprocity in all areas of life.

Sherwin Bailey takes the idea a step further: "Sexual intercourse establishes and nourishes a new, organic, biune relation in which man and woman give themselves to one another entirely and without stipulation, yet so that while their independence is broken down, the individuality of each is enhanced and developed. . . . Their sexual union both constitutes and symbolizes this unique, organic relation which in its essential nature is in no way comparable to a partnership, being founded upon love and not upon mutual agreement."[15] Bailey overstates his point, for it is indeed a partnership nonetheless.

His emphasis on the fundamental nature of the one-flesh union is apparently confirmed by the importance which Jesus and Paul attach to Genesis 2:24. They both suggest that the establishment of the one-flesh union is the first purpose for which men and women are brought together by God in marriage. Nowhere in the New Testament is any prominence assigned to procreation as such, whereas the great Pauline conception of marriage is the analogue of Christ's union with His church—a truly relational analogy of the highest order conceivable. Thus the unitive end of marriage takes precedence. While sexual intercourse is the powerful and exclusive symbol of a couple's union, and every renewed act confirms that union, Otto Piper suggests that once a union is established, the sense of oneness is confirmed even by the gentlest touch. Nevertheless, the unity established and maintained by the sexual bond is the major objective and indelible feature of Jesus' insistence that the union not be dissolved by divorce: "What therefore God has joined together, let no man put asunder (Matthew 19:6). God is in the bond between them; in His purpose the union is of a permanent nature.

The one-flesh idea allows marriage to be seen primarily for what it is —a relationship of equal partners in a full complementarity of being and doing. Sexual union is the basic symbol of the unity as well as the actual enactment of it. In the comprehensive nature of sexual expression, the entire person is given in the act. So complete is the surrender that Paul can say, "The wife does not rule over her own body, but the husband does; likewise the husband does not rule over his own body, but the wife does" (1 Corinthians 7:4). That the total self is surrendered in intercourse renders any attempt to do less a perversion, a parody of sexuality.

Sex is not like other human needs, such as hunger or thirst. Something happens between two people when they have sexual intercourse. The same thing does not happen when they have lunch together—or do anything else together for that matter. Dan Sullivan points out that sexual mutuality is *the* means of inter-personalization. An inverse proof can be found in the fact that all forms of sexual perversion require a depersonalized milieu in which to operate. This is true despite the claim of homosexual "couples" to have a personalized union. We answer this by saying that theirs is only a one-dimensional relation and thereby a denial of sexual differentiation in its fundamental purpose, a denial of the order of Creation, a denial of fulfillment through duality in unity. It is necessarily devoid of the full inter-personalization that God intends. When Paul summarily condemns homosexuality in Romans 1:24-27, he speaks of it as being contrary to natural use. There Paul's use of the expression "natural relations" is far broader than what the body is capable of "doing naturally." He refers rather to the purpose God implanted in the nature of the man-woman relation. Anything else in God's eyes is unnatural, regardless of what may seem natural in the eyes of man. However cleverly it may be argued that homosexuality is imprinted in a given human personality, however argued that it is neither sin nor sickness, Scripture inescapably declares that: (1) it cannot express the purpose of sexuality which the Scriptures set forth, (2) it is nowhere commended or condoned as compatible in any way with this fundamental purpose, and (3) it is specifically condemned in both the Old and New Testaments.

A writer such as W.R.D. Fairbairn can agree that the primary aim of sexual desire is person-to-person relationship, that authentic sexual desire is inherently a total self-giving. While sexuality invests the whole person, sexual conduct itself can be isolated and made to express only the mutilation of the sexually differentiated self. It is with this in mind that we come to the somewhat confusing but powerful exposition of Paul in 1 Corinthians 6:13-20:

"The body is not meant for immorality, but for the Lord, and the Lord for the body. . . . Do you not know that your bodies are members of Christ? Shall I therefore take the members of Christ and make them members of a prostitute? Never! Do you not know that he who joins himself to a prostitute becomes one body with her? For, as it is written, 'The two shall become one [flesh].' But he who is united to the Lord becomes one spirit with him. Shun immorality. Every other sin which a man commits is outside the body; but the immoral man sins against his own body. Do you not know that your body is a temple of the Holy Spirit within you, which you have from God? You are not your own; you were bought with a price. So glorify God in your body."[16]

Sherwin Bailey asks if there is not a radical contradiction in Paul's statement that the most irresponsible sexual act—for this is why he uses prostitution rather than simple fornication as his example—makes a couple who are not husband and wife "one-flesh"? For certainly fornication with a prostitute lacks every condition necessary for the establishment of a true one-flesh union! There is neither the intention of fidelity to a life partnership nor the recognition of responsibility to each other or to the community as in biblical marriage. But let's refer directly to Bailey:

"St. Paul contrasts two kinds of union. There is, first, that of the believer with Christ, expressed in the metaphor of the body and its members—a spiritual, metaphysical union analogically exemplified in the true *henosis* of husband and wife: 'he that is joined unto the Lord is one spirit'. Second, there is union with a harlot—a parody of the true *henosis* and so of the marriage between the heavenly Bridegroom and his bride. St. Paul, therefore, can set before the Corinthians two alternatives: union with Christ or union with a prostitute. *The Christian who has intercourse with*

a harlot becomes thereby a member, so to speak, of the Devil's community;
this shocking travesty of the 'one flesh' union is the analogue of the 'mar-
riage' between the Evil One and those who have surrendered their lives to
him."[17]

Paul, as Bailey indicates, draws a shocking analogy, but one worthy of contrast with the analogy of Christ and His church. As sexual union in Christian marriage is a true analogy of the heavenly Bridegroom and His bride, so sexual union with a prostitute is a parody, hence a true analogy of the diabolical bridegroom and his bride! Bailey, once again, is most precise and illuminating:

"His use of 'body' *(soma)* instead of 'flesh' *(sarx)* shows how well St. Paul understood the significance of sexual union. The 'body' is not simply the physical organism, but the total self; 'one flesh' and 'one body' are synonymous. Intercourse therefore is much more than a mere physical act which takes place on the periphery, as it were, of personal experience; it involves and affects the whole man and the whole woman in the very centre and depth of their being, so that afterwards neither can ever be as if they had never come together. This is true even of fornication, which cannot be excused or dismissed as something insignificant, done in complete detachment, and from which no consequences follow . . . the fallacy, as common now as it was among the Corinthians, that casual and promiscuous intercourse is 'natural' and means nothing."[18]

We can allow with Paul, then, that sexual intercourse always establishes a one-flesh union. It is clear, however, that in every case the character of the union will be determined by the character of its constitutive act. Thus, says Bailey, a distinction can be drawn between two sharply contrasted states of one-flesh. When there is consent to love and take responsibility for another, and also the knowledge and approval of the community, there is a true union in conformity with the divine law. This includes what is known as common-law marriage. But false, invalid one-flesh union is effected by all forms of casual, nonresponsible fornication or adultery. Here we would agree with Bailey that even in such a false union, its redemption through subsequent marriage validates what was formerly invalid. Now there is growth in love and in responsibility that was not previously possible. Bailey draws the implication:

"Sexual intercourse is an act of the whole self which affects the whole self; it is a personal encounter between man and woman in which each does something to the other, for good or for ill, which can never be obliterated.

. . . It cannot, therefore, be treated simply as sensual indulgence. Fornication . . . is the expression of an attitude of mind in which God, other persons, and the self are all involved. . . . In their coming together they either affirm or deny all that sexual intercourse means. In the one case they become knit together in a mysterious and significant *henosis* and fulfill their love as husband and wife; in the other they merely enact a hollow, ephemeral, diabolical parody of marriage which works disintegration in the personality and leaves behind a deeply-seated sense of frustration and dissatisfaction—though this may never be brought to the surface of consciousness and realized. So profound, however, are the consequences of sexual intercourse that they can only be adequately expressed by saying that every act initiates or maintains a state of 'one flesh' which either affirms or negates its own inner meaning."[19]

To this understanding it can be added that every sexual act is an accurate reflection of, and a judgment upon, the whole relation which exists between two people. Perhaps as a means of maintaining the sense of one-flesh and also because there is both danger and frustration in incontinency, Paul says, "The husband should give to his wife her conjugal rights, and likewise the wife to her husband. For the wife does not rule over her own body, but the husband does; likewise the husband does not rule over his own body, but the wife does" (1 Corinthians 7:3, 4). Immorality, as we are seeing, is a perversion of the relationship of sexuality and personhood which man bears within himself. It attempts to separate sexuality from the rest of personality, denying it as an expression of the whole man. It is not possible to separate a person from his sexuality; the sexual desires of a person are no less than expressions of the self. It is not physical flesh, then, which has sexual desires, but the whole self. In the phrase "The husband does not rule over his own body, but the wife" (and vice versa 1 Corinthians 7:4), lies the implication that in sexual union one whole self is surrendered to another whole self.

Back to the problem of 1 Corinthians 6:13-20. That the Christian is one body with his wife can take place only in correspondence with the fact that he himself is one spirit with the Lord. But in intercourse with a prostitute no such correspondence is possible. For at the consummation of the encounter husband and wife become one body, belonging wholly to one another, thus mutually attesting their humanity as completed. This is not, then, a neutral sphere of indifferent occurrence. For the Christian a decision has been made; as he belongs to Christ, so he belongs to the woman who is his wife. He cannot proceed to contradict the fact that he belongs to Christ by becoming one body with a prostitute.

At this point the thinking of Teilhard de Chardin has a very relevant bearing. In *The Phenomenon of Man* he asks, ". . . at what moment do lovers come into the most complete possession of *themselves,* if not when they say they are *lost* in each other?" He saw that the truest and deepest self is discovered, disclosed, and fulfilled at the moment of orgasm, when one can literally "come" into one's self as well as into the beloved. He says that it is only sexual union "that is capable of uniting living beings in such a way as to complete and fulfill them, for it alone takes them and joins them by what is deepest in themselves." Dan Sullivan adds the comment: "In this idea of unique self-fulfillment in the moment of authentic, total self-loss, we have the ground of the personalist conception of human sex." This also verges on the scriptural view as well.[20]

Now, why in Paul's exposition does the "one spirit" with Christ exclude the "one body" with a prostitute? Obviously, says Karl Barth, because Christ is the faithfulness of God in Person, whereas the prostitute personifies human unfaithfulness against God. This is similar to Bailey's suggestion that becoming "one body" with the prostitute is becoming a member of the devil's community. This a Christian cannot do in the freedom given him by Christ. He would become something other than the temple of the Holy Spirit, and could not then glorify God in his body. There would be only a sorry distortion of the completion between man and woman in marriage. The climax of the encounter would be denial of any real encounter. It is fellowship in the form of the betrayal of true fellowship, for one does not seek a woman thus in her whole being. It is a process of dehumanization, of depersonalization. But let there be no mistake—even in this distortion the completion is real enough. A mutual offering takes place; male and female become one-flesh. But, as betrayers of their humanity and of God's design for unity in duality, they mutually void that true unity, and shame each other.

In this passage the argument is based upon the significance of the body not as a thing apart from the real self, but essentially one with it. Sexual activity involves the whole man, and unites not merely two physical organisms but two persons. It is on this basis that the apostle condemns sexual irregularities for the damage they cause to the integrity of the persons involved in them. What he says of the prostitute applies to any extramarital sex. His reference to prostitutes is simply the most concrete and vivid example available at that time and place.

The Greek word *soma* (body) is used in the sense of the self objectified. The *soma* is in reality the vehicle of expression for the personality. All of which is to say that much of the description of *soma* (body) is parallel to that of *sarx* (flesh). There is indeed a close identification, although of course that identification is not complete. Mereleau-Ponty's words are very much to the point: "The body can symbolize existence because it brings it into being and actualizes it. . . . It may be said that the body is the 'hidden form of being ourselves' . . . personal existence is the taking up and manifestation of a being in a given situation. . . . In this way the body expresses total existence, not because it is an external accompaniment to that existence, but because existence comes into its own in the body."[21]

In identifying believers as the temple of God, the apostle uses both the word *soma* (body) and the personal pronoun, as we note in the following verses. The Corinthians are reminded, "Do you not know that *you* are God's temple and that God's Spirit dwells in *you?*" (1 Corinthians 3:16, italics added). Later on, in his second letter to the Corinthians, Paul says, "For *we* are the temple of the living God" (2 Corinthians 6:16, italics added). Twice now he has used the personal pronoun. But between these two he asks, "Do you not know that *your body* is a temple of the Holy Spirit within you, which you have from God?" (1 Corinthians 6:19, italics added). Here the word *soma* (body) is interchangeable with the personal pronoun. There can be little question but that *soma* is here used to denote man's whole personality in relationship to God. Man is related to God as a whole being; he is to be redeemed, not only as a soul independent of the body, but as a *soma*, which includes both. When man is redeemed as a whole person, then his relationships are renewed and he becomes indeed the dwelling place for the Spirit of God.

The sexual relation, in Maulnier's phrase, is "a reaching out of the spirit through the body." Nowhere do flesh and spirit meet so closely as in sexual intercourse. Nowhere do the meanings of body and spirit merge so profoundly. Although the actual sexual union is clothed in mystery, it is through the body that I apprehend another as a person, or that another becomes aware of me as a person.

The Christian affirms that man constitutes a vital unity, flesh and spirit together as one being. When God came into the world and sought a direct encounter with man, He chose to do so by assuming a human body. It was in Jesus Christ—truly God, yet truly Man—that He revealed Himself to us. That His body is inseparable from His Person is evidenced in the bodily Resurrection of our Lord. As Jesus said after He appeared to His disciples,

"See my hands and my feet, that it is I myself; handle me, and see; for a spirit has not flesh and bones as you see that I have" (Luke 24:39). Jesus, too, saw the indivisible unity of flesh and spirit. It was in the body that He suffered for our redemption, in the body that He rose for our justification, in the body that He ascended to the Father's right hand, and in the body that He shall descend once again.

Robert Grimm quotes the cogent words of A.M. Henry: "Sin makes man carnal, including his spirit, while grace makes man spiritual, including his flesh."[22] Our body, with all its perplexing functions, becomes through the grace of God a temple of the Holy Spirit. It is the body redeemed by the Lord, and therefore belonging to Him. As the body mediates the life of man, it mediates the personal response of man to God. It is on such a ground that the apostle directs his imperative, "So glorify God in your body" (1 Corinthians 6:20). And it is this intimate association of body with spirit that Paul has in mind when he writes, "I appeal to you therefore, brethren, by the mercies of God, to present your bodies as a living sacrifice, holy and acceptable to God, which is your spiritual worship" (Romans 12:1). Notice carefully: ". . . your bodies . . . your spiritual worship." Yes, "your bodies"—in other words, your whole physical existence as a person. Remember, when Jesus offered up His body on the cross, He "gave" Himself. To whom shall we offer our bodies, our very selves?

Continuing to speak about fornication, Paul says, "Shun immorality. Every other sin which a man commits is outside the body; but the immoral man sins against his own body" (1 Corinthians 6:18). Henry Alford is among those holding the view that this is comparative, that there are sins done in and by the body which abuse the body, yet which are still outside the body—i.e., introduced from without, and sinful not in their act but in their effect. "But," he says, "fornication is the alienating that body which is the Lord's, and making it a harlot's body—it is sin against a man's own body, in its very nature—against the verity and nature of his body; not an effect on the body from participation of things without, but a contradiction of the truth of the body, wrought within itself."[23]

All relationships between men and women are sexual in that they are relationships between sexually differentiated persons. There are degrees of personal involvement, degrees of physical involvement. As to the physical, some relationships are nonspecific, i.e., with little or no involvement. No one would consider these to be intimate. Other relationships are physically more specific, more involved, and to some degree intimate. As to the personal aspects, some relationships have a low degree of need-fulfillment, whether in emotional, social, or spiritual spheres. Other relationships have a relatively high degree of fulfillment in these and other spheres. Some relationships are more binding, others less binding, depending upon the degree of intimacy achieved. All relationships between the sexes may be characterized anywhere from a very low degree of obligation and responsibility to a high degree. It is impossible to separate the personal from the sexual. For sexual expressions symbolize the personal intensity and depth of any given relationship between the sexes. Thus we see that sexual integrity is very much a part of personal integrity; the two are inseparable.

William Banowsky has this to say: "Until we have reliable data to the contrary, we may infer from what we observe generally in ordinary life that sheer quantity of sexual experience does not provide the release for which people hope—clearly, it does not enrich the quality of gratification. The physical act itself decreases in quality of satisfaction to whatever extent a couple is incapable of symbolizing through it the deeper values which they hold in common. Because, as an act of self-indulgence, sexual intercourse yields diminishing returns, persons who begin by using sex purely for physical release often end by searching for new sources of titillation and for new partners, as in the game of wife trading. It thus becomes easy for people to find themselves chained to the need for variety in the source of stimulation, and less free from sexual tension."[24]

Banowsky then cites the words of Karl Menninger, in *Love Against Hate*, which run counter to the superficial claims of the promiscuous: "It is an axiom in psychiatry that a plurality of direct sexual outlets indicates the very opposite of what it is popularly assumed to indicate. Dividing the sexual interest into several objectives diminishes the total sexual gratification. . . ."

On every hand there is supporting evidence that God knew precisely what He was doing when He appointed the one-flesh relationship between two persons to express their total life partnership from the simplest aspects of it to the most sublime. We heartily agree with Banowsky's appeal: "We urge a larger view of sex, a view that enriches life, rather than a narrower one that diminishes it. . . . We call for a more ardent sexuality and a restoration of the intensities that ennoble us." This is all possible within God's design, *but only Christians can celebrate such sexuality!*

As New Testament light falls with ever-increasing brilliance upon the orders of Creation, it becomes evident that sexual fulfillment is designed to be dependent upon the marriage relation, even as marriage fulfillment is designed to be dependent upon the sexual relation. As man is first and foremost a spiritual creature, the spiritual is meant to transcend the physical and psychological aspects of sexual union. We understand, too, that God designed sex so as to fuse it together with the highest emotion of which man is capable—*love*—and with the highest commitment of which man is capable—*marriage*. Marital love is the most intense and demanding form of loves, for it is the love of two persons in a total relationship of responsible caring. Marriage also is the most intense form of total-life commitment, inasmuch as it demands an exclusive, enduring union of complete mutuality and complementarity. When this is their purpose, a couple share sexually with no other; hence, what they hold in common is special. Their sexuality becomes a chief reinforcement of an exclusive commitment in love.

The sexual relation is ultimately a profound test of personal integrity and responsibility. Is it not subject to man's intelligence and volition? Is it not given him as a sacred trust? Is it not a gift of God with a purpose to fulfill, given to man in order that he might know and choose this fulfillment? The Christian cannot ignore the fact that God will bless or withhold blessing according to whether or not sex is incorporated into a couple's obedience to His plan. So you see, for the Christian this is not an empty ideal; it is a moral imperative!

Since man at his highest is spirit, flesh must serve spirit. But only in a commitment to God through Jesus Christ is it possible for flesh to serve spirit, rather than spirit serving flesh. In the intimate correlation between sex and marriage, marriage is a divine calling to two people. Sex is a gift incorporated within that calling. The two belong together. Marriage and sex stand in a reciprocal relation—designed of God to be that way. Sex needs marriage to give it ultimate meaning and value; marriage needs sex to give it an exclusive and profoundly intimate bond. Marriage dignifies sex as more than a mere function of the body—making it instead a symbolic expression of a life partnership. Marriage purifies sex and keeps it from becoming irresponsible or exploitative. Marriage transforms the physical into something more than physical. But similarly, sex extends the means through which marriage gives expression to love and tender care. Husband and wife are not sexual performers but intimate partners. Into their sexual intimacy a husband and wife bring all the meaning and value they attach to their whole marital life together. Marriage would be deprived without the gift of sex, and the gift of sex would be meaningless, in terms of its ultimate value, apart from the stability, the responsibility, and the mutuality which marriage brings to it.

Marriage is the consummation of a growing relationship of love and personal commitment; it is the consummation of two people's commitment to a life together. Similarly, sexual intercourse is the consummation of a growing physical intimacy. In God's design, these twin consummations are meant to converge at the point of marriage. The commitment of love is matched by the commitment of sexual intimacy. Paradoxically, sex is restricted to marriage—not to withhold a good thing, but to enhance the meaning of marriage.

Ebbie Smith makes the observation that the one-flesh relationship is established by marriage, and yet is a relationship that grows in marriage. It grows in expanded dimensions and in meanings as it is experienced. This is realized as the two become one, molded after the likeness of Christ. This is not explicitly validated by specific verses of Scripture, but it is clearly implied from the fact that the relationship of the Christian to his Lord is a maturing one. It involves a receptive heart and an obedient life. Sanctification is a progressive transformation of life—life that grows constantly both in character and in capacity as it approximates the likeness of Christ, and what Paul calls "the measure of the stature of the fulness of Christ" (Ephesians 4:13).

Robert Grimm places our subject in proper context: "But sex, operating through the action of the hormones, involves the entire personality. The whole being is profoundly affected. Hormonal sexuality now becomes psychic sexuality. At this point the distinction between man and the animal clearly emerges. For man, sexual pleasure is something he shares with a partner he has deliberately chosen. His responses are under his conscious control, his actions are explained and interpreted by words. In human sexuality, therefore, the instinctual elements become subservient to the psychic elements in the personality; biological sex is under the rule of the conscience. In this setting, sexuality becomes a function of relationship, a medium of exchange and reciprocity between two persons. It becomes the dynamic force which enables the personality to attain its goal—to exist for others, to love. In this sense, we can truly say that our sexuality does not belong to us at all. It belongs to that other person in and through whom it fulfills itself."[25]

Sexual intercourse, says Sherwin Bailey, "is an act which engages and expresses the whole personality in such a way as to constitute a unique mode of self-disclosure and self-committal. By engaging in it, a man and woman become 'one flesh'—mutually involved for good or ill in a relation of profound significance and consequence."[26] The one-flesh union is so profound, so intimate, so enduring that only marriage can encompass it. Scripturally, monogamy is demanded, not by specific proof texts, but by the recognition that this one-flesh union is the total union of marriage; a total relationship can exist only in the form of monogamy. Fidelity, which is part of totality means accepting an unlimited and lifetime liability, working out the blessings and burdens of sexual life in a lifetime partnership. As William Wylie remarks, "Because I can never do anything more intimate than this with anyone, I am yours in the most intimate possible union. . . . Only to the person who can claim the whole of us can we give such a complete commitment, and only exclusive sexual intercourse can rightly symbolize and interpret such total commitment."[27] Simply, the one-flesh union is bound by its shared secret and it lives in the context of permanency.

Viewed developmentally, sex in the one-flesh union moves toward a progressive integration of the several dimensions of personal existence. *Biologically*, sex appeases passion and reduces tension. *Psychologically*, sex discloses otherwise unexpressed aspects of our selfhood. *Socially*, sex is a unitive factor in the paired relationship. *Ethically*, sex manifests the necessary interdependence between fulfillment and responsibility. *Theologically*, sex points to the mystery of a union divinely purposed and illustrative of that between Christ and His church. These meanings acquire varied emphases at different times and seasons in any given couple's experience. For the most part these meanings are not experienced consciously at the time. But for the Christian couple who have deeply sought for the essential significance, there will be an increasing integration of these meanings as their sexual expression matures. Nor is it difficult to see that marriage safeguards sex from its own passionate instability. Marriage provides the setting in which sex can prove its stability, its lasting power and its fidelity to the high calling of God and to the partner's welfare. This setting means, too, that gratitude and fulfillment survive the brief moments of ecstasy. Those moments are only the concentrated expression of a continuing relationship which outlasts all mere moments of disappointment as well as of ecstasy.

Surely, the Christian couple has every reason to see their marriage as the expression of one flesh, one spirit, one love! Their goal is to fulfill the divine ideal of an exclusive, indissoluble union. Such a vocation can be fulfilled only as a couple lives in the enabling power of God who called them to this special union. The purpose of God can be fulfilled only in the power of God. But, then, God never calls a couple to one-flesh union without extending to them the enabling power of His Holy Spirit. It is a radical calling, yet the resources are available in God. Physically, the one-flesh union is made up of acts and intervals, the greater proportion devoted to life in the intervals. There are concentrated moments when all that is valued in the relationship is brought into physical focus, there to be expressed in a profound way. But it is life in the intervals that speaks most continually of the real union of persons. What ultimately matters is that acts and intervals are integrated into a single meaningful pattern.

In the early beginnings of marriage, acts are perhaps more meaningful than intervals. But as the life partnership grows and matures, the intervals contain the ever more meaningful content of the personal union. A couple is not sexually coupled all the time; in fact, the time occupied is very minor in relation to the time occupied in a multiplicity of other activities. Sexual desire follows and is followed by periods of no sexual desire. The sexual unity transcends the sexual moments of desire. These moments are special, celebrative acts which symbolize a couple's greater and continuous unity. They experience their unique unity in terms of being *one flesh, one spirit, one love.*

Students of behavioristic psychology know the power of positive reinforcement. Sex is one of the strongest primary reinforcers. Thus when it is associated with one person in a delightful union, a strong attachment is first established, then positively reinforced. A word of caution is apropos. Two extremes in expectation are to be avoided. First, a couple may *expect too much* from sexual intercourse. They must realize that sexual intercourse cannot bring about a complete relationship between two persons, nor can it provide all the satisfactions of life. It is not a substitute for the myriad other expressions of love and unity. It is but one means—albeit the most intimate and powerful—incorporated within the larger context of a couple's life partnership. Second, a couple may *expect too little.* This occurs when they restrict the meaning to physical gratification. Then it is not accepted as the symbol of all that is meaningful in their total union. For such a couple sex must come to represent far more. The concept of one-flesh in all its symbolism and meaning can be a bright new discovery. Christian sexual life under the sanctions of God, incorporated within His purposes, is the way to blessing and satisfaction and the celebration of life in Christ.

8

Celebrating the Mystery

A writer recently said, "Modern man has shifted the fig leaf from his genitals to his face. He's lost the mystery of his sexuality and in the process he has lost his own identity." In succeeding to expose every imaginable facet of sexual behavior, modern man has at the same time succeeded in diminishing any sense of sacred mystery. But humanity cannot be stripped of its mystery, try as man may, and sex is a dimension of that mystery. In attempting to humanize sex, contemporary man has dehumanized sexuality from being expressive of the whole personality. For all the new access to sex, sexual meaning has become diminished. The new freedom has introduced chains of its own. It has not produced what it promised, and the world seems none the happier for the sexual revolution. In the face of it all, Christian theology calls for a return to the sense of mystery, for only then will there be a sense of celebration.

It is the fallacy of all psychological analyses of sexuality, and certainly of hedonistic philosophies, that they pretend to explain human sexuality in naturalistic terms while divesting it of all mystery. But the best trained of theological minds confess to standing before an ineffable mystery, and make no apology for that fact. Paul himself declared this mystery to the Ephesians. Jeremy Taylor, in the seventeenth century, saw that marriage is "the symbolical and sacramental representation of the greatest mysteries of our religion." Otto Piper in our day says, "The Biblical view of sex revolves about two fundamental ideas: reverence for the mystery of sex, and the sanctification of marriage as the God-appointed goal of the sexual relationship."[1]

The inner secret of sex is a mystery which cannot be described objectively. It is more than merely something previously unknown or withheld from us. Rather, it presupposes a purpose of God for which something is withheld from general knowledge only that it might be revealed to the right persons at the right time. The sexual mystery is a secret whose disclosure is solely in the hands of two persons in that special relationship of husband and wife. Their personal destiny which they determine together is something that can be shared between two, but never with a third. For every couple revelation of the inner secret is uniquely theirs, exclusive in nature, a revelation that dare not be profaned or it is lost altogether. Although the mystery is thus revealed, it remains a mystery, a shared secret that never loses its sublime nature. It can be described objectively, or functionally, only to a limited extent, and then never in the way the couple experiences it. For at the peak of the sexual union all consciousness of difference may vanish. A loss of self-consciousness may take place, and a sense of oneness may prevail over the sense of separateness.

Otto Piper puts it concisely: "The sexual act leads to a new and deepened understanding of oneself which is characterized by three features: it is an intuitive knowledge given in and with the sexual experience; it discloses what was thus far hidden from the individual; and its subject matter is one's Self seen in the mutual relationship in which it stands with the partner's Self."[2] The sexual act conveys knowledge apart from which the full meaning of the unity of the flesh cannot be comprehended.

William Hamilton proposes the following: "If it is true that sexual intercourse mediates and makes possible an intimate form of personal knowledge, it is obvious that a very special status must be given to the first experience of the sexual act . . . a decisive importance attaches to the first time this mutual and intimate knowledge was ever shared. A man, for example, would seem to be bound in an irrevocable way, because of this interchange of knowledge, to that woman who first helped him understand himself as a man."[3] This is just why Jesus teaches no sexual intercourse with anyone other than one's mate, before or after marriage. Hamilton also asserts that sex reminds us that we are alone, that sexual union only leads to and recalls our basic separateness, that we are unable to fulfill ourselves and that we need another. This other, he says, is most creatively defined as a husband or wife with whom the sexual life can be explored and understood in openness and honesty, in continuation and completeness.

It is Otto Piper's observation that though the mystery of sex has been disclosed in the first sexual encounter, a couple never fully loses the awareness of its secret. No matter how continuously over the years they experience their intimate union with each other, they feel the mutual mystery of it all. They also sense the mystery that something so unknowable as another self is being united with their self in a way that can never be fully known to either.

One can gain an intimation of the mysterious nature of sexual knowledge by observing the manner in which the sexes make advances toward each other. The reserved nature of a young man's first approach to a girl is not so much caused by lack of self-confidence as by an awareness that he is confronted with a secret that demands a delicate and sensitive courting. That secret is not readily his. A certain reserve on the part of the young woman expresses the same instinctive feeling. The girl's reserve indicates her unwillingness to allow anyone to penetrate her secret, to know her mystery, who does not properly appreciate what he is to experience. It must be more than merely a transient experience, leaving her robbed of the opportunity to someday make an exclusive revelation within a responsible and permanent union. With maturing self-identity, this mystery of sexual integrity becomes more valued.

As a couple attains sexual experience with one another, they enter into something formerly inaccessible. Sexual desire is heightened by what is veiled, and initially possessed only by imagination. The male is aroused to sexual desire when he perceives portions of the female body which normally are covered. But arousal occurs only under certain conditions. Since the unclothed parts of the body do not by themselves stimulate sexual feelings —the nude in art is beyond the realm of sexual stimulation—it is rather the unveiling or unclothing that arouses the excitement. Think, if you will, of the way modern advertising exploits the sexually exciting positioning and dress of a beautiful young woman. She is not pictured simply to show her beauty, but is posed to impress the beholder with the realization that parts of her body commonly concealed are now deliberately bared for his eyes. He fantasizes that she is baring her body as a personal invitation to him to think further in those terms. What is bared carries the suggestion of what is not yet bared, but waits for his response. This is why there is a far more effective erotic response to partial unveiling than to, say, a whole beach full of barely clad young women whose state of undress has nothing whatever to do with their partially unveiling themselves for the eyes of a man. Of course, in some instances eroticism enters intrusively when this is the obvious effect sought by a particular young woman. And fantasy being what it is, there is always an underlying eroticism related to any state of undress which lies somewhat beyond what is regarded as the conventional.

The New Testament clearly condemns any penetration of the mystery of another's sexuality outside the marital bond, for it regards this the robbing of another's sexual secret. While concealment is the individual's form of protection, especially the woman's, responsible behavior is the concern of both the man and the woman he confronts.

Quite naturally, sexual curiosity is difficult to bridle and forms a perfectly natural part of psychosexual development. Imagination tends to build upon past perceptions, going on to form a mental construct equal to whatever pull of sexual desire may be present. But the Christian does well to seek to come to terms with this temptation by being especially careful in the matter of exposing himself to what he knows is tempting. He does well to heed the words of Henry Thoreau:

"We should treat our minds as innocent and ingenious children whose guardians we are . . . be careful what objects and what subjects we thrust on their attention. . . . Every thought that passes through the mind helps to wear it and tear it, and to deepen the ruts, which, as in the streets of Pompeii, evince how much it has been used. How many things there are concerning which we might well deliberate whether we had better know them."

Just in passing it should be mentioned that the practice of petting is a penetration of the sexual secret. It violates another person's sexual integrity. Jesus warned about looking that is lusting, and certainly petting, whatever else it stands for, is nothing less than looking by means of one's hands. Those who pet should know what is involved, in what all too commonly is regarded as innocent "presexual" involvement.

Sexual intercourse may be defined as a surrender of one's private identity to another for the sake of creating a single corporate identity. This leads to the matter of privacy as the context for sexual intercourse. Sometimes it is assumed that sexual acts are shameful and hence are to be hidden. What a gross distortion! It is guilt from the hidden works of sinful man projected onto the pure and worth-giving acts of man.

Actually, two considerations determine the insistence upon privacy for the sexual consummation. First, the implication is that such acts between husband and wife are personal in the highest sense and intimate in the most protected sense. Personal meanings are concentrated and intensified by excluding all other personal relationships from an intrusive role. Second, in privacy a couple is free to think of that unique union which is fully experienced by themselves and shared by no other. Here in the seclusion of their own intimate world of two, separated from all the other worlds in which they live out their daily existence, their full and free expression of mutual love can refresh and renew them. In privacy the unique sacramental meaning of their union is expressed, uncomplicated by any extraneous considerations. The One who is the Mediator of true openness, He alone is present at the celebration. From that intimate world they can leave to participate in the larger world of persons and relationships, knowing that they have once again reconsecrated themselves to each other by means of the gift they alone share. No interlopers here! Even the children must know that there is a sacred mystery preserved in this intimacy. Growing children are thus assured that one day they, too, shall have the privilege of protected intimacy—this exclusive, sacramental world of personal meaning. The fullest openness to each other is experienced in the context of the least openness to the world of persons outside themselves.

Because such a secret is shared in sexual intercourse, each partner can feel with respect to the other, "You enhance my being, you add to what I am; you cause me to have a deeper sense of both *I*-ness and *we*-ness." In becoming one-flesh, a couple participates in that unity which cannot be reversed ontologically. There is an indissoluble bond which is irrevocable even when infidelity makes an open break between the partners. There is no reversing the knowledge of the shared secret. (Infidelity, incidentally, occurs the very moment when one does not feel himself or herself bound by the secret, and seeks to share it with another.) As Herbert Doms has expressed it, two human beings who have shared the sex act can no longer act toward one another as if they had not done so. The unity achieved transcends the biological domain. It reflects their shared participation in a profoundly significant secret.[4] Otto Piper expresses it beautifully:

"A distinctive feeling of well-being suffuses both persons at the completion of the sexual act. The man experiences release from tension and a sense of satisfaction because finally the restless striving of his will and desire has found its respite through this person. The woman too feels enriched by the assurance that she has encountered the person who gives meaning to her womanhood. Both partners are happy in the joyful certainty of mutual blessedness and of belonging together. This sense of belonging together implies on the part of the man the jealous wish to possess his partner for himself alone; while on the part of the woman there is the desire to bind him to herself in permanent union."[5]

One reason parents have difficulty instructing their children in sexual understanding is that they are aware of the mystery, the form of knowledge which is gained only in the act of intercourse itself, and which cannot be taught objectively. How does one adequately impart this knowledge which in its finest, fullest sense is existential?[6]

Erich Fromm contends that complete rational knowledge is possible only of *things*, that we cannot know our fellow man or ourselves rationally because we are not merely objects. He writes, "There is, however, another path to knowing man's secret. This path is not that of thought, but of *love*. Love is active penetration of the other person in which my desire to know is stilled by union. In the act of fusion I know you, I know myself. . . . I know in the only way in which knowledge of that which is alive is possible for man—by the experience of *union*, not by any knowledge our thought can give. The only way to full knowledge lies in the act of love; this act transcends thought, it transcends words." Thus a psychoanalyst of high repute, an acknowledged agnostic, says precisely what the Scriptures indicate. Sexual knowledge is existential; it is knowledge communicated in the enactment of sexual union.[7]

The Hebrew term for coitus is *yadá*, "to know." In Genesis 4:1 we read, "Now Adam knew Eve his wife, and she conceived and bore Cain." Similarly, Rebekah is described, in Genesis 24:16, "The maiden was very fair to look upon, a virgin, whom no man had known." In light of the very explicit language elsewhere in the Old Testament concerning sexual intercourse (*see* Ezekiel 16 and 23, for example), *yadá* is hardly a mere euphemism for intercourse. Intercourse provides a language of the body, a nonverbal medium of communicative exchange that enables a couple to explore the mystery which is sexual union and communion. This strange expression, *to know*, is used interchangeably of the man and of the woman (the latter usage in Genesis 19:8; Luke 1:34 KJV), and points to the hidden element in sex which does not come to light except in intercourse.[8]

At the moment the woman was given to him Adam became aware of his existence as a man. For Eve the experience was similar. Each had need of the other to achieve self-awareness in sexual distinctiveness. "To know" in Hebrew thought did not signify simply an intellectual recognition of another person, but involvement and participation with that person in experiences calculated to reveal each one's true identity. This was particularly true of sexual union. In giving of one's body in the sexual encounter, one comes to a new awareness of the mystery of one's own personal identity and the other's. Man gets in touch with himself, and thus is able to reveal himself truly to another. Self-disclosure invites self-disclosure, so that the process is truly reciprocal. The intimate self-disclosure through sexual intercourse invites self-disclosure at all other levels of personal existence. This is an exclusive revelation unique to the couple. They know each other as they know no other person. This unique knowledge is tantamount to laying claim to another in genuine belonging. What the couple knows and shares between themselves alone is reinforcing to their whole marital relation. And when a couple reserve their sexual revealing for one another alone, then indeed sex is controlled rather than controlling. The nakedness and physical coupling is symbolic of the fact that nothing is hidden or withheld between them. When this disclosure is made within the covenant of Christian marriage, there can be mutual trust and acceptance.

Up to this point we have emphasized only one purpose which sexual intercourse serves within the covenant of marriage, namely, the establishment and nurture of the one-flesh union. It is only in recent times that the church has recognized the unitive along with the procreative function. Recent statements by major denominational study commissions indicate the general acceptance of the unitive, relational purpose as a prominent, if not the most prominent, function.

Perhaps it would be better to say, with Seward Hiltner, that marital sex has different aims rather than primary and secondary aims. Its chief biological purpose is procreation; its chief ontological purpose is unitive and relational; its chief personal purpose is integration and fulfillment. The unitive, relational purpose takes precedence simply because it is essential to the very establishment of marriage. To put it in the order which it serves, we might say that marital sex is: (1) creative, (2) recreative, and (3) procreative. A relationship is created at the beginning, it is continually recreated, and out of it there may or may not come the procreative. In the Creation accounts, sex is seen in the context of personal relation; in fact, offspring are not even mentioned. Not that the place of children in marriage is minimized in any sense, but simply that when God is talking about the man and his wife, the relational bond is uppermost.

The second of the three purposes is the *recreative*. Sexual intercourse functions as a renewing, reconstituting force in marriage. Reuel Howe comments that "the woman and man in married love may come together freely and unashamedly in the communion of the flesh and spirit in the experience of recreation."[9] Herbert Doms reminds us that the human spirit can never communicate itself adequately in a single act. In his delightful book *What God Has Joined Together*, Gustave Thibon writes, "It is the miracle of true human love that it can use the force of sexuality, basically alien and centrifugal to the final destiny of the soul, to nourish all that is most delicate in the interior life."[10]

Paul writes, in 1 Corinthians 7:3-5, "The husband should give to his wife her conjugal rights, and likewise the wife to her husband. . . . Do not refuse one another except perhaps by agreement for a season, that you may devote yourselves to prayer; but then come together again, lest Satan tempt you through lack of self-control." Note the equality of rights; there is no hint of "husband's rights, wife's duties." In any long-term continence either party might be tempted, while for both partners sexual intercourse is a means of recreating, renewing, and reconstituting their intimate life partnership.

The third of the three purposes is *procreative*. Ernest White sums it up well: "There is no denial in the New Testment of the purpose of procreation. The subject is practically ignored! The emphasis is almost entirely upon the relational aspect of marriage. The procreative purpose appears to be tacitly assumed and accepted without elaboration. The inference can be drawn that a proper sexual union was expected to be fruitful but not to the exclusion of other purposes and functions in sexual relationship. Certainly there is no indication as to the degree of fruitfulness that is expected. . . . The responsibility in sexual union comes from two directions. The first lies in the fact that when a person accepts another in sexual union, he becomes responsible for that person in sexuality and in *all* of the development of personality. In other words, the *whole* person must be accepted in both inner development and social setting. The second approach to responsibility lies in the very fact of potential procreation, whether it becomes a reality or not."[11]

It might be added that one of the earliest texts in Genesis finds God commanding Adam and Eve, "Be fruitful and multiply, and fill the earth and subdue it" (Genesis 1:28). This is spoken of in the context of God's blessing upon man before the fall. It is also spoken at the beginning of the human race, when to fill and replenish the earth was the major task. In our time the problems of overpopulation require other decisions, lessening the relative importance of procreation. Surely, this is no longer the primary justification of sexual relations for married couples. In fact, if this were the primary justification, what of couples who cannot have children? We can say that for them the primary purpose of sexual relations is intact, namely, the unitive purpose which establishes and nurtures their union.

Within the relational purpose the place of pleasure is assured, contrary to the church's understanding for so many centuries. For most churchmen today this would pose no problem. God is most surely the Author of pleasure. Like many other qualities attendant to man's existence, pleasure in itself is amoral; it is moral or immoral depending upon the use to which it is put. While man may abuse it, God utilizes pleasure in all of human life. It is part of the celebration of life under God. Sexually, God utilizes pleasure to bind a couple together in the enjoyment and enhancement of their common life. He thus assures that union will take place. One is reminded of the quip of William Graham Sumner, the American sociologist, "Who would subject himself to the indignities of parenthood, if the sex act were not pleasurable?" Pleasure is God's bonus, His gift of ecstasy and joy. The fullness of pleasure, untainted by any guilt of exploitation or the violation either of the integrity of another person or of God's purpose itself, becomes the great reinforcement of a couple's deepest values. Their pleasure is both physical and personal.

Seward Hiltner takes note of an important connection: "Implicit in the Christian view is the conviction that in their full human dimensions, intensity and steadfastness are likely to support and enhance each other. A movement toward full human intensity in sex will increase steadfastness; and a movement toward full human steadfastness will increase intensity. Therefore these should be concomitant characteristics of the sex life." That sex is presumed to have intensity implies that any attempt to make it casual would be to distort its inherent meaning. Similarly, that sex is presumed to have steadfastness implies that it requires more than transient, impersonal contacts. Sex is less than sex whenever it is limited to the meeting of two bodies.

Hiltner sums up his position with reference to intensity: "Intensity is desirable from each of the relevant perspectives: biologically, in the intense pleasure of the encounter and the orgasm; psychologically, in the discovery of unsuspected depths in the self; socially, in the depth of discovery of another; ethically, in the integration of fulfillment and responsibility; and theologically, in the deepening sense of the mystery. The arbitrary or permanent exclusion of any aspect of intensity foreshortens the meaning of sex."

Hiltner also sums up his position on steadfastness: "Steadfastness is also desirable from each of these perspectives: biologically, in the form of physical fidelity to another; psychologically, in the sense of movement toward depth and not merely toward breadth or thrill; socially, in the constant recognition of new depth in the other and, by implication, in all other persons potentially; ethically, in the responsibility that, far from destroying fulfillment, goes along with it; and theologically, in the growing conviction that true faithfulness is its own reward."[13]

Fidelity is a movement toward depth and intensification. Fulfillment and responsibility are integrated as a relationship matures in time and in mutual commitment. Fidelity brings its own reward, and sexual fidelity, representing as it does interpersonal fidelity, is a constant indicator of the unchanging covenant between God and His people. Fidelity and intensity are thus interdependent, supporting and enhancing each other. And one of the ensuing confidences is that sexual partners can fail without fear. Where so much more than physical sex is experienced, each is free to relax in the knowledge that sexual moments, be they highly satisfying or not at all, are but moments within the larger meaning and history of an enduring relationship. How truly it has been said that life for man consists in commitments rather than experiences, and that sex is one of the powers behind his commitments. In a permanent marital commitment, even sex itself is reinforced and released to greater heights. There is less chance of inhibitions arising out of the fear that one partner is not giving himself as wholeheartedly as the other. Out of the deeper, more assured sense of commitment there arises a greater sexual satisfaction, while out of the greater sexual satisfaction there arises a gratitude that strengthens the commitment. So we are compelled to conclude that marriage can never stand in a neutral place so far as sexual indulgence is concerned. Either marriage is the one appropriate context for sexual union, and hence the *friend* of sex, or marriage is the *enemy* of the sex that would not restrict itself to marriage.

William Hamilton does not let us forget that the sexual relation not only symbolizes personal relation; it is a judgment upon it as well. A married couple who have been feeling cool and distant to one another, who perhaps have a disagreement dividing them, can be challenged and made contrite and reconcilable by participating in the sexual act. It reminds them of the unity and selflessness upon which their union was founded. At the same time, one of the reasons why even the most consistent libertine ultimately ends with a sense of despair is that no one can stand the awful judgment that results from consistently engaging in an act that symbolizes a relationship not present. Sexual intercourse confronts a couple simultaneously with the relational ideal which they are called to realize, and the quality of life which they are actually living in the present. Any incompatibility between the ideal and the actual is experienced as a tension which disturbs their intercourse in subtle yet powerful ways. The indication is that they are failing to work out satisfactorily all that one-flesh union implies. They must therefore pay careful heed to the quality of their relation as it is disclosed to them in their coming together sexually, for the sexual act will invariably be either a joyful affirmation of their common life, or a revelation of its defects and disturbances.

So, properly experienced within marriage and its commitment to fidelity, the sexual relation brings a sense of well-being, complete identity, joy unbounded, perfect mutuality, freedom in responsibility, fulfullment of purpose, and an indescribable unity of being. Wrongfully experienced outside this commitment, it brings a sense of unfulfilled unity, of a meaningless investment of self, guilt in transgressing the law of God, possibly even physical revulsion, since sex is experienced as nothing more than physical connection. There will follow a sense of having squandered something precious, of giving away something that was unique, and of having gained nothing of abiding value from the most intimate of acts. Rather than union, the succeeding shock of separation is the most vivid remembrance. In wrongful sex there is no assuaging of personal problems, no comfort of inner hurts, no assurances, no true joy or sense of well-being. But in marriage, even when the physical fails to bring the expected satisfaction, when its pleasure is temporarily frustrated, it still can serve to bring humility, acceptance, a deepened sense of interdependence, and the need for love above all else. Karl Barth wraps it up in a choice statement:

"Marriage is 'chaste,' honourable and truly sexual when it is encompassed by the fellowship of the spirit and of love, but also of work and of the whole of life with all its sorrows and joys, and when this total life experience justifies at the right time and place this particular relationship. When the relationship is fulfilled in this context, when the fulfillment is demanded and sustained by the environment of total coexistence, then and only then is it right and salutary. If it does not take place in this context, it is neither chaste, right nor salutary. To use our earlier phrase, coitus without coexistence is demonic."[14]

Following Immanuel Kant and Martin Buber, it has become common for the theology of sexuality to take cognizance of the difference between *persons* and *things*. We are meant by God to value and love persons, to use and benefit from things. It is remarkably easy, however, to reverse this —to love and value things while using people for our own ends. So if sex becomes only a pleasure, a means to one's own satisfaction by using another, then any person who can provide this pleasure necessarily becomes a thing, an object. He is neither valued nor loved for himself, but for what he can supply. John Macmurray said, "To use another person for your own ends is to violate his personality by making an object of him. And in violating the integrity of another, you violate your own." To use another person for whatever purpose is to reduce that person to an object of utilitarian value only. Thus a person is valuable if useful, but if no longer useful, then not valuable and hence dispensable. This is the Playboy syndrome; a person who serves my pleasure is not my partner but my plaything. Sex is recreational only. A.D. Lindsay said, "If we let ourselves use other people as a means only, we soon become grossly insensitive to their quality." Indeed, it can only be so. When married partners are committed to caring for one another, to serving one another in love, then they transcend their natural inclination to use one another. No longer do they make the other the object of their own self-gratification. Every person is a unique, irreplaceable center of conscious experience, not a pawn that may be used, exploited, manipulated, enjoyed for awhile and then cast aside. And nowhere does the dignity of man cry out more vehemently against such abuse of personhood than in the realm of sexual exploitation.

Only persons can stand in relation. Another person, however, stands over against me, as one who is equal, as one who exists in his own right. My attitude must be one of respect and responsibility. So with those whose reality and significance we recognize as we do our own, we move into personal relation. When I step over the bounds of my separate singleness into relation with another, then my mate is one into whose life I enter, even as he enters into mine. Though only momentary, our human life consists in our personal encounters. True, I may so forget my humanity as to treat another person as a thing, as someone whose human dignity I can outrage, whose sexual integrity I can violate, whose essential worth I can repudiate. But in so doing I debase myself as well. On the other hand, to love is the most remarkable of all encounters. Here we can agree with Nicholas Berdyaev that love "is the ontological basis of the marriage union." Without love, there can be nothing but legalized cohabitation devoid of all inner validity.[15]

Love is greater than sexual desire, inasmuch as love means desire reaching out after the whole person. One cannot love by abstracting out certain attractive personal features as if they alone mattered. This is the ground of fidelity. One does not first abstract out just the attractive features, to build a relationship on these. Neither does one abstract out the unattractive features later on as ground for rejecting the person. Love is desire for and acceptance of the whole person. This is what is contained in Martin Buber's saying, "Love is responsibility of an I for a Thou." Apart from this true marital love, all forms of sexual love are incomplete since they do not engross the total personality. And as Harry Overstreet urged, love is not the possession of the person, but the affirmation of the person. On a more spiritual plane, the comment of Helmut Thielicke is even more relevant, that since the other person stands in his own individual relationship to God, he can never be completely reduced to his relationship to me. Therefore I can never wholly possess the other person. This we do well to remember always.

Love leads men and women to redirect their lives, centering their satisfactions in the creative growth of each other. They live in and for each other. Love overcomes the egoism that otherwise would obstruct a one-flesh union. Love also constrains one to acknowledge the unconditional significance of the other. As Vladimir Solovyev points out, the center of man's existence is thus transferred beyond the limits of his own person and the fusion of two existences is effected. Hence it is love that forms the ontological basis of the one-flesh unity.

Rollo May takes up the matter of love as personal, shown in the love act itself. Man is the only creature who makes love face-to-face, who copulates looking at his partner. Oh, indeed, he can turn his head or even assume other positions for variety's sake, but these are variations on a theme —the theme of making love vis-à-vis each other. As May continues, this opens the whole front of the person—all the parts which are the most tender and most vulnerable—to the kindness or cruelty of the partner. The man can thus see in the eyes of the woman the nuances of delight or awe. It is the posture of the ultimate baring of one's self. It not only stamps the love act as irrevocably personal, with all the implications of that fact, one of which being that the lovers can speak if they wish, but the looking is fraught with intensity; it brings a heightened consciousness of personal relationship. We experience what we are doing—which may be play, or exploitation, or sharing of sensuality, or, indeed, loving. The norm signified by this position is personal, and any meaning other than that is a deviation therefrom. As May contends, we have to block off something, exert some effort to do so, to make it not personal.

Chastity is the term given to describe sexual abstinence outside of marriage, whether prior to or concomitant with marriage. Chastity is the negation of both premarital and comarital sex. But this suggests that chastity is essentially a negative principle when it is not. Chastity does not refer to the repressing of legitimate, natural desires, nor does it mean their denial. Rather, it means keeping sex in the right place for the right person at the right time. In a positive sense it means sex serving its intended purpose, controlled, not controlling. It means that sex was made for man, not man for sex, that sexuality is one dimension of man's obedience to God and his fulfilling of God's purpose. Thus we are considering what may be regarded as a negative means but a positive end. Still in a positive vein, chastity is to be seen within the larger principle expressed by Johann von Goethe: "It is only with renunciation that life, properly speaking, can be said to begin." To this Dietrich Bonhoeffer adds, "The essential element in chastity is not the renunciation of pleasure, but the directing of one's whole life to one end." In other words, sex can facilitate personal growth or inhibit it, can support one's life purposes or detract from them. If a person's one end is the fulfillment of God's will, then chastity is essential to that fulfillment. It is singular to man's humanity that he is the only animal capable of chastity—capable of renouncing present pleasures for future benefits that are more enduring. And in order to be a chaste person, his concern isn't so much *what not to do* because it is wrong, but *what he is privileged to do* because it is right. So chastity is a discipline that keeps marital love pure and holy. It guards the dedication of husband and wife to each other. It also guards the unity they are pledged to achieving together. It preserves the highest values of God's gift and intention. Chastity, in other words, leads on to celebration at the most fulfilling moment. And just as it is natural for man to have passions and desires, so it is natural for him to have control over them. The same God who gave us passions and desires enables us to control and direct them to their highest use.

Sexual permissiveness is regarded by many as a basic human freedom. But for Christians it is a question of liberty or lordship. Freedom is only meaningful in terms of the specific purpose it serves. To be free *from* is meaningful only in terms of its correlate, to be free *for*. If sexual freedom means freedom to violate God's appointed order for sexuality, it is not a God-given freedom, but merely the freedom of creaturely choice. Freedom in Christ is a precious gift, but it is not freedom to be irresponsible. It is never freedom just for freedom's sake. Freedom to be promiscuous is no longer freedom to fulfill God's purpose; one freedom cancels out the other. The new freedom only starts as freedom; it soon becomes a new bondage to passion and to undisciplined desire. For the Christian, true freedom is to obey the highest command, to fulfill the highest purpose, to escape the destructive, defeating consequences of freedom's abuse.

Consistent with God's purpose for sexuality, all deviations from this purpose are explicitly proscribed. Of the ten basic moral commandments specifically given to man, the seventh is "You shall not commit adultery" (Exodus 20:14). The tenth is specifically directed to men and reads, "You shall not covet your neighbor's wife" (Ecclesiastes 20:17). Now, this by itself appears ambiguous, but Leviticus 18:20 is more explicit, ". . . you shall not lie carnally with your neighbor's wife, and defile yourself with her." Two chapters later, in Leviticus 20:10, the penalty for this disobedience is death. Deuteronomy 22 and Numbers 5 tell of severe penalties—from divorce to death—for sexual unfaithfulness. The commands, but not the penalties, are reiterated in the New Testament.

God's holy nature is unchanging. In the New Testament, the words *adultery* and *fornication* are largely interchangeable. The word for fornication is used broadly for any instance of sexual intercourse between two people not married to each other. The word for adultery has the same broad meaning, although primarily restricted to sexual unfaithfulness within marriage. It seems clear that Jesus extended the meaning of the seventh commandment to include all instances of sexual unchastity. When Jesus speaks of exclusive and enduring marriage with sexual behavior limited to that, He adds, "Not all men can receive this precept, but only those to whom it is given" (Matthew 19:11).

The practical guide to behavior in the Old Testament is the Book of Proverbs. The reader should look up the following: Proverbs 5:18-23; 6:23-29, 32; 7:16-19, 21, 22. Progressing through the books of the New Testament the reader should look up 1 Corinthians 6:9-20; 7:1-9, 36-38; Galatians 5:16-19, 24; Ephesians 5:3; 5:6, 12; Colossians 3:5, 6; 1 Thessalonians 4:3-8; Hebrews 13:4; 1 Peter 2:11; 2 Peter 2:9, 10, 14, 18-20; Jude 4-7; Revelation 21:8; 22:15. It is difficult to find situation ethics in the explicit passages noted above. God's Word is wholly consistent with itself.

A word of Karl Barth is especially helpful here: "The command of God claims the whole man . . . and in so doing it is the decisive sanctification of physical sexuality and the sex relationship. It sanctifies man by including his sexuality within his humanity, and challenging him even in his bodily nature and therefore in his sexual life. . . . Because his being in its totality is at stake, physical sexuality and the sex relationship cannot remain outside the scope of God's command."[16]

Law and love are two approaches to Christian sex ethics which are sometimes placed in opposition to one another. They really are not contradictory but complementary. Neither is ever true at the expense of the other, nor does one ever usurp the place of the other. Love, more explicitly, does not abolish law. Legalism errs by mistaking the rules for the vital principle, but that does not lead us to abandon the rules which are essential to the achievement of God's aim. Negative rules have a positive aim. Legalism on the contrary squeezes out love, and love is the primary virtue. Thus we must distinguish between the valid place of rules, and the untenable stance of legalism. Those who oppose law to love usually misunderstand the nature of both, for they are essentially allies. This is brought out splendidly by Oliver R. Barclay.[17]

God's command deals with content as an unchanging element in Christian ethics. There are certain things which are always right, others which are always wrong. This does not say that there are not also things which are sometimes right within certain contexts, wrong in others. But stress must be placed on the fact that there are indeed absolute Christian standards, eternally valid, as unchanging as the moral nature of God and His purposes for man. In this sense God addresses us from outside our history, and our response is to His call for obedience. Romans 7:12 NEB declares, "The law is in itself holy, and the commandment is holy and just and good." Paul could not say that the Christian is beyond or outside the bounds of law. Bishop John A. T. Robinson insists that the Christian ethic can never be presented as law plus love, or law qualified by love. For though law has its place, that place is at the boundaries and not at the center. But Robinson provides only a mere construct. C.F.D. Moule contends that the Ten Commandments are not the basis of Christian morals on which an ethic of love builds. But he, too, fails to see the necessary interdependence of law and love, or the way in which each defines the other. Bishop Robinson argues that persons matter more than principles, therefore principles can never dictate to persons. But only a false dichotomy sets principles over against persons. Scripture does not. It cannot be said that persons take priority over principles; in the economy of God's order, principles antedate persons. Not that principles thereby take precedence; but principles and persons form one integral consideration in the order of the Almighty. Furthermore, to decide an issue for one's self is not the same as deciding an issue on one's own. One still decides for himself when confronted with the absolute of God's command and the nature of personal choice. Another false dichotomy, impressive only at first hearing, says, "Law induces fear, love induces freedom; freedom is found only in love." But this is not so; it is like talking about "free love"; but free love is like Grape Nuts—neither grapes nor nuts. Free love is neither love nor free.

A growing number of writers are emphasizing love as the guiding principle of sex relationships. Love, as everyone will concede, is the primary Christian virtue. But the question we must ask is this: On what authority, or for what reasons, should we always put love first? By the logic employed by the love-alone advocates we might ask: If we can reject law in the Christian life, why not reject love as well? Has one more authoritative grounds than the other? Is one truer to Scripture? Jesus spoke of love as a *new commandment* (John 13:34; 15:12). Does it not seem incongruous to the love-alone advocates that Jesus *commands* love? And if love is but a summary of prudential reasons for certain behavior, love amounts to no more than good advice which lacks any base of authority. Love becomes, on this basis, an ambiguous guide. Love's path is not self-evident, and there is great uncertainty whenever love is made the final arbiter of what is right. Sentiment and desire can cloud the issue, for love is subjective and individual and therefore inadequate to issues which are not individual but social in nature. Nor can love alone penetrate to the underlying purposes of God in the order He has established for moral behavior. There is a certain naïveté in the supposition that love has a kind of built-in homing device leading us infallibly to its true goal. How could this be a safe guide for sinful, selfish, and fallible creatures? To know anything at all about the agape love of God is to know how imperfectly any of us shall ever reflect it. Human love is too greatly affected by desire, passion, novelty, projection, and illusion. As Oliver Barclay suggests, love for men must be secondary to love for God. And it was Jesus who said, "If you love me, you will keep my commandments" (John 14:15). Love for God cannot divorce itself from delight to do His will, or else that love is little more than sentimentality. Love, scripturally perceived, is adequately defined only in terms of God's law. On balance, law must incorporate love, and love must incorporate law. To quote Barclay, law "is essential in order to give backbone to the life of love ruled by the Spirit of God."[18]

So far as the moral law is concerned (not the statutes and ordinances of the old covenant), the Old Testament looks forward, not to the abolition of the law, but to the time when it will be written on our hearts (*see* Jeremiah 31:31-34). Jesus and the apostles repeatedly affirm the divine and permanent character of the law, as, for instance, in the Sermon on the Mount (Matthew 5:17-19). At the same time our Lord shows that what God intends is not merely keeping certain rules, but sustaining the attitude and spirit which they represent—not only no murder, but no hate; not only chastity of deed, but of thought. To suggest that because the New Testament stresses the spirit rather than the letter gives us liberty to void the letter is illogical. Jesus said, "Whoever then relaxes one of the least of these commandments and teaches men so, shall be called least in the kingdom of heaven; but he who does them and teaches them shall be called great in the kingdom of heaven" (Matthew 5:19). We are called by grace to do more, not less than the law requires. Christian morality is not mere law-keeping, but equally it is not lawlessness either. It is the apostle of love himself who defines sin as *lawlessness* (1 John 3:4). The danger of legalism must not weaken our love for and obedience to God's commands. Rules are not the controlling principles of Christian life, but they are still true, the basic morality to be obeyed. They are secondary to love, but not contrary to it. The law of love is not a substitute for the moral law, but a summary and a fulfillment of it. It may be only the framework, says Barclay, but it is still part of the whole structure of Christian morality. To renounce the law is to renounce the Lawgiver. The commandments are a means to constructive ends, to the good of man—this is their aim, and only a rebel can suppose otherwise. The reason that love needs law is illustrated by the editors of Inter-Varsity publications in Britain. In Piccadilly Circus, London, a statue was erected as a memorial to the seventh Lord Shaftesbury, the great evangelical philanthropist and social reformer of the nineteenth century. The statue was intended to represent the Angel of Christian Charitable Love. Interestingly, it has been universally thought to represent Eros—love between the sexes. This confusion about the meaning of love is not altogether untypical of the human creature wherever he is found and at whatever point in history. Therefore, love needs the careful definitions and boundaries of the law. That God has supplied.

The remainder of this chapter will be devoted to a six-part conceptualization of the meanings of sex for Christian couples, meanings anchored in our understanding of the one-flesh union. The first five concepts, when taken together, find their crowning significance in the sixth—*celebration*.

Each of the six is a positive aspect with roots in the distinctively Christian perspective. Each is an aspect of personal and spiritual response to the physical act, elevating it to the place of God's highest purpose.

1. *Sex as symbolic*

By symbolic we mean that sexual relation expresses personal values which transcend the purely physical values. Man is the only animal who can see something sacred in this common physical sign. It is in view of the sacred meanings which man perceives that his choices are informed— including the choice to withhold the sexual encounter in anticipation of what will be the larger commitment of marriage. The context is important and that means the sacred context of man's relationship to God and to his human partner. For not only is the will and purpose of God for his own life significant at this point, but his perception of the will of God for his would-be partner. Every aspect of the sexual relation is symbolic of deeper personal meanings. This is not to deny or ignore the purely physical values, but along with these values to share the symbol of total oneness in love and trustful commitment. The physical symbolizes the unity, commitment, and love a couple share. It also symbolizes their oneness in the redeeming grace of God, their participation together in the calling of God to marriage, and their united service for Him. Highest of all, the relation of the divine Bridegroom to His earthly bride is symbolized by their union with each other.

I once counseled a man who in the course of his story recounted having visited a prostitute. When he asked her what her name was, she contemptuously gave him a nickname. Another attempt to learn something about her only brought a quick rebuff. The only thing she wanted him to know of herself was stated in one sentence. "Mister, you can kiss me anywhere but on the lips."

There is profound significance in this poignant declaration, and it illustrates our point vividly. This girl was in the business of selling her body for the use of any man who paid the price. Sex for her was commercial; her body was the commodity. The customer could do with it as he pleased —but with one important limitation. What was she saying? She was affirming herself as a person with self-respect. She was attempting to detach her personhood from the use of her body in the sexual encounter. She had a sacred preserve, however, inasmuch as she loved a man. For the one she loved she saved her lips. This was the symbol of her love and commitment, to give her lips to her lover. To all others she gave her body, but to him alone she gave her lips.

The Christian has a different symbolism. The lips may touch another and say thereby, "I'm fond of you." Or perhaps, "I'm so glad to see you." But the body is given sexually only to the one who is loved deeply and exclusively in the union of marriage. For the Christian husband or wife, the sexual use of the body is symbolic of the total commitment between two persons. For the prostitute, there remained only a lesser possibility.

A student recently told me of her promiscuity over a period of two years. She bitterly recounted the diminishing value and meaning of her sexual experience. In tears she asked, "Do you think I can ever forget the cheapness which sex now represents? Can I ever marry and have sex with meaning?" Gladly I could tell her that Jesus Christ forgives and blots out our past indiscretions. More than that, I could suggest that because sex was experienced without personal meaning, it could be experienced in marriage as a totally new thing—as that which is spiritually meaningful, symbolic of all the meanings attaching to her marital committment, and profoundly sacramental.

2. Sex as sacramental

Deeper far than mere symbolism, the mystery of a couple's union is sacramental. While rejecting the Catholic notion of marriage as a sacrament in which saving grace is received, Protestants in recent times have seen the distinctly sacramental nature of married sexual partnership in Christ. The outward act stands for an inward spiritual reality. As the type of Christ and His bride, there is a spiritual mystery incorporated into the intercourse of Christian husband and wife. A special sanctity attaches to God's gift and the recognition of His special blessing. But the truly sacramental aspect is found in the words of Paul, "This is a great mystery, and I take it to mean Christ and the church" (Ephesians 5:32).

3. Sex as communicative

Interestingly, the word *intercourse* means "communication" and also "sexual relations"; we speak of "social intercourse" and "sexual intercourse." Sherwin Bailey comments: "All relation is based upon, and sustained by, communication, and love is no exception; but its content is such that verbal communication alone is insufficient to convey all that must be said. Hence the unspoken dialogue enacted by lovers which leads up to, and finds its conclusion in, coition."[19] Take Elton Trueblood's comment: "One of the most significant things to say about sexual intercourse is that it provides husband and wife with a language which cannot be matched by words or by any other act whatsoever. Love needs language for its adequate expression and sex has its own syntax."[20]

Sex is indeed a language all its own, and it cannot be enhanced by complicating it with other language. Other forms of speech can only be distracting. A couple can afford to relax in this understanding, and not feel a need to communicate verbally, as if this were a necessity to the overall communicative aspect of their intimate coming together. This is developed by Allan Fromme:

"The language of the body has a quality of unmatched validity. . . . A man's and a woman's hands reach out and touch. Silently they eloquently speak of their mutual awareness. . . . This is exactly why sex is necessary for the deepest expressions of love. The affection we feel in a relationship is strongest when we act it out, when we use our body. The use of the body by a man and woman for the purpose of seeking and expressing satisfaction in each other is what we mean by sex. . . . In this physical communication of love, the lovers are relating their ideal of acceptance and satisfaction in the most personally valid form. . . . Like any true language, it has a vocabulary for its expression. Sometimes one of them feels like loving, the other like being loved; sometimes one takes the active role, sometimes the other. Sometimes they are frolicsome, imaginative, serious, playful, tender, stormily passionate. . . . The love of man is incomplete without this sexual expression. . . . The body is as much a part of the individual as the mind, the emotions; the personality expresses itself through all its elements."[21]

A concluding statement, very much to the point, comes from Sherwin Bailey, whose careful analysis of our subject has been so helpful: "Part of the importance of sexual intercourse is that it affords husband and wife a medium for those mutual disclosures for which no words can be found; the senses become the channel of communication for all that lies too deep for utterance and yet must somehow be told. Such intercourse is necessarily pleasurable because of what it expressed, and not because it is a means of sensual gratification."[22]

We are reminded of the question once put to Mozart, "What are you trying to express by your music?" He replied, "If I could express it in words I wouldn't need music." Sexual intimacy has a full repertoire of meanings which communicate themselves in an act that transcends words. It is the language of love and commitment to life partnership.

4. *Sex as gift*

It must be emphasized that sex is one of God's gifts and as such is good in itself and to be received with thanksgiving. All God's gifts are good and sex is not the least of those good gifts. It is a bonus from the abounding grace of God. Of course, a gift calls forth gratitude to the giver, and true gratitude is shown when the gift is used in accordance with the giver's intent. For the Christian who sees sex as God's gift, that gift is also regarded as a sacred trust—not his own to do with it as he wills, but his to hold and to use as a trust from God. Christian couples are trustees, entrusted with that which is given as a stewardship. Their stewardship is fulfilled as they fulfill the purpose of the Giver. Now, what a couple receives they also give to one another as a gift. Paul Tournier says, "The sexual bond is the gift of the supreme secret, supreme intimacy, of the finest, most personal secret, one's own body. . . . There is inscribed in the human soul a law of all or nothing in love. The gift of one's body is only the sign of this decision to make a complete gift of self which will imply also the mutual gift of all one's secrets. . . . When you love and feel yourself loved you can express yourself. You discover yourself by expressing yourself, at the same time that you discover the other partner."[23] Meaningfully, Ralph Waldo Emerson wrote, "Riches and jewels are not gifts, but apologies for gifts. The only true gift is a portion of thyself." Surely it's true that we have only that part of another person which is given us in love; and what a person gives us in love is not less than himself. The integrity of such a gift of self lies in the quality of its undivided and enduring nature. David Mace tells of an experience from his own marriage counseling. A wife described to him how, in loving anticipation of their intercourse, her husband would always say on behalf of them both, "For what we are about to receive, may the Lord make us truly grateful." Husband and wife are both givers and receivers. So there may be mutual thankfulness for that which is received and that which is given.

5. *Sex as offering*

So close to our last category as to be almost synonymous, we turn our attention to sex as offering. Whenever a gift of God is recognized as such, it is to be offered back to Him in thanksgiving. It thereby attains its highest meaning and beauty. A gift is offered back in fulfillment of its design and purpose. The offering of self which husband and wife make to each other is elevated in virtue of the fact that they offer themselves and their sexual

relation back to God. This is part of the offering of their total life partnership to Him. Thus it is that a couple can pray about their sexual relation
as they might pray about any other aspect of their life in Christ, asking
God's blessing and the sense of His presence and grace. Even when the
purely physical satisfaction is deficient, they may experience joy and meaning, for still it is an offering to each other and to God. Sherwin Bailey
remarks, "In the immediacy of intercourse there can be consciousness of
none but the beloved, but the act itself must take place in the context of
a common God-centered life and must be offered to Him—in intention
beforehand, in thanksgiving afterwards—as husband and wife silently acknowledge the Author of their love."[24] As Gibson Winter puts it, "Sexual
offering expresses the depth and fulness of the consent and decision. Word
and body are given in promised commitment. Word and body join in the
fulfillment of promise."[25] The reciprocal nature of offering-response is
described by Erich Fromm: "The culmination of the male sexual function
lies in the act of giving; the man gives himself, his sexual organ, to the
woman. At the moment of orgasm, he gives his semen to her. . . . For the
woman the process is not different, although somewhat more complex. She
gives herself too; she opens the gates of her feminine center; in the act of
receiving, she gives."[26] Several of the concepts in this analysis converge in
the remarks of Prentiss Pemberton: "Anything less than this mystical
symbolism fails to express all that is meant by the communication between
the sexes which belongs in genuine sexual love." He continues, saying that
"the power to offer one's self is the cornerstone of Christian sexual communication . . . an interchange begun and carried through as offerings and
responses. It is precisely at this point that faith in the revealed purpose for
mating gives the Christian man power to offer himself rather than demand.
This is the revolutionary new dynamic which man as a spiritual being can
bring into the sexual dialogue. This strength to offer, not to demand, means
that the man's entire sexual fulfillment centers not in his capacity to attain,
but in his mate's capacity to respond to his offering. This focuses the
consummation of sex where it belongs, not in the individual resources of
either mate, but in the profound blending of these separate forces. This
blending is achieved when each can honestly offer to the other, evoking
a powerful mutual response. The response is thus the eager and appreciative
reaction of one who realizes that the other's promise is unfulfilled until
accepted and redeemed. In many marriages, sex occurs only as demand and
obligation." Not so in the truly Christian marriage![27]

6. *Sex as celebration*

Man is the only creature who celebrates. It is the highest expression of which he is capable, and to it he brings all his faculties—mind, emotions, and body. God summons man as a total, integrated person to celebrate life in its fullest. Celebration is possible when there is a sense of wholeness about a person's life, wholeness in his relationships both to God and to his fellows. Vogt Von Ogd goes so far as to suggest, "Indeed, perhaps the Christian is the only one who can celebrate life, precisely because he does celebrate all of it." When sexuality is properly incorporated in the whole of life, expressive of its true ends, it is a dimension of man's celebration of life in God. And it is to this celebration of our sexuality that God summons us. [28]

Currently there is a strong and continuing upsurge of the predication that it is our Christian birthright to celebrate life in Christ, and that this touches all of life. As Harvey Cox would say, it is "saying yes to life." The Christian is life-affirming. Here we are reminded of the Apostle Paul's enjoining us to "do all to the glory of God." He encourages us to "glorify God in your body." What is it to glorify God in one's bodiliness—including his sexuality—if it isn't to celebrate His good gifts and His gracious purposes?

Celebration links us to the past and the future in a rich continuity of life. In its more accustomed historical sense, a celebration is the symbolic reenactment of a meaningful event, a reconstitution of certain essential symbols which stand for an event of extraordinary meaning. Celebration points to a reality which extends a past event into the living present. More than that, it reaffirms values that are meant to endure. So in a way that is powerfully reinforcing to the celebrants, the meaning of an event is *reoccasioned*. Celebrations become occasions of vivid recollection of things most highly valued. Sexual celebration is a recurrent sign, marking out in time a covenant union once established and meant to endure throughout a couple's lifetime. Each occasion of sexual intercourse makes possible a renewed consciousness of the valued commitments of the marital bond. The covenant of marriage is reaffirmed. It is in this sense that we can say that sex apart from marriage can never be a celebration.

Though subject to the eroding effects of familiarity and repetition, a couple's sexual intimacy is elevated above ordinariness when viewed as celebration. The central event of their union which is commemorated, and the covenant between them which is reaffirmed, can never be considered a commonality, however recurrent its enactment. It evermore transcends the ordinary. Besides, each celebration carries forward the potential for a growing, ever-greater intimacy. Von Ogd indicates this dimension of celebration: "In celebration, life is continually readjusted to its principle centers of reference." Sexual celebration continually readjusts a couple's life to their covenant commitment. Therefore, Christian couples never relinquish their roles as celebrants of a God-given relationship. Nor is there any sense in which a male priesthood has been ordained for this celebration! No, both partners equally and mutually play their respective roles. Perhaps nowhere in all of human experience is there a more marked difference between a *charade of noncommunication* and a celebration of deepest meaning than in the exercise of human sexuality!

In celebration, Christian couples move from the *indicative*—what God gives—to the *imperative*—the commanding nature of their response. God is both Origin and Object! Sexual celebration is a transcendent experience!

One closing thought on celebration is suggested by the words from a source no longer remembered: "In their celebration a couple should hear the echo of the Creator's joy in seeing the fulfillment of one of His purposes for man. They may let their thoughts soar to the heights of God's enjoyment in His creation." This is the echo of Eden, "And God saw everything that he had made, and behold, it was very good" (Genesis 1:31). Now God invites us, yes, summons us to enter into His delight in what He has created!

Here, then, is the celebration of *love* in its most powerful symbol. Included is the remembrance of God's unspeakable love for man in Christ. Here, too, is the celebration of *union* in its most powerful symbol as well. Included in this is the remembrance of the union of Christ with His bride. If it speaks of an enduring commitment between a man and his wife, much more does it speak of God's unconditional and unchanging commitment to us—a commitment sealed in the blood of His Son! As husband and wife are called back to the recollection that they are bound together in a unity of life, so too are they reminded that together they are bound in a unity of life in God through Jesus Christ.

Celebration in its highest sense speaks of lives open and responsive to One who stands in relation to them as Creator, Redeemer, and Lord of all. It speaks of purity of heart and motive between partners. Such celebration happens only where there is freedom of spirit, for to be a true celebrant is to be free from the burden of guilt, free from meaninglessness and futility, free from any sense of squandering a precious gift on selfish ends, free from the tyranny of passion. As is nothing else, sexual celebration is dependent upon the quality of the total marital relationship. Sex becomes the most searching test of that quality. No wonder sex by itself, apart from marital bonds, stands so starkly as the symbol of personal impoverishment! This depressing sense cannot be assuaged by regarding sex as recreational, the Hugh Hefners of this world to the contrary! What God has joined together—sex and marriage—no man can, in an ultimate sense, put asunder!

A biblical theology of sexuality is equivalent to a theology of marriage. To celebrate sex is to celebrate the totality of marriage; to celebrate marriage is to celebrate the totality of sex.[29] To disjoin the two diminishes them both to less than what God designed them to be. As marriage represents a sacred covenant, so sex is the seal of that covenant. To every Christian couple, therefore, God's Word comes as a solemn yet joyous affirmation of sexual union in beauty and holiness. This is God's appointed bond for the most intimate and sacred of human relationships. To every Christian couple His summons is this: *Put your relationship in its entirety under the lordship of Jesus Christ, and in fulfillment of your life together, celebrate your sexuality!*

"For everything there is a season, and a time for every matter under heaven . . . a time to embrace, and a time to refrain from embracing. . . . He has made everything beautiful in its time; also he has put eternity into man's mind . . ."(Ecclesiastes 3:1-11).

Notes

INTRODUCTION

1. Rollo May, *Love and Will*. N.Y., W. W. Norton & Co., 1969, p. 87.
2. Ibid., p. 313.
3. D. P. Verene, *Sexual Love and Western Morality: A Philosophical Anthology*. N.Y., Harper & Row, Pub. 1972, p. 289.
4. Ibid., p. 290.
5. In the writer's reading, the idea of celebration of sexuality has only appeared in literature of the past decade. While the idea may be found earlier, the concept is very recent. I recall the concept only in the writings of Robert Bonthius, Harvey Cox, and David Augsburger. It is a key concept in the development of this present book.
6. Harvey Cox, *A Feast of Fools: A Theological Essay on Festivity and Fantasy*. Cambridge, Mass., Harvard Univ. Press. 1969, pp. 7-10.
7. Harvey Cox, *Sex, Family and Society in Theological Focus*. N.Y. Association Press. 1966, p. 16.
8. Emil Brunner, *The Divine Imperative: A Study in Christian Ethics*. Phila., The Westminster Press. 1947, p. 341.
9. Robert Osborn, "Sex and the Single God," *Christian Century*. Vol. LXXXIII, No. 36, Sept. 7, 1966, p. 1080.

CHAPTER 1

1. Derek Wright, "The New Tyranny of Sexual Liberation," *Life*, Nov. 6, 1970.

2. John W. Petras, *Sexuality in Society*. Boston, Allyn and Bacon, Inc. 1973, p. 116.

3. Cf. Howard S. Becker, *Outsiders*. Glencoe, Ill. Free Press, 1963; Kai T. Erikson, *Wayward Puritans*. N.Y. John Wiley. 1966.

4. Kingsley Davis, "Sexual Behavior," *Contemporary Social Problems*. R.K. Merton and R.A. Nisbet, eds., N.Y. Harcourt, Brace, and World, 1966.

5. Herbert A. Otto, ed. *The Family in Search of a Future*. N.Y., Appleton-Century-Crofts, 1970, p. 9.

6. Edward C. Hobbs, Ibid., p. 35.

7. Virginia Satir, Ibid., p. 62.

8. Ben N. Ard, Jr., "Sexuality as a Personal and Social Force," in *The New Sexuality*. Herbert A. Otto, ed., Palo Alto, Science and Behavior Books, Inc. 1971, pp. 14-22. Cf. also: Wayland Young, *Eros Denied: Sex in Western Society*. N.Y., Grove Press, 1964, p. 357. Incidentally, no one who reads widely in this subject is unaware of the influence of Albert Ellis. The mood being described recalls Ellis's "The Case Against Religion," *Mensa Bulletin* 38, Sept. 1970, pp. 4, 5.

9. S. Jeffrey Garfield, Sander I. Marcus, and Elizabeth Garfield, "Premarital Sex From an Existential Perspective," *The New Sexuality*. pp. 247, 248.

10. Ibid., p. 261.

11. Rosalyn Moran, "The Singles in the Seventies," *Intimate Life Styles: Marriage and Its Alternatives*. eds, JoAnn S. and Jack R. DeLora, Pacific Palisades, Calif., Goodyear Pub. Co., 1972, p. 344.

12. "Games Singles Play," *Newsweek*, July 16, 1973, pp. 57, 58.

13. Otto, *Family in Search*. p. 188.

14. Cf. Mervyn Cadwallader, "Changing Social Mores," *Current*. Feb. 1967, p. 48. Robert N. Whitehurst coined the word *unmalias*, a condensation of "unmarried liaisons."

15. Ira L. Reiss, "How & Why America's Sex Standards Are Changing," *Intimate Life Styles*. p. 109.

16. Harvey Cox, *The Secular City*. N.Y., The Macmillan Co., 1965, pp. 206, 207.

17. Margaret Mead, "Marriage in Two Steps," *Redbook*. July, 1966 p. 84.

18. Ibid., p. 85.

19. Ibid., p. 85.

20. Michael Scriven, "Putting the Sex Back into Sex Education," *Phi Delta* 49, 1968.

21. Virginia Satir, "Marriage as a Statutory Five Year Renewable Contract." Paper presented at the American Psychological Association Annual Convention, 1967.

22. Mervyn Cadwallader, "Marriage as a Wretched Institution," *Atlantic Monthly*, 218, 1966; pp. 62-66.

23. Robert H. Rimmer, *The Harrad Experiment*. Los Angeles, Sherbourne Press, 1966. Cf. also Robert H. Rimmer, *The Harrad Letters*. N.Y. New American Library, 1969.

24. John F. Crosby, *Illusion and Disillusion: The Self in Love and Marriage*. Belmont, Calif., Wadsworth Publishing Co., 1973, p. 99.

25. Otto, *Family in Search*. p. 37.

26. Ibid., p. 39.

27. Crosby, *Illusion and Disillusion*. p. 86.

28. Morton Hunt, "The Future of Marriage," *Intimate Life Styles*. p. 402.

29. Albert Ellis, "Group Marriage a Possible Alternative?" *Family in Search* pp. 85-97.

30. John A.T. Robinson, *Honest to God*. Phila., Westminster Press. 1963, p. 118.

31. This idea is developed by the controversial writer, Karl Bednarik, in his chapter "The Crisis of Eros" in *The Male in Crisis*, N.Y., Alfred A. Knopf, 1970, pp. 47-108.

32. Cf. the book of my departmental colleague, Ronald Enroth, and Gerald E. Jamison, *The Gay Church*. Grand Rapids, William Eerdmans Pub. Co., 1973. Cf. also the issues debated in *Is Gay Good? Ethics, Theology and Homosexuality*. ed. W. Dwight Oberholtzer. Phila., The Westminster Press. 1971.

33. Cf. Jessie Bernard, *The Future of Marriage*. N.Y., The World Publishing Co., 1972.

CHAPTER 2

1. Derrick Sherwin Bailey, *Sexual Relation in Christian Thought.* N.Y., Harper
    & Bros. Pub., 1959.
2. Derrick Sherwin Bailey. *Sexual Ethics.* N.Y., The Macmillan Co., 1962, p.
    9.
3. Ibid., p. 19.
4. Ibid., pp. 19, 20
5. Ibid., p. 20.
6. The term *lust* was indiscriminately applied to intercourse in marital relations
    and in fornication. The King James Version continues Augustine's usual
    word, *concupiscence.* Long, intricate Latinized words have an ominous ring
    to them, perhaps because of the mysterious complexity. Thus "concupis-
    cence" or "masturbation" seem negatively connotative.
7. Bailey, *Sexual Relation.* p. 49.
8. Ibid., p. 49.
9. Ibid., p. 53. Augustine had tried following Manichaeism for nine years.
10. Ibid., p. 102.
11. Seward Hiltner, *Sex and the Christian Life.* N.Y., Association Press, 1957,
    p. 56.
12. The foregoing and many of the historical references are taken from the
    extensive material found in *Sex in History.* G. Rattray Taylor, N.Y., Harper
    & Row, 1973.
13. Cf. E.R. Dodds, *The Greeks and the Irrational.* Berkeley, Univ. of Calif.
    Press, 1951.
14. Cf. O. Kiefer, *Sexual Life in Ancient Rome.* N.Y., Barnes & Noble, 1934;
    Paul Brandt, *Sexual Life in Ancient Greece.* London, Routledge & Kegan
    Paul, 1932.
15. Cf. D. P. Verene, *Sexual Love and Western Morality.*
16. Andrew R. Eikhoff. *A Christian View of Sex and Marriage.* N.Y., The Free
    Press, 1966, p. 25.
17. Ernst Troeltsch, *The Social Teaching of the Christian Churches.* London,
    George Allen & Unwin, 1949, Olive Wyon, tr., Vol. I, p. 129.

CHAPTER 3

1. Cf. Ernest C. Messenger, *The Mystery of Sex and Marriage in Catholic Theology*, Vol. II in *Two in One Flesh*, 2nd ed., Westminster, Md., The Newman Press, 1950, p. 152.
2. Cf. major works on the rise of romantic love: Clive. S. Lewis, *The Allegory of Love*. London, Oxford Univ. Press, 1936; Denis de Rougemont, *Love in the Western World*, Montgomery Belgion, tr., N.Y., Harcourt, Brace and Co., 1940; Morton Hunt, *The Natural History of Love*. N.Y., Alfred A. Knopf, 1959; Charles Williams, *He Came Down From Heaven*.
3. Bailey, *Sexual Relation.* p. 163.
4. Cf. full account in H.D. Traill and J.S. Mann, *Social England*. London, Cassell, 1909. Also J.D. Unwin, *Sex and Culture*. London, Oxford Univ. Press, 1934.
5. Taylor, *Sex in History.* p. 38.
6. Ibid., p. 42.
7. Ibid., p. 52, 53.
8. Ibid., p. 69.
9. Morton Hunt, *The Natural History of Love*. N.Y., Alfred Knopf, 1959, p. 230.

CHAPTER 4

1. The foregoing is taken from Oscar E. Feucht, ed. *Sex and the Church*. St. Louis, Mo., Concordia Publishing House, 1961. This is Volume V in the Marriage and Family Research Series, issued by the Family Life Committee of the Lutheran Church, Missouri Synod. This is the work of four authors and a research team of eighteen. It is part of a highly commendable endeavor of a major denomination producing excellent sex education materials on all levels. It is only to be regretted that in a volume of some 250 pages, only 23 pages are devoted to "A Christian Interpretation of Sex," and this is devoid of theological references.
2. Hunt, *Intimate Life Styles.* pp. 222-224.
3. Ibid., p. 227.

4. Feucht, *Sex and the Church.* p. 86.

5. Eickhoff, *Sex and Marriage.* pp. 28, 29.

6. Bailey, *Sexual Relation.* p. 173.

7. E. L. Hebden Taylor, *The Reformational Understanding of Family and Marriage.* Nutley, N.J., The Craig Press, 1970, p. 10.

8. Ibid., p. 16.

9. Manfred Kuhn, "American Families Today: Development and Differeniation of Types," in Howard Becker and Reuben Hill, *Family, Marriage and Parenthood.* Boston, D.C. Heath & Co., 1955, p. 134.

10. G. Rattray Taylor, Ibid., p. 174. He quotes the earlier work of H.G. Graham on the social life in Scotland.

11. The foregoing material is taken in part from Edmund S. Morgan, *The Puritan Family.* rev. ed. 1966, N.Y., Harper & Row Pub. and Edmund S. Morgan, *The New England Quarterly,* Vol. XV, 1942, pp. 591-607. See also Charles F. Adams, "Some Phases of Sexual Morality and Church Discipline in Colonial New England," *Massachusetts Historical Society Proceedings,* XXVI, pp. 477-516.

12. Cited in Floyd Mansfield Martinson, *Family in Society.* N.Y., Dodd, Mead & Co., 1970, p. 28, 29.

13. Reported in George E. Howard, *A History of Matrimonial Institutions.* Chicago. Univ. of Chicago Press, 1904, II, p. 152.

14. Arthur Schlesinger, Jr. "An Informal History of Love, U.S.A.," *Love, Marriage, Family: A Developmental Approach.* Marcia E. Lasswell & Thomas E. Lasswell, eds. Glenview, Ill., Scott, Foreman & Co., 1973. p. 15.

15. Hunt, *History of Love.* p. 235. He cites Emil Oberholzer, Jr., in *Delinquent Saints: Disciplinary Action in the Early Congregational Churches of Massachusetts.* N.Y., Columbia Univ. Press, 1956.

16. Arthur W. Calhoun, *A Social History of the American Family: Colonial Period,* Vol. I. N.Y., Barnes & Noble, Inc., 1960, p. 146.

17. Hunt, *History of Love.* p. 252.

18. Ibid., p. 310.

19. May, *Love and Will.* p. 39.

20. Schlesinger, *Love, Marriage, Family.* p. 19.

21. Hiltner, *Christian Life.* p. 64.

22. Contemporary philosophers whose personalistic insights are helpful to Christian studies, and whose work reflects the earlier conceptions of Kant, would include John Macmurray in England, Peter Bertocci in America, both of whom will be referred to further on.

23. Immanuel Kant, *Lectures on Ethics*, Louis Infield, tr. London, Methuen & Co., Ltd., 1930, pp. 162-175.

24. Cf. "The Sexual Renaissance in America", *Journal of Social Issues*. April, 1966 (special journal issue); *The Encyclopedia of Sexual Behavior* edited by Albert Ellis and Albert Abarbanel (N.Y., Hawthorn Books, 1961) is the most complete and authoritative source of its kind available. For recent positions of church bodies, cf. *Foundations for Christian Family Policy* (The Proceedings of the North American Conference on Church and Family). Published for the Canadian and National Council of Churches, National Council of Churches of Christ in the U.S.A., 1961. Cf. also *Sexuality and the Human Community*, The General Assembly of the United Presbyterian Church in the United States of America, 1970. In some quarters the Roman Catholic position is undergoing renewal, as expressed by the president of Notre Dame University: "Both [Puritanism among Protestants and Jansenism among Catholics] regarded sex with suspicion, in some ways identifying it with concupiscence and sin. Under this scheme of moral values, it was impossible to integrate sex into any healthy philosophy of life. Sex became shameful instead of sacred; it was something divorced from any reasonable consideration of man's personal or social development. . . . Nor need we disguise the pleasure that God designed to ease the burdens and responsibilities of married life, and to highlight the perfect communication of marital love." (Theodore M. Hesburgh, "Sex Education and Moral Values," in *Social Hygiene Papers: A Symposium on Sex Education.* N.Y., American Social Hygiene Assoc., Nov. 1957., pp. 18-21.)

CHAPTER 5

Note: The author's eclectic approach includes drawing upon insights from dialectical theology. This is not to be construed to mean that the author accepts the presuppositions of this theology, nor that he is to be in any way classified as neo-orthodox. Brunner is the theologian whose work on the image of God has made the most significant impact on the thought of our time. His views on this subject are closer to those of Calvin than is generally conceded. With David Cairns, the present writer is more in agreement with Calvin and Brunner on the *Imago Dei* doctrine than with other writers. But in the chapter following, it is with Karl Barth that the author must agree as having the most perceptive insights in our time.

1. David Cairns, *The Image of God in Man*. London. SCM Press, Ltd., 1953, p. 16, 19.

2. Karl Barth, *Church Dogmatics*. III, 2. Edinburgh, T. & T. Clark, 1960, p. 72. Cairns, correctly discerning Brunner's position, writes: "Brunner indeed rejects the conception of man as a substance which can exist independently, and to which a relation to God can be added as an accident. But to claim this is not to deny that man can be truly a substance. The proper antithesis here is not between substance and act, but between persons and things, or between person-substances and thing-substances. If personal being is reduced to decision or act or relation, the objection is perfectly justified that one cannot think of a decision which is not the decision of a subject." (*Image*, p. 190.) Paul Tillich comments that "any ontology which suppresses the dynamic element in the structure of being is unable to explain the nature of a life-process and to speak meaningfully of the divine life."

3. G. C. Berkouwer, *Man: The Image of God*. Grand Rapids. Wm. E. Eerdmans Pub. Co., 1962, p. 29.

4. Helmut Thielicke, *The Ethics of Sex*. N.Y., Harper & Row, Pub., 1964, p. 31. (Italics added)

5. Everett F. Harrison, ed. *Baker's Dictionary of Theology*. Grand Rapids. Baker Books, 1960, p. 339.

6. Emil Brunner, *Man in Revolt*. Phila. The Westminster Press, 1947, p. 92.

7. Brunner, *Revolt*. p. 92.

8. Carl F.H. Henry sees the image as the precondition of relationship, but leans too far toward equating the image with man's human attributes. Thielicke, in contrast, holds that the image has an ontological element of this kind, but fallen man is not defined by this element. Taking a more personalistic view, he claims that the Reformers saw the image exclusively as relation. But neither is this the case, though both Luther and Calvin must be credited with understanding the relational aspect. As Berkouwer puts it in balance, "it is one thing to say that the relation to God is of the essence of the image, but quite another to make the image itself consist merely of a relation." Cf. Berkouwer, *Man*. p. 139. Cairns says of Calvin and the *Imago Dei*: "It is a theme to which he has given greater attention than any great theologian since Augustine, and his contribution is even greater than Augustine's. Indeed, little that is radically new and important on the subject has been said since

Calvin. He conceives the image dynamically, and brings it into relation to God as Augustine does, and as every sound doctrine of the image must do." (*Image.* p. 144.)

9. Emil Brunner, *The Christian Doctrine of Creation and Redemption.* Dogmatics, V. II. Phila. The Westminster Press, 1952, p. 58.

10. The relation of every man to God is one of confrontation, or encounter. Encounter implies personal endowments, but always endowments in response. Man's unique nature is thus endowment-in-response. Neither endowments nor confrontation are lost to sinful man; rather, sin has brought about the disablement of response. Cairns sees this clearly: "This confrontation is compatible with a very profound ignorance of God on the part of man, and also compatible with a will opposed to God. Thus when Christ saves, He saves what had been in His presence all the time, though as Augustine says, 'Its misfortune was not to be with Him as He was with it.' " (*Image.* pp. 188, 189.)

11. Cf. standard works on Reformed theology, such as Calvin, Bavink, Hodge, Berkouwer, Berkhof. Esp. cf. John Murray, "Common Grace," *Westminster Theological Journal.* Nov., 1942, pp. 1-28.

12. Eichrodt speaks of man's "spiritual superiority, which expresses itself not only in his higher rational endowment, but above all in his capacity for self-consciousness and self-determination; in short, in those capacities which we are accustomed to regard as typical of personality." Virtually all Christian writers up to Aquinas conceived the image of God exclusively as man's power of reason—reason as rationality inclusive of will. Brunner noted that man's reason is, from the first, implanted in man for the purpose of receiving God's Word.

13. Niebuhr writes, "Man contradicts himself within the terms of his true essence. His essence is free self-determination. His sin is the wrong use of his freedom and its consequent destruction. . . . The Christian estimate of human evil is so serious because it places evil at the very center of human personality: in the will." (Reinhold Niebuhr, *The Nature and Destiny of Man.* N.Y., Charles Scribner's Sons. 1941. Vol. I, p. 16.) Now, in speaking of "will," we recall Tillich's caution: "Freedom is not the freedom of a function (the 'will') but of man, that is of that being who is not a thing but a complete self and a rational person. It is possible, of course, to call the 'will' the personal center and to substitute it for the totality of the self. . . . One should speak of the freedom of *man,* indicating that every part and every function which constitutes man a personal self participates in his freedom." (Paul Tillich, *Systematic Theology.* Vol. I. Chicago. The Univ. of Chicago Press, 1951, p. 183.)

14. Tillich's expression is telling: "He 'possesses' himself in the form of self-consciousness." (Ibid., p. 170.) Niebuhr adds, "Self-consciousness represents a further degree of transcendence in which the self makes itself its own object in such a way that the ego is finally always subject and not object." (*Nature and Destiny*, p. 14.) Kierkegaard said, "The determining factor in the self is consciousness, i.e. self-consciousness."

15. "The dynamic character of being implies its tendency to transcend itself. . . . Therefore it is impossible to speak of being without also speaking of becoming. Becoming is just as genuine in the structure of being as is that which remains unchanged in the process of becoming." (Tillich, *Theology.* p. 181); Niebuhr adds, "The obvious fact is that man is a child of nature, subject to its vicissitudes, compelled by its necessities, driven by its impulses, and confined within the brevity of the years which nature permits its varied organic form . . . The other less obvious fact is that man is a spirit who stands outside of nature, life, himself, his reason and the world." (*Nature and Destiny.* p. 3.) To Heidegger the fundamental characteristic of human existence is anxiety. The fear of death, the end of existence, is the fundamental state of the human being. Is this not a manifestation of self-transcendence combined with God-consciousness, or the cry for that Other which lies outside one's self and in whom one has ultimate existence?

16. Early in the theological development of this book it should be noted that the author's theological position is intended as a biblical refutation to certain popular positions held in our day. The following are some of the books which are antithetical to the evangelical interpretation found in this book: *Christian Morals Today* by John A. T. Robinson, *Situation Ethics* by Joseph Fletcher, *Sex and the New Morality* by Frederic C. Wood, *The Christian Response to the Sexual Revolution* by David R. Mace, *Honest Sex: A Revolutionary New Sex Guide for the Now Generation of Christians* by Rustum and Della Roy, *Towards a Quaker View of Sex* by Alastair Heron, ed., *Ethics in a Christian Context* by Paul Lehmann, *Making Sexuality Human*, a recent "theology of sex" by Norman Pittenger, and Richard F. Hettlinger's *Living With Sex: The Student Dilemma.* Not one of these books measures up to orthodox biblical theology or ethics. Typical of contemporary writers who condemn Christian sexual morality by selecting writings from the Reformers and earlier theologians, while ignoring recent Protestant thought, is Demosthenes Savramis's *The Satanizing of Woman: Religion Versus Sexuality* (N.Y., Doubleday & Co., 1974.) On the positive side, it should be noted that Christian college men and women are finding practical guidance from writers such as Walter Tro-

bisch, David Augsburger, Herbert Miles, Letha Scanzoni, Peter Bertocci, and
Evelyn Duvall.

CHAPTER 6

1. Laymen wishing to read the material from which this chapter is adapted will
   find it readily accessible in Karl Barth, *Church Dogmatics: A Selection*. Trans.
   and ed. by G. W. Bromiley. N.Y., Harper & Row, 1962, and Karl Barth, *On
   Marriage*. Phila., Fortress Press, 1968. Insofar as biblical anthropology deals
   with the man-woman relation, Barth stands alone. What one finds of contemporary conceptualization in Brunner, Piper, Bailey, or Thielicke is there
   already in Barth, explicitly or implicitly, and more profoundly so. An illustration of the neglect of Barth is the otherwise fine volume *Sex and the Church*,
   issued by the Family Life Committee of the Lutheran Church, Missouri
   Synod. The name of Karl Barth does not once appear. Actually, little that is
   objectionable in Barth's theology is in evidence in these sections. His ponder-
   ous sentences, carried over into the English translation, combined with the
   frequent excurses in small print, probably account for the lack of acquaintance
   of many with Barth.

2. Barth, *On Marriage*. pp. iii, iv.

3. Thielicke, *Ethics*. p. 3.

4. Some scholars, including von Rad, hold that not only the spiritual, personal
   attributes are created in God's likeness, but the entire living human being,
   body included.

5. With this conceptualization Brunner and Thielicke are in substantial agreement. Both Barth and Brunner hold with the older orthodoxy that "Let us
   make man in our own image" refers to the Trinity. This is denied by others,
   as in the Interpreter's Bible.

6. Karl Barth, *Church Dogmatics*. III, 4, Edinburgh, T & T Clark, 1960, p. 163.

7. Barth, *Dogmatics*. III, 2. p. 324. It is a major limitation of Barth's understanding of *Analogia relationis* that he equates the man-woman relation with the
   Imago Dei. We can only go so far as to say that the man-woman relationship
   is a major aspect of the divine image.

8. Barth suggests that *partner* is perhaps the best modern rendering of the word *helpmate.*

9. Cited in David R. Mace, *The Christian Response to the Sexual Revolution.* Nashville, Abingdon Press. 1970, p. 97 (italics added).

10. Barth, *Dogmatics.* III, 4., p. 150.

11. William P. Wylie, *Human Nature and Christian Marriage.* London, Student Christian Movement Press, Ltd., 1958, p. 53.

CHAPTER 7

1. Dietrich Bonhoeffer, *Creation and Fall: A Theological Interpretation of Genesis 1-3.* London, SCM Press Ltd., 1959, p. 33.

2. Ibid., p. 44.

3. Ibid., pp. 45, 46.

4. Ibid., p. 61.

5. Ibid., p. 62.

6. Ibid., p. 63.

7. Thielicke, *Ethics.* p. 8.

8. Brunner, *Revolt.* pp. 348, 349.

9. M. Merleau-Ponty, *Phenomenology of Perception.* tr. Colin Smith, London, Routledge & Kegan Paul, 1962, pp. 166, 167.

10. Brunner, *Revolt.* p. 352.

11. Niebuhr, *Nature and Destiny.* p. 239.

12. Ernest White in his excellent book, *Marriage and the Bible* makes this his proper starting point. The present writer is indebted to his analysis.

13. H. Wheeler Robinson, "Hebrew Psychology," *The People and the Book.* ed. Arthur S. Peake. Oxford, Clarendon Press, 1957. p. 362.

14. William S. Banowsky, *It's Playboy World.* Old Tappan, N.J., Fleming H. Revell Co., 1969, pp. 73-79.

15. Derrick Sherwin Bailey, *The Mystery of Love and Marriage.* N.Y. Harper & Bros. Pub., 1952, p. 67.

16. The RSV is quoted here with one exception, the addition of the word *flesh* in the phrase "two shall become one flesh." It is strange that this omission is found in the RSV in every other instance where the term is found (Mark 10:2-12; Matthew 19:3-11; Ephesians 5:22f.).

17. Bailey, *Mystery.* p. 51. (italics added)
18. Ibid., pp. 51,52.
19. Ibid., pp. 53, 54.
20. Dan Sullivan, "Sex and the Person," *Commonweal.* Vol. LXXXIV, No. 17, July 22, 1966, p. 461.
21. Merleau-Ponty, *Perception.* pp. 164-166.
22. Robert Grimm, *Love and Sexuality.* David Mace, N.Y. Association Press, 1964, pp. 44, 45.
23. Henry Alford, *The Greek Testament.* London, Rivington's Pub., 1865, II, p. 518.
24. Banowsky, *Playboy World.* p. 89.
25. Grimm, *Sexuality.* p. 33.
26. Bailey, *Sexual Ethics.* p. 21.
27. Wylie, *Human Nature.* pp. 65, 66.
28. In the development of my theological premises in these central chapters, I wish to express my gratitude for the privilege of reading two unpublished papers by esteemed colleagues, one a study on sexuality by Dr. Ray S. Anderson, the other a study of *soma* in 1 Corinthians 6:12-20 by Dr. Robert H. Gundry. My concepts were also sharpened by aspects found in Ebbie C. Smith, *The One-Flesh Concept of Marriage: A Biblical Study.* Unpublished ThD dissertation, 1960. Southwestern Baptist Theological Seminary, Fort Worth, Texas. The holistic view of one-flesh presented in this book is congruous with that of the major writers in the field of sex ethics, such as Barth, Brunner, Thielicke, Piper, Bailey, Hiltner, and a host of others.

CHAPTER 8

1. Otto A. Piper, *The Biblical View of Sex and Marriage.* N.Y., Charles Scribner's Sons. 1960, p. 13. This is a completely revised version of *The Christian Interpretation of Sex* which appeared in 1941. The most substantial contribution of this book is the chapter "The Hidden Meaning of Sex," to which the writer acknowledges his indebtedness.
2. Ibid., p. 35.
3. Cf. William Hamilton, *Faith, Sex and Love.* National Student Council of the YMCA and YWCA, 291 Broadway, New York, N.Y., 1954.

4. Cf. Herbert Doms (tr. G. Sayer), *The Meaning of Marriage*. London, 1939.

5. Piper, *Biblical View*. p. 41.

6. One of the finest and latest books on sex education from a Christian perspective is Letha Scanzoni's *Sex is a Parent Affair*. Her book *Sex and the Single Eye* is also one of the best for young people.

7. Erich Fromm, "Man is Not a Thing," *The Saturday Review*. March 16, 1957, p. 10.

8. Cf. Paul Haupt, "To Know—To Have Sexual Commerce," *Journal of Biblical Literature*, XXXIV (1914), pp. 71–76.

9. Reuel Howe, *The Creative Years*. Greenwich, Conn., Seabury Press, 1959, p. 98.

10. Gustave Thibon, *What God Has Joined Together*. Chicago, Henry Regnery Co., 1952, p. 116.

11. Ernest White, *Marriage and the Bible*. Nashville, Tenn., Broadman Press, 1965, pp. 19, 21.

12. Hiltner, *Christian Life*. p. 88.

13. Ibid., pp. 86, 87.

14. Barth, *Dogmatics*. III, 4, p. 133.

15. Nicholas Berdyaev, *The Destiny of Man*. tr. Natalie Duddington. London, G. Bles, 1937, pp. 302ff. Thielicke assents to this, Brunner dissents, erroneously supposing fidelity to be something other than and apart from love in its truest sense. (Cf. Emil Brunner, *The Divine Imperative*, p. 357.)

16. Barth, *Dogmatics*. III, 4, p. 132.

17. Oliver R. Barclay, ed. *A Time To Embrace: Essays on the Christian View of Sex*. London, Inter-Varsity Fellowship, 1964, pp. 51-60.

18. Ibid., p. 56. Since this is a book on the theology of sexuality, the ethics being largely implicit in the theology, it might serve a purpose to comment on books which the reader might turn to for ethical questions. As for the New Morality, Situation Ethics and Contextual Ethics, one who requires a not-too difficult book will do well to see *God, Sex and You* by Merville O. Vincent. Somewhat more difficult is *The New Theology and Morality* by Henlee Barnette. For advanced students one of the finest books is Paul Ramsey's *Deeds and Rules in Christian Ethics*. With this one might take *Norm and Context in Christian Ethics* edited by Gene H. Outka and Paul Ramsey. Also cf. *The Morality Gap* by Erwin W. Lutzer.

19. Bailey, *Sexual Ethics*. p. 103, 104.

20. Elton and Pauline Trueblood, *The Recovery of Family Life*. N.Y., Harper & Row, Pub., 1953, p. 54.

21. Allan Fromme, *The Ability to Love.* N.Y., Farrar, Straus & Co., 1965, pp. 72, 73.
22. Bailey, *Mystery.* p. 60.
23. Paul Tournier, *Secrets.* J. Embry, tr. Richmond, Va., John Knox Press, 1965, p. 47.
24. Bailey, *Mystery.* pp. 59,60.
25. Gibson Winter, *"Sex, Family and Society in Theological Focus,* ed. John Charles Wynn, Association Press, N.Y., 1966, p. 218.
26. Erich Fromm, *The Art of Loving.* N.Y., Harper & Row Pub. Co., 1956, p. 23.
27. Prentiss L. Pemberton, *Dialogue in Romantic Love.* Valley Forge, Pa., Judson Press, 1961, p. 33.
28. Vogt Von Ogd, *Modern Worship.* New Haven, Yale Univ. Press, 1927, p. 29.
29. Here I must disagree with Paul King Jewett's criticism of Barth for seemingly confusing man's creation as male and female with the institution of marriage. (Cf. Paul King Jewett, *The Doctrine of Man: The Divine Image; Man as Male and Female.* Pasadena, Calif., Fuller Theological Seminary Bookstore, 1973. Published as course syllabus. p.p. 28-30b.) Whereas Jewett feels that Barth obscures the point that the Christian view of human sexuality is not all one and the same with the Christian view of marriage, Jewett himself seems unduly to separate the two. Together with Barth and Bailey, I would stress the point that the most fundamental male-female relationship is marriage because obviously the most comprehensive. And while Jewett finds support in Barth for understanding that Genesis 2:19-24 is not the first wedding, I must heartily disagree. This passage, taken as a whole, is not merely man and woman in social relation. On the contrary, the passage is indivisible; the relation is not complete until the two are joined in such a way that the commentary refers to them as "one flesh." While there are dimensions of sexual identity and interaction other than that of the one-flesh union, sexuality indeed finds its *telos* in the marital union. Hence the theology of sexuality is the sexuality of marriage in its fullest definition.